Contents

Dedication

Keith Randell (1943–2002)

The *Access to History* series was conceived and developed by Keith, who created a series to 'cater for students as they are, not as we might wish them to be'. He leaves a living legacy of a series that for over 20 years has provided a trusted, stimulating and well-loved accompaniment to post-16 study. Our aim with these new editions is to continue to offer students the best possible support for their studies.

CHAPTER 1

Dissent and revolution 1917

Russia witnessed two revolutions in 1917. The February Revolution was essentially the collapse of tsardom from within, whereas the October Revolution was a seizure of power by Lenin's Bolshevik Party from the Provisional Government, which had replaced the tsar. This chapter considers these interlocking topics:

★ The structure of government 1917

★ Russia at war 1917

★ The February Revolution 1917

★ The Dual Authority and continued dissent

★ The October Revolution 1917

Key dates

1914–17	Russia at war	1917	
1915 August	Nicholas II took command of the Russian armies	April 4	Lenin issued his April Theses
		July 3–6	'July Days' uprising
1917		September 1	Kornilov's abortive march on Petrograd
February 18 to March 4	February Revolution	September 25	Bolsheviks gained a majority in Petrograd soviet
February 28	Provisional Government claimed authority	October 9	Petrograd soviet set up the Military Revolutionary Committee
March 1	Petrograd soviet issued Order Number 1	October 24–25	Bolshevik Rising
March 4	Tsar's abdication proclaimed	October 26	Bolsheviks established *Sovnarkom*
April 3	Lenin returned to Petrograd	October 27	Bolsheviks took power under Lenin

The structure of government 1917

> ▶ *What were the main features of the tsarist system of government?*

The following sections describe the main features of the tsarist system of government.

The tsar

The peoples of the Russian Empire were governed by one person: the tsar (emperor). In 1917, the reigning tsar was Nicholas II, who had come to the throne in 1894. By law and tradition, the tsar was an absolute ruler whose authority was exercised through three official bodies:

- the Imperial Council, a group of honorary advisers directly responsible to the tsar
- the Cabinet of Ministers, which ran the various government departments
- the Senate, which supervised the operation of the law.

These bodies were appointed, not elected, and they did not govern; their role was merely to give advice. They had no authority over the tsar, whose word was final in all governmental and legal matters. In practice, the tsar governed through the Cabinet of Ministers appointed by him. This concentration of power in the hands of a privileged élite was the reason why Russians who wanted their country to reform and modernise were unhappy with the tsarist system.

The *duma*

In 1906, Nicholas II had agreed to the creation of a *duma* (parliament). Although this was made up of two houses, an upper appointed chamber and a lower elected chamber, the *duma* had no real power, as had been made clear at the time of its creation when Nicholas had reasserted that he remained the final authority in all governmental and state matters. Nevertheless, although this had not been the tsar's intention, the *duma*, in which all the political parties were represented, provided a forum for criticism of government policies. This was particularly significant after 1915 when the *duma* members became increasingly hostile towards the government's handling of the war (see page 7).

Opposition parties

It was not until 1906 that political polities were legally permitted, and by 1917 a significant number of them had come into being. These belonged to one of two main categories: liberals, who wanted to reform the tsarist system, and revolutionaries, who wanted to overthrow it.

Liberal parties

Octobrists

The Octobrists were a party of moderates who urged the tsar to honour the October Manifesto that he had issued in 1906, promising a range of freedoms. They were basically loyal to the tsar and his government and believed that the tsarist system was capable of being improved by measured reform. They regarded the establishment of the *duma* as a major constitutional advance.

Kadets (Constitutional Democrats)

The Kadets, the largest of the liberal parties, wanted Russia to develop as a constitutional monarchy in which the powers of the tsar would be restricted by a democratically elected constituent (national) assembly. They believed that such a body, representative of the whole of Russia, would be able to settle the nation's outstanding social, political and economic problems.

Revolutionary parties

The Social Revolutionaries (SRs)

The Social Revolutionary Party began as a movement among the **Russian peasantry**, but also gained recruits from among the **urban workers**. It had two main wings, Left Social Revolutionaries, who claimed that only a policy of terrorism could bring necessary change to Russia, and Right Social Revolutionaries, who, while believing in revolution, were prepared to work with other parties for an immediate improvement in the conditions of the workers and peasants.

The Social Democrats (SDs)

The Social Democrats had come into being in 1898. Their aim was to achieve revolution in Russia by following the ideas of Karl Marx (1818–83), the German revolutionary, who had advanced the idea that human social development was shaped by **class struggle**, a process that operated throughout history. He referred to this process as the **dialectic**, whose final stage would be the violent overthrow of the **bourgeoisie** by the **proletariat**. In 1903, the SDs had split into two separate Marxist parties:

- the Mensheviks, who believed in a broad coalition of all the Russian progressive parties to work to bring down tsardom
- the Bolsheviks, led by Vladimir Lenin (see page 17), held that only their dedicated party of Marxist believers had the necessary commitment and understanding to achieve genuine proletarian revolution. At the beginning of 1917, most of the leading Bolsheviks, including Lenin, were in exile because of their revolutionary activities.

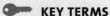

KEY TERMS

Russian peasantry Agricultural workers, who made up over 80 per cent of the population.

Urban workers Factory workers who, while comprising only four per cent of the population, were economically and politically significant.

Class struggle A continuing conflict at every stage of history between those who possessed economic and political power and those who did not, the 'haves' and the 'have-nots'.

Dialectic The dynamic force that drives the class struggle forward.

Bourgeoisie The owners of capital, the boss class, who exploited the workers but who would be overthrown by them in the revolution to come.

Proletariat The exploited industrial workers who would triumph in the last great class struggle.

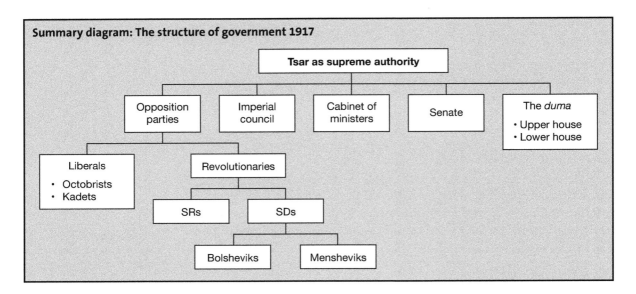

Summary diagram: The structure of government 1917

2 Russia at war 1917

► *Why had widespread opposition to tsardom developed by February 1917?*

War is a time when the character and structure of a society are put to the test in a particularly intense way. The longer the war lasts, the greater the test. During the years 1914–17, the political, social and economic institutions of Russia proved ultimately incapable of meeting the demands that war placed on them.

When Russia went to war against Germany and Austria-Hungary in 1914, Tsar Nicholas II had become the symbol of the nation's resistance in its hour of trial. Had the war gone well, there is little doubt that the tsar's reputation and authority would have become unchallengeable. But the war did not go well. Military and economic failures led to mounting political crises which ultimately proved to be the undoing of tsardom. The impact of the war on Russia is best analysed in six main areas:

- inflation
- food supplies
- transport
- the army
- the role of the tsar
- the role of Rasputin.

Inflation

The war destroyed Russia's financial stability. Between 1914 and 1917 war costs meant that government spending increased from 4 million roubles to

30 million. Increased taxation at home and heavy borrowing from abroad were only partially successful in raising the capital Russia needed. The **gold standard** was abandoned, which allowed the government to put more banknotes into circulation. In the short term this enabled wages to be paid and trade to continue, but in the long term it made money practically worthless since the rouble no longer had a genuine value. The result was rapid **inflation**, which had become particularly severe by the beginning of 1917. Between 1914 and 1916 average earnings had doubled while the price of food and fuel had quadrupled (see Table 1.1).

Table 1.1 Wartime inflation 1914–17, expressed in terms of the price index (to a base of 100 in July 1914)

	Price index	Banknotes in circulation
July 1914	100	100
January 1915	130	146
January 1916	141	199
January 1917	398	336

Food supplies

As the war continued, peasants found it impossible to sustain agricultural output. One reason for this was the **requisitioning** of farm horses and fertilisers by the military. There was the additional problem that inflation made trading unprofitable and so the peasants stopped selling food and began hoarding their stocks instead.

What increased the problems for the ordinary Russian was that the army had first claim on the limited amount of food being produced. The military also had priority use of the transport system. It commandeered the railways and the roads, with the result that the food supplies that were available could not be distributed easily to civilian areas. Hunger bordering on famine was a constant reality for much of Russia after 1915. Shortages were at their worst in the towns and cities. **Petrograd** suffered particularly badly because of its remoteness from the food-producing regions and because of the large number of refugees who swelled its population and increased the demand on its dwindling resources. By early 1917, bread rationing meant that Petrograd's inhabitants were receiving less than a quarter of the amount that had been available to them in 1914.

Transport

It was the disruption of the transport system that intensified Russia's wartime shortages. The attempt to transport millions of troops and masses of supplies to the war fronts created unbearable pressures. The signalling system on which the railway network depended broke down; blocked lines and trains stranded by engine breakdown or lack of coal became commonplace. A graphic example of the confusion was provided by the northern port of Archangel. So great was the

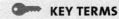

KEY TERMS

Gold standard The rouble had a fixed gold content, giving it strength when exchanged with other currencies.

Inflation A decrease in the value and purchasing power of money.

Requisitioning State-authorised seizure of property or resources.

Petrograd For patriotic reasons, the German name for St Petersburg was changed to the Russian form soon after the war began.

pile-up of undistributed goods there that they sank into the ground beneath the weight of new supplies.

Elsewhere there were frequent reports of food rotting in railway trucks that could not be moved. One of the tsar's wartime prime ministers later admitted: 'There were so many trucks blocking the lines that we had to tip some of them down the embankments to move the ones that arrived later.' By the end of 1916, Petrograd and Moscow were receiving only a third of their food and fuel requirements. Before the war, Moscow had received an average of 2200 wagons of grain per month; by January 1917, this figure had dropped to below 700. The figures for Petrograd told a similar story; in February 1917 the capital received only 300 wagonloads of grain instead of the 1000 it needed.

The army

By 1917, the war was going badly for Russia. A critical factor was that the army was severely hampered by a lack of equipment. This was not because there had been underspending on the military. The problem was poor administration and liaison between the government departments responsible for supplies. Despite its takeover of the transport system, the military was as much a victim of the poor distribution as the civilian population. In the first two years of the war, the army managed to obtain its supply needs, but, from 1916, serious shortages began to occur. **Mikhail Rodzianko**, the president of the *duma*, having undertaken a special fact-finding study in 1916 of conditions in the army, reported to the *duma* on what he described as 'the great evil' of widespread disorganisation, which was costing the nation the lives of its soldiers and denying it ultimate victory.

The suffering that the food shortages and the dislocated transport system brought to both troops and civilians might have been bearable had the news from the war been encouraging or had there been inspired leadership from the top. There had been occasional military successes, such as those achieved on the south-western front in 1916 when a Russian offensive brought Austria–Hungary to the verge of collapse. But the gains made were not followed up and were never enough to justify the ever-lengthening lists of dead and wounded. The enthusiasm and high morale with which Russia had gone to war in 1914 had turned by 1917 into pessimism and defeatism. Ill-equipped and underfed, the 'peasants in uniform' who composed the Russian army began to desert in increasing numbers.

The role of the tsar

Central to Russia's military failures was Tsar Nicholas II himself. The strong central leadership that the war effort desperately needed was not being provided. This related directly to a critical decision that Nicholas had made in 1915 when he formally took direct command of Russia's armed services. The intention had been to rally the nation around him as the representative of the Russian

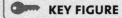

KEY FIGURE

Mikhail Rodzianko (1859–1924)

A tsarist loyalist who tried to persuade Nicholas to introduce essential reforms.

people, but it also made him a hostage to fortune. As commander-in-chief, Nicholas II was now personally responsible for Russia's performance in the war. If things went well, he would take the credit; if they went badly, he would be to blame. And things did go badly. Under his command, Russia sustained a series of military reverses that were seldom broken by a major victory. That the tsar still claimed to rule by divine right made his military failures seem even more glaring.

The growth of opposition

The result of the tsar's fateful decision in 1915 to take personal control of the army was clearly evident two years later. The majority of *duma* members and the high command by now shared the view that he was an inept political and military leader, incapable of providing the inspiration that the nation needed. It is significant that the first moves in the February Revolution in 1917, the event that led to the fall of tsardom, were not made by the revolutionary parties. Instead, the aristocracy and the army, and the civil servants, who, at the outbreak of the war in 1914, had been the tsar's strongest supporters, were, by the winter of 1916, too wearied by his incompetence to wish to save him or the system he represented.

The *duma* recalled

In August 1914, the *duma* had shown its total support for the tsar by voting for its own suspension for the duration of the war. But within a year, Russia's poor military showing had led the *duma* to demand that it be recalled. Nicholas II had bowed before the pressure and allowed the *duma* to reassemble in July 1915. From then on the *duma* became a platform for increasingly vocal critics of the tsar and his government for their mishandling of the war.

One major political mistake made by Nicholas and his ministers was their refusal to co-operate fully with the non-governmental organisations such as the **Union of *Zemstva*** and the **Union of Municipal Councils**, which at the beginning of the war had been willing to work with the government in the national war effort. These elected bodies formed a joint organisation, ***Zemgor***. The success of this organisation both highlighted the government's own failures and hinted that there might be a workable alternative to tsardom.

The 'Progressive Bloc'

A similar political blindness characterised the tsar's opposition to the *duma*'s urging that he replace his incompetent cabinet with 'a ministry of national confidence' with members drawn from the *duma*. Nicholas' rejection of this proposal destroyed the last opportunity he would have of retaining the support of the politically progressive parties. Milyukov, leader of the Kadets, complained that the tsar and his advisers had 'brushed aside the hand that was offered them'.

 **KEY TERMS**

Union of *Zemstva* A set of patriotic rural local councils.

Union of Municipal Councils A set of patriotic urban local councils.

Zemgor The joint body which devoted itself to helping Russia's war wounded.

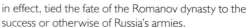

Profile: Nicholas II

1868	Born into the Romanov house
1894	Became tsar on the death of his father, Alexander III
	Married Princess Alexandra, a German princess
1906	Opened the first *duma*
1913	Led the celebrations of 300 years of Romanov rule
1915	Took over personal command of the Russian armed forces
1917	Abdicated on behalf of the Romanov dynasty
1918	Murdered with his family in Yekaterinburg

The character of Nicholas II is important in any analysis of revolutionary Russia. The evidence suggests that, although he was far from being as unintelligent as his critics asserted, his limited political understanding prevented him from fully grasping the nature of the events in which he was involved. When he attempted to be strong, he simply appeared stubborn.

The tsar made a number of crucial errors in his handling of the war, the most significant being his decision in 1915 to take direct command of Russia's armed forces. This, in effect, tied the fate of the Romanov dynasty to the success or otherwise of Russia's armies.

In 1914 there had been a very genuine enthusiasm for the tsar as representative of the nation. Within three years that enthusiasm had wholly evaporated, even among dedicated tsarists. The fall of Nicholas was the result of weak leadership rather than of savage oppression. He was not helped by his wife's German nationality or by court scandals, of which Rasputin's was the most notorious. But these were minor affairs which by themselves would not have been sufficient to bring down a dynasty. What fatally undermined the tsarist system which he led was his alienation of those who should have been his natural supporters, the aristocratic members of the *duma*, the leaders of the army and the progressive but non-revolutionary parties. Their desertion of him was the beginning of the February Revolution.

Denied a direct voice in national policy, 236 of the 422 *duma* deputies formed themselves into a 'Progressive Bloc', which began criticising the government's handling of the war. Initially, the bloc did not directly challenge the tsar's authority, but instead tried to persuade him to make concessions. Nicholas, however, was not willing to listen to the bloc. The result was that, as he and his government showed themselves to be increasingly incapable of running the war, the bloc, from having been a supporter, became a focus of political resistance. It was another of tsardom's self-inflicted wounds.

The government continued to shuffle its ministers in the hope of finding a successful team. In the year 1915–16, there were four prime ministers, three foreign secretaries, three ministers of defence and six interior ministers. It was all to no avail. None of them was up to the task.

The role of Rasputin

Gregory Rasputin was the man on whom much of the hatred of the tsarist system came to be focused. This was because he appeared to represent the corruption that had overtaken the royal court and government. By any measure his rise to prominence in Russia was an extraordinary story, but its true significance lay in the light it shed on the nature of tsarist government.

 KEY FIGURE

Gregory Rasputin (1872–1916)

A wandering monk believed by the credulous to have supernatural powers; by coincidence, 'rasputin' also means 'lecher' in Russian.

Rasputin was a self-ordained *starets* (holy man) from the Russian steppes, who was notorious for his sexual depravity which made him fascinating to certain women. His reluctance to wash himself or his clothes seemed to add to the attraction he had for them. Many fashionable ladies in St Petersburg, including the wives of courtiers, boasted that they had slept with him. Unsurprisingly, his behaviour made him bitterly hated at the imperial court to which he was officially invited. Outraged husbands and officials detested this upstart peasant. But, since he enjoyed royal favour, they could not get rid of him. As early as 1907 Rasputin had won himself an introduction to the tsar and his wife, Alexandra. The Empress Alexandra was desperate to cure her son, Alexei, the heir to the throne, of his **haemophilia**. Hearing that Rasputin had extraordinary gifts of healing, she invited him to court where he did, indeed, prove able to help Alexei, whose condition eased considerably when he was with him.

Rasputin did not, of course, have the miraculous powers that the more superstitious claimed for him, but he was a very good amateur psychologist. He realised that the pushing and prodding to which Alexei was subjected when being examined by his doctors only made the boy more anxious and feverish. Rasputin's way was to speak calmly to him, stroking his head and arms gently so that he relaxed. This lowered Alexei's temperature and eased his pain. It was not a cure, but it was the most successful treatment he had ever had. Alexandra, a deeply religious woman, believed it was the work of God and that Rasputin was his instrument. She made the 'mad monk', as his enemies called him, her confidant, someone in whom she placed a special trust.

Scandal inevitably followed. Alexandra's German nationality had made her suspect and unpopular since the outbreak of war, but she had tried to ride out the storm. She would hear no ill of 'our dear friend', as she called Rasputin in letters to Nicholas, and obliged the tsar to maintain him at court. Since Nicholas was away at military headquarters for long periods after 1915, Alexandra and Rasputin effectively became the government of Russia. Even the staunchest supporters of tsardom found it difficult to defend a system which allowed a nation in the hour of its greatest need to fall under the sway of the **'German woman'** and a debauched monk.

Alexandra was indeed German, having being born a princess in the house of Hesse. However, after marrying Nicholas, she had tried sincerely to make Russia her adopted country. She converted to the **Orthodox Church** and endeavoured to learn and apply Russian customs and conventions. This accounted for little after 1914, when, despite her undoubted commitment to the Russian cause, her enemies portrayed her as a German agent. Rodzianko, desperate to prevent Russia sliding into political chaos and military defeat, warned the tsar that Rasputin's presence at court and influence over the tsarina and the government threatened disaster. Rodzianko's warning was backed by a member of the royal family, Grand Duke Nicolai Mikhailovich, who wrote to the tsar (see Source A).

KEY TERMS

Haemophilia A genetic condition where blood fails to clot, leaving the sufferer with painful internal bleeding, which can be life threatening.

'German woman' The description used by anti-tsarists to suggest that Alexandra was spying for Germany.

Orthodox Church Russia's established state religion and traditionally one of the bulwarks of tsardom, supporting the idea that tsars ruled by divine right.

Why is it significant that the letter in Source A was written by a member of the royal family?

SOURCE A

From an extract of a letter to Tsar Nicholas II of 1 November 1916 from Grand Duke Nicolai, quoted in Richard Pipes, *The Russian Revolution 1899–1919*, Collins Harvill, 1990, p. 256.

You trust Alexandra; that is quite natural. Still what she tells you is not the truth; she is only repeating what has been cleverly insinuated to her. If you are not able to remove this influence [Rasputin's] from her, at least protect yourself from constant systematic manoeuvres attempted through the intermediacy of the wife you love. Believe me, if I insist so much on your freeing yourself from the chains that have been forged I do so only in the hope of saving you and saving the throne of our dear country.

Such appeals went unheeded. Nicholas II's long absences from Petrograd after he became commander-in-chief allowed Rasputin to interfere with, if not direct, government policy. This had the result against which the tsar's supporters, such as Rodzianko and the grand duke, had warned. The tsar's reputation declined further and his government fell into increasing disrepute.

SOURCE B

Why were so many people in Petrograd ready to believe the stories about Rasputin's scandalous behaviour, such as that depicted in this postcard?

One of the many pornographic postcards that circulated in Petrograd in 1917. The Russian word on the card, *samoderzhavie*, means 'holding'. It is used here as a pun to suggest Rasputin's hold on Russia as well as his physical holding of the empress. Despite this cartoon and all the scurrilous things said about Rasputin and Alexandra, there is no reliable evidence that they were ever lovers in a sexual sense.

The murder of Rasputin

In December 1916, in a mixture of resentment and a genuine wish to save the monarchy, a group of aristocratic conspirators murdered Rasputin. His death was as bizarre as his life. Poisoned with arsenic, shot at point-blank range, battered over the head with a steel bar, he was still alive when he was thrown, trussed in a heavy curtain, into the River Neva. His post-mortem showed that he had water in his lungs, and so must have still been breathing when he was finally submerged under the icy waters.

Rasputin's importance

From time to time there have been various attempts to present Rasputin in a more sympathetic light, but any new evidence that appears seems to bear out the description of him as an essentially disruptive force. Where he does deserve credit is for his achievement in reorganising the army's medical supplies system. He showed the common sense and administrative skill that Russia so desperately needed and which his aristocratic superiors in government so obviously lacked. It was his marked competence that infuriated those who wanted him out of the way. Yet, no matter how much the reactionaries in the court and government might rejoice at the death of the upstart, the truth was that by the beginning of 1917 it was too late to save tsardom. Rasputin's extraordinary life at court and his murder by courtiers were but symptoms of the fatal disease affecting the tsarist system.

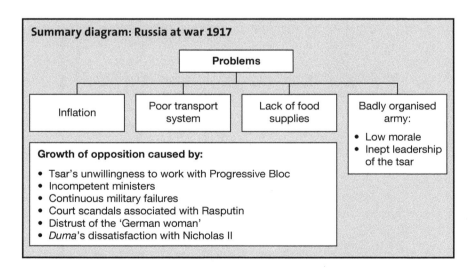

The February Revolution 1917

▶ *Were the events of February 1917 a collapse at the top or a revolution from below?*

KEY TERMS

Okhrana The tsarist secret police.

System of dating Until February 1918, Russia used the Julian calendar, which was thirteen days behind the Gregorian calendar, the one adopted in most Western countries by this time. This book uses the older dating for the events of 1917.

? What picture of the unrest in Petrograd at the start of 1917 emerges from the description in Source C?

Character of the revolution

The rising that came in February 1917 was not the first open move against the tsar or his government. During the preceding year there had been a number of challenges. The Octobrists in the *duma* had frequently demanded the removal of unwanted ministers and generals. What made February 1917 different was the range of the opposition to the government and the speed with which events turned from a protest into a revolution. Rumours of the likelihood of serious public disturbances breaking out in Petrograd had been widespread since the beginning of the year. An **Okhrana** report in January 1917 provides an illuminating summary of the situation (Source C).

SOURCE C

From an extract of an *Okhrana* report, January 1917, quoted in Ronald Hingley, *The Russian Secret Police*, Hutchinson, 1970, p. 74.

There is a marked increase in hostile feelings among the peasants, not only against the government but also against all other social groups. The proletariat of the capital is on the verge of despair. The mass of industrial workers are quite ready to let themselves go to the wildest excesses of a hunger riot. The prohibition of all labour meetings, the closing of trade unions, the prosecution of men taking an active part in the sick benefit funds, the suspension of labour newspapers, and so on, make the labour masses, led by the more advanced and already revolutionary-minded elements, assume an openly hostile attitude towards the Government and protest with all the means at their disposal against the continuation of the war.

On 14 February, Rodzianko, the *duma* president, in the first of a series of telegrams to the tsar, warned him that 'very serious outbreaks of unrest' were imminent. He added ominously, 'there is not one honest man left in your entourage; all the decent people have either been dismissed or left'. It was this desertion by those closest to the tsar that unwittingly set in motion what proved to be a revolution.

According to the **system of dating** in imperial Russia, the revolution occupied the period from 18 February to 4 March 1917. A full-scale strike was started on 18 February by the employees at the Putilov steel works, the largest and most politically active factory in Petrograd. During the next five days, the Putilov strikers were joined on the streets by growing numbers of workers, who had been angered by rumours of a further cut in bread supplies. It is now known that these were merely rumours and that there was still enough bread to meet the capital's basic needs. However, in times of acute crisis, rumour often has the same power as fact.

The course of events

It also happened that 23 February was International Women's Day. Thousands of women came on to the streets to join the protesters in demanding food and an end to the war. By 25 February, Petrograd was paralysed by a city-wide strike which again began at the Putilov works. Factories were occupied and attempts by the authorities to disperse the workers were hampered by the growing sympathy among the police for the demonstrators. There was a great deal of confusion and little clear direction at the top. Events which were later seen as having had major political significance took place in an atmosphere in which political protests were indistinguishable from the general outcry against food shortages and the miseries brought by war.

SOURCE D

> What do the slogans carried by the protesters suggest about the problems faced by women in Petrograd? **?**

Some of the demonstrators at the 1917 International Women's Day. On the banner is written: 'As long as women are slaves, there will be no freedom. Long live equal rights for women.'

The breakdown of order

The tsar, at his military headquarters at Mogilev, 790 km (490 miles) from Petrograd, relied for news largely on the letters received from Empress Alexandra, who was still in the capital. When he learned from her about the disturbances, Nicholas ordered the commander of the Petrograd garrison, **General Khabalov**, to restore order. Khabalov cabled back that, with the various contingents of the police and militia either fighting each other or joining the demonstrators, and his own garrison troops disobeying orders, the situation was uncontrollable.

Khabalov had earlier begged the government to declare martial law in Petrograd, which would have given him the power to use unlimited force

 KEY FIGURE

General Khabalov (1858–1924)

Arrested after the fall of the tsar on the grounds that he had tried to suppress the people, but later released without charge.

against the demonstrators. But the breakdown of ordinary life in the capital meant that the martial law proclamation could not even be printed, let alone enforced. More serious still, by 26 February all but a few thousand of the original 150,000 Petrograd garrison troops had deserted.

The *duma* provisional committee

Faced with this near-hopeless situation, Rodzianko, on behalf of the *duma*, informed the tsar that only a major concession on the government's part offered any hope of preserving the imperial power. Nicholas, again with that occasional stubbornness that he mistook for decisiveness, then ordered the *duma* to dissolve. It did so formally as an assembly, but a group of twelve members disobeyed the order and remained in session as a 'provisional committee'. This marked the first open constitutional defiance of the tsar. The twelve were made up of landowners, industrialists and lawyers who had been part of the Progressive Bloc. As well as Kadets and Octobrists, there were two SR members. It was one of the SRs, **Alexander Kerensky**, who then made the boldest move yet, when, speaking for the provisional committee, he called for the tsar to stand down as head of state or be deposed.

The Petrograd soviet

On that same day, 27 February, another event took place that was to prove as significant as the formation of the provisional committee. This was the first meeting of the 'Petrograd **Soviet** of Soldiers', Sailors' and Workers' Deputies', which gathered in the Tauride Palace, the same building that housed the provisional committee. The moving force behind the setting up of the soviet were the Mensheviks, who, under their local leader, Alexander Shlyapnikov, had grown in strength in Petrograd during the war.

These two self-appointed bodies – the provisional committee, representing the reformist elements of the old *duma*, and the soviet, speaking for the striking workers and rebellious troops – became the *de facto* government of Russia. This was the beginning of what became known as the **Dual Authority**, an uneasy alliance that was to last until October. On 28 February, the soviet published the first edition of its newspaper *Izvestiya* (*The News*) in which it declared its determination 'to wipe out the old system completely' and summon a constituent assembly, elected by **universal suffrage**.

The tsar abdicates

The remaining ministers in the tsar's cabinet were not prepared to face the growing storm. They used the pretext of an electricity failure in their government offices to abandon their responsibilities and to slip out of the capital. Rodzianko, who up to this point had struggled to remain loyal to the tsar's government, then advised Nicholas that only his personal abdication could save the Russian monarchy. On 28 February, Nicholas decided to return to Petrograd, apparently in the belief that his personal presence would have a

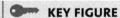

calming effect on the capital. However, the royal train was intercepted on its journey by mutinous troops who forced it to divert to Pskov, a city and important depot 290 km (180 miles) from Petrograd. It was at Pskov that a group of generals from *stavka*, the Russian army's high command, together with the representatives of the old *duma*, met the tsar to inform him that the seriousness of the situation in Petrograd made his return both futile and dangerous. They, too, advised abdication.

Nicholas tamely accepted the advice. His only concern was whether he should also renounce the throne on behalf of his son, Alexei. This he eventually decided to do. The decree of abdication that Nicholas signed on 2 March nominated his brother, Grand Duke Michael, as the new tsar. However, Michael, unwilling to take up the poisoned chalice, refused the title on the pretext that it had not been offered to him by a Russian constituent assembly.

By default, the provisional committee, which had renamed itself the Provisional Government, thus found itself responsible for governing Russia. On 3 March, the new government officially informed the outside world of the revolution that had taken place. On the following day, Nicholas II's formal abdication was publicly announced. Thus it was that the house of Romanov, which only four years earlier in 1913 had celebrated its tri-centenary as a divinely appointed dynasty, came to an inglorious end.

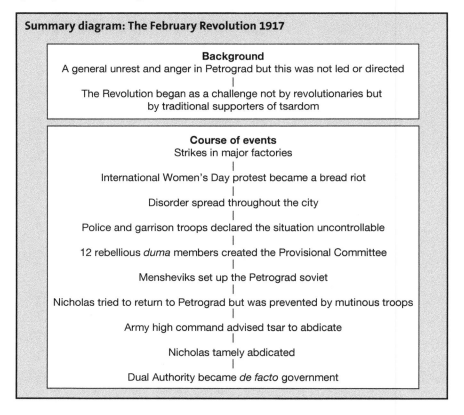

Summary diagram: The February Revolution 1917

Background
A general unrest and anger in Petrograd but this was not led or directed
|
The Revolution began as a challenge not by revolutionaries but
by traditional supporters of tsardom

Course of events
Strikes in major factories
|
International Women's Day protest became a bread riot
|
Disorder spread throughout the city
|
Police and garrison troops declared the situation uncontrollable
|
12 rebellious *duma* members created the Provisional Committee
|
Mensheviks set up the Petrograd soviet
|
Nicholas tried to return to Petrograd but was prevented by mutinous troops
|
Army high command advised tsar to abdicate
|
Nicholas tamely abdicated
|
Dual Authority became *de facto* government

4 The Dual Authority and continued dissent

▶ *What were the basic weaknesses of the Provisional Government?*

The Provisional Government, led by **Prince Lvov**, which picked up the reins of authority after the tsar's abdication, was really the old *duma* in a new form. From the beginning it suffered from the two characteristics that weakened it throughout the eight months of its existence:

● It was not an elected body, having come into being as a rebellious committee of the old *duma*, which had defied the tsar's order to disband. In consequence, it lacked legitimate authority and had no claim on the loyalty of the Russian people. Lacking this, it would be judged entirely on how well it dealt with the nation's problems.
● Its authority was limited by its unofficial partnership with the Petrograd soviet in the Dual Authority.

The Soviet did not set out to be an alternative government. Initially, it regarded its role as supervisory, checking that the interests of the soldiers and workers were understood by the new government. However, in the uncertain times that followed the February Revolution, the Provisional Government often seemed unsure of its own authority. This uncertainty tended to give the soviet greater prominence.

SOURCE E

? Why was the presence of the Bolsheviks in the soviet meetings so significant?

A packed meeting of the Petrograd Soviet in March 1917. Initially huge numbers of soldiers and workers, sometimes as many as 3000, attended the early meetings, but by the autumn this had dropped to a few hundred. However, the Bolsheviks kept up their numbers, which gave them a predominant influence in the soviet.

The ability of the Petrograd soviet to restrict the Provisional Government's authority was evident from the outset. In one of its first moves as an organisation, the soviet had issued its 'Order Number 1', which declared that, in military matters, the orders of the Provisional Government were to be obeyed 'only when they do not contradict the orders and decrees of the soviet'. What the order meant was that the decrees of the Provisional Government were not binding unless they were approved by the Petrograd soviet.

The Bolsheviks return

Once the Bolsheviks, most of whom had been in exile, learned of Nicholas II's abdication, they rushed back to Petrograd. Among the first to arrive were Josef Stalin and **Lev Kamenev**. These two prominent party spokesmen took the view that, in the aftermath of the February Revolution, the Bolsheviks should co-operate with the Provisional Government, and the other revolutionary and reforming parties. However, this accommodating approach would dramatically change once Lenin had returned.

Lenin's return in April 1917

Lenin arrived in Petrograd on 3 April. The manner of his return from exile in Switzerland was a remarkable story in itself. Lenin's wife, Krupskaya, recorded it (see Source F).

SOURCE F

From K.K. Krupskaya, *Reminiscences of Lenin*, Lawrence & Wishart, 1933, p. 336.

*The moment the news of the February Revolution was received, Ilyich [Lenin] was all eagerness to get back to Russia. As there were no legal ways of travelling, illegal ways would have to be used. But what ways? From the moment the news of the Revolution was received, Ilyich had no sleep. His nights were spent building the most improbable plans. Naturally the Germans gave us permission to travel through Germany in the belief that Revolution was a disaster to a country, and that by allowing **emigrant internationalists** to return to their country they were helping to spread the Revolution in Russia. The Bolsheviks, for their part, considered it their duty to bring about a victorious proletarian revolution. They did not care what the German bourgeois government thought about it.*

Krupskaya's account is instructive. In the hope that the tsar's fall would be the prelude to the collapse of the Russian armies, the German government arranged for Lenin to return to Russia in a sealed train across occupied Europe. Since the outbreak of war in 1914, the German foreign office had given regular financial support to Lenin and the Bolsheviks, in the hope that if they achieved their revolutionary aims they would pull Russia out of the war. It just so happened that, for quite different reasons, what Lenin wanted – the withdrawal of the Russian armies from the war – was precisely what the Germans wanted.

 KEY FIGURE

Lev Kamenev (1883–1936)

Held various key positions under Lenin between 1917 and 1924.

According to Source F, why had the attitudes of the Bolsheviks and the Germans coincided at this point?

 KEY TERM

Emigrant internationalists Russian revolutionaries living in exile.

However, it made no difference to anti-Bolsheviks that the German reasons were military and Lenin's were political. They considered the German government and the Bolshevik Party to be co-operating in a common cause, the defeat of Russia.

There is no doubting the great significance of Lenin's return to Petrograd in April. Before then, the Bolsheviks, led by Kamenev and Stalin, had accepted the formation of the Dual Authority as part of a genuine revolution. They had been willing to work with the other reformist parties. Lenin changed all that. In his speech on his arrival at Petrograd's Finland Station on 3 April, he declared that the events of February, far from giving Russia political freedom, had created a **parliamentary-bourgeois republic**. He condemned the Provisional Government and called for its overthrow in a genuine revolution.

The April Theses

The following day Lenin issued his April Theses, in which he spelt out future Bolshevik policy. To the bewilderment of those Bolsheviks who had expected to be praised for their efforts in working with the other revolutionary groups, Lenin condemned all that had happened since the fall of the tsar. He insisted that, since the Bolsheviks were the only truly revolutionary proletarian party, they must:

- abandon co-operation with all other parties
- work for a true revolution entirely by their own efforts
- overthrow the reactionary Provisional Government
- struggle, not to extend freedom to all classes, but to transfer power to the workers
- demand that authority pass to the soviets, which based on the Petrograd model, had been set in place by workers and soldiers in many other Russian cities and towns.

Lenin had ulterior motives in demanding that the soviets take over government. Although he rejected much of what the soviets had done, he saw them as a power base. Circumstances had made them an essential part of the structure of post-tsarist government. Lenin calculated that the soviets – the Petrograd soviet in particular – offered his small Bolshevik Party the means by which it could obtain power in the name of the proletariat. By infiltrating and dominating the soviets, the Bolshevik Party would be in a position to take over the state.

The essence of Lenin's argument was summed up in two provocative Bolshevik slogans that he coined: 'Peace, Bread and Land' and 'All Power to the Soviets'. But these were more than slogans. They were Lenin's way of presenting in simple, dramatic headings the basic problems confronting Russia:

- 'Peace' – the continuing war with Germany.
- 'Bread' – the chronic food shortages.
- 'Land' – the disruption in the countryside (see page 21).

(see page 21)

KEY TERM

Parliamentary-bourgeois republic A contemptuous term for the Provisional Government, which in Lenin's eyes had simply replaced the rule of the tsar with the rule of the reactionary *duma*.

Lenin asserted that as long as the Provisional Government stayed in power these problems could not be solved because the ministers governed only in the interests of their own class. They had no wish to end the war, which brought them profits, or supply food to the Russian people, whom they despised, or reform the land-holding system, which guaranteed their property rights and privileges. That is why Lenin demanded 'All Power to the Soviets'. The current ministers must be swept aside and replaced with a government of the soviets. Only then would the people's needs be addressed.

Lenin's analysis was shrewd and prophetic; the Provisional Government's failure to deal with the three principal issues he had identified would lead to its eventual downfall.

The Provisional Government and the war

From the outset, the Provisional Government was in a troubled position. The main problem was the war. For the Provisional Government after February 1917 there was no choice but to fight on. The reason was not idealistic but financial. Unless it did so, it would no longer receive the supplies and **war-credits** from the Western allies on which it had come to rely. Tsardom had left Russia virtually bankrupt. No Russian government could have carried on without large injections of capital from abroad. But the price Russia had to pay was not merely financial. To keep the Western loans coming, it had to guarantee to carry on the war. Making peace was not an option.

The strain that this obligation imposed on the Provisional Government eventually proved unsustainable. Its preoccupation with the war prevented the government from dealing with Russia's social and economic problems. It was a paradoxical situation: in order to survive, the Provisional Government had to keep Russia in the war, but in doing so it destroyed its own chances of survival.

Emergence of Kerensky

The Provisional Government represented the progressive landowners, industrialists and professional classes. They were all patriots, but some members had misgivings about continuing the war. However, at no time did the government as a body contemplate withdrawing from it. This would have mattered less had the Russian armies been successful, but the military situation continued to deteriorate, eroding the support the government had initially enjoyed. Lvov stayed as nominal head of the government but it was Kerensky who became the major influence. As war minister, he campaigned for Russia to embrace the conflict with Germany as a crusade to save the revolution. He toured the front, appealing passionately to the troops to be prepared to lay down their lives for Russia. 'Forward to the battle for freedom. I summon you not to a feast but death.'

The attempt to turn the war into a national crusade took no account of the real situation. The truth was that Russia had gone beyond the point where it could

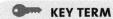

KEY TERM

War-credits Money loaned on easy repayment terms, mainly by France and Britain, to Russia to finance its war effort.

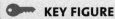

KEY FIGURE

**General Kornilov
(1870–1918)**

Distinguished by his bravery
as a soldier, he was a fierce
patriot who hated the Russian
revolutionaries.

fight a successful war. Yet Kerensky persisted. In June, a major offensive was
launched on the south-western front. It failed badly. The Russian forces were no
match for the Austrians, who inflicted heavy losses. Whole Russian regiments
mutinied or deserted. The commander on the south-western front, **General
Kornilov**, called on the Provisional Government to halt the offensive and direct
its energies to crushing the 'political subversives', his term for the Bolsheviks, at
home. This appeal for a tougher policy was taken up by the government. Early in
July, Lvov stood down as prime minister, to be replaced by Kerensky. Kornilov
became commander-in-chief.

The government's troubles were deepened by events on the island of Kronstadt
– an island naval base 30 km (20 miles) west of Petrograd across the Bay of
Finland – where sailors and workers defied the central authorities by setting
up their own separate government. Such developments tempted a number of
revolutionaries in Petrograd into thinking that the opportunity had come for
them to bring down the Provisional Government. The attempt to do so became
known as the 'July Days'.

The July Days

By the summer of 1917, the government was no longer in full control of events.
The most ominous signs were:

- the establishment of soviets throughout Russia
- worker control of factories
- widespread seizure of land by the peasants
- the creation of breakaway **national minority governments** – most notably
  in Ukraine.

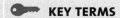

KEY TERMS

**National minority
governments** A number
of Russia's ethnic peoples
exploited the Provisional
Government's difficulties
by setting up their own
governments and claiming
independence.

**All-Russian Congress
of Soviets** A gathering of
representatives from all the
soviets formed in Russia since
February 1917.

In the first week of July, large-scale demonstrations occurred in Petrograd.
Public protests were not uncommon; they had been almost a daily happening
since February. But, in the atmosphere created by the news of the failure of
the south-western offensive and the government's mounting problems, the
demonstrations of early July turned into a direct challenge to the Provisional
Government. The rising itself was a confused, disorderly affair. In the course
of three days the demonstrators fell out among themselves; those members of
the soviet who seemed reluctant to make a real bid for power were physically
attacked. The disunity made it relatively easy for the Provisional Government
to crush the rising. Troops loyal to the government were rushed from the front.
They duly scattered the demonstrators and restored order.

It is not entirely clear who started the rising of 3–6 July. A month before, at the
first **All-Russian Congress of Soviets**, Lenin had declared that the Bolshevik
Party was ready to take power, but the delegates had regarded this as a general
intention rather than a specific plan. There were also a number of non-Bolshevik
revolutionaries in the soviet who, for some time, had been demanding that the
Petrograd soviet take over from the Provisional Government.

Leon Trotsky later referred to the July Days as a 'semi-insurrection' and argued that it had not been begun by the Bolsheviks. In saying this, he was trying to absolve them from the blame of having started a rising that failed. The explanation offered afterwards by the Bolsheviks was that they had come heroically to the aid of the workers of Petrograd and the sailors of Kronstadt, who had risen spontaneously against the government.

The consequences of the uprising

While the true origins of the July Days may have been unclear, the results were not. The failed uprising revealed that the Bolsheviks were still far from being the dominant revolutionary party and that the Provisional Government still had sufficient strength to put down an armed insurrection. This last revelation did much to raise the spirits of the Provisional Government and brought particular credit to Kerensky as war minister. Two days after the uprising had been crushed, he became prime minister. He immediately turned on the Bolsheviks. *Pravda* was closed down and many of the Bolshevik leaders, including Trotsky and Kamenev, were arrested. Kerensky also launched a propaganda campaign in which Lenin and his party were branded as traitorous agents in the pay of Germany. Lenin fled to Finland. A fortnight after the July Days, the Bolshevik Party appeared to have been broken as a political force. What enabled the Bolsheviks to survive were the critical misjudgements made by the Provisional Government over the land question and the Kornilov affair.

The land question

Land shortage was a chronic problem in Russia. The February Revolution had led the peasants to believe that they would soon benefit from a major land redistribution, which the government would introduce after taking over the landowners' estates. When the government made no such moves, the peasants in many parts of Russia took the law into their own hands and seized the property of local landlords. Disturbances in the countryside occurred daily throughout 1917 in what amounted to a national peasants' revolt.

The Provisional Government had no real answer to the land problem. While it was true that it had set up a land commission with the supposed aim of redistributing land, this was a mere gesture. The reality was that the government's heart was never in land reform. The majority of its members came from the landed classes who had little enthusiasm for a policy that threatened their own interests. While they were quite willing for the estates of the fallen monarchy to go to the peasants, they had no intention of losing their own possessions in a state land grab.

Lenin adroitly turned the government's embarrassment over land to his advantage. Earlier, he had declared that it was pointless for the Bolsheviks, the party of the workers, to make an alliance with the backward peasantry. Now, however, faced with the fact of peasant land-seizures throughout Russia, he

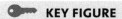

KEY FIGURE

Leon Trotsky (1879–1940)
A leading Bolshevik who was later to become Stalin's arch opponent (see page 71).

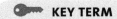

KEY TERM

Pravda The Russian word for truth; the chief Bolshevik newspaper, dating from 1912.

claimed that the special circumstances had produced a situation in which the peasants were a truly revolutionary force. He adopted the slogan, 'Land to the Peasants', indicating that the Bolsheviks recognised the peasant land-seizures as perfectly legitimate. As intended, this produced a considerable swing to the Bolsheviks in the countryside.

The Kornilov affair

In August, Kerensky's government became involved in a crisis that undermined the gains it had made from its handling of the July Days, and allowed the Bolsheviks to recover from their humiliation. By late August, the advance of German forces deeper into Russia began to threaten Petrograd itself. Large numbers of refugees and deserters flocked into the city, increasing the disorder there. General Kornilov, the new commander-in-chief, declared that Russia and the government stood in grave danger of a socialist-inspired insurrection.

Kornilov was an army officer who had never accepted the February Revolution. He believed that before Russia could fulfil its national duty of defeating Germany, it must first destroy the enemies within. 'It's time', he said, 'to hang the German supporters and spies, with Lenin at their head, and to disperse the Soviet.' He informed Kerensky that he intended to bring his loyal troops to Petrograd to save the Provisional Government from being overthrown.

Accounts tend to diverge at this point in their description of Kerensky's response. Those who believe that he was involved in a plot with Kornilov to destroy the soviet and set up a dictatorship argue that Kerensky had at first fully supported this move. It was only afterwards, when he realised that Kornilov also intended to remove the Provisional Government and impose military rule, that he turned against him. Other commentators, sympathetic to Kerensky, maintain that he had not plotted with Kornilov and that his actions had been wholly consistent. But, however the question of collusion is decided, it was certainly the case that Kerensky publicly condemned Kornilov's advance. He ordered him to surrender his post and placed Petrograd under martial law. Kornilov reacted by sending an open telegram (see Source G).

SOURCE G

From an extract of Kornilov's appeal, 26 August 1917, quoted by Richard Pipes, *The Russian Revolution*, Collins Harvill, 1990, p. 460.

People of Russia! Our great motherland is dying. The moment of death is near. I, General Kornilov declare that under pressure of the Bolshevik majority in the soviets, the Provisional Government is acting in complete accord with the plans of the German General Staff. It is destroying the army and is undermining the very foundations of the country.

? According to Kornilov in Source G, what role were the Bolsheviks currently playing in Russia?

Fearful that Kornilov would attack, Kerensky called on all loyal citizens to take up arms to defend the city. The Bolsheviks were released from prison or came out of hiding to collect the weapons issued by the Provisional Government to all who were willing to fight. By this strange twist in the story of 1917, the Bolsheviks found themselves being armed by the very government they were pledged to overthrow. In the event, the weapons were not needed against Kornilov. The railway workers refused to operate the trains to bring Kornilov's army to Petrograd. When he learned of this and of a mass workers' militia formed to oppose him, Kornilov abandoned the advance and allowed himself to be arrested.

Bolshevik gains

It was the Bolsheviks who benefited most from the failure of the attempted coup. They had been able to present themselves as defenders of Petrograd and the revolution, thereby diverting attention away from their failure in the July Days. What further boosted the Bolsheviks was that, despite the obvious readiness of the people of Petrograd to defend their city, this could not be read as a sign of their belief in the Provisional Government. Indeed, the episode had damaged the Provisional Government by revealing its political weakness and showing how vulnerable it was to military threat. Kerensky later admitted that the Kornilov affair had been 'the prelude to the October Revolution'.

Summary diagram: The Dual Authority and continued dissent

Provisional Government	Petrograd soviet
Initial co-operation	
But order Soviet Order Number 1 restricts government authority	

Bolshevik impact

Lenin's April Theses ends co-operation

Lenin's slogan 'Bread, Peace and Land'
illustrates Provisional Government's problems

Food shortages – Continuation of the War – Peasant land seizures

July Days Rising a Bolshevik failure

but

Bolsheviks saved by government's mishandling of
Kornilov affair

The October Revolution 1917

▶ *What developments put the Bolsheviks in a position to seize power in October 1917?*

The political shift in Petrograd

So considerable were the Bolsheviks' gains from the Kornilov affair that by the middle of September they had a majority in both the Petrograd and Moscow soviets. However, this should be seen not as indicating a large swing of opinion in their favour, but rather as a reflection of the changing character of the soviets. In the first few months after the February Revolution the meetings of the soviets had been fully attended. Over 3000 deputies had packed into the Petrograd soviet at the Tauride Palace. But as the months passed enthusiasm waned. By the autumn of 1917 attendance was often down to a few hundred. This worked to the Bolsheviks' advantage. Their political dedication meant that they continued to turn up in force while the members of other parties attended only occasionally. The result was that the Bolshevik Party exerted an influence out of proportion to its numbers, most notably in its over-representation on the various soviet subcommittees.

Broadly, what happened in Petrograd following the Kornilov affair was that the Petrograd soviet moved to the political left while the Provisional Government shifted to the political right. This made some form of clash between the two bodies increasingly likely. Lenin put it as a matter of stark choice: 'Either a soviet government or Kornilovism. There is no middle course.'

Lenin's strategy

From his exile in Finland, Lenin constantly appealed to his party to prepare for the immediate overthrow of Kerensky's government. He claimed that the Provisional Government, incapable of ending the war or solving the land issue, was becoming increasingly reactionary. This meant that the Bolsheviks could not wait long; they must seize the moment while the government was at its most vulnerable. In a sentence that was to become part of Bolshevik legend, Lenin wrote on 12 September: 'History will not forgive us if we do not assume power.' Lenin's sense of urgency arose from his concern over two events that were due to take place in the autumn, and which he calculated would seriously limit the Bolsheviks' freedom of action:

- the meeting of the All-Russian Congress of Soviets in late October
- the election for the Constituent Assembly in November.

Lenin was convinced that the Bolsheviks would have to take power before these events occurred. If, under the banner 'All Power to the Soviets', the Bolsheviks could topple the Provisional Government before the Congress of Soviets met, they could then present their new authority as a ***fait accompli*** which the congress would have no reason to reject.

The elections to the Constituent Assembly presented a different problem. The assembly was the body on which all progressives and reformers had set their hopes. Once it came into being, its moral authority would be difficult to challenge. Lenin told his party that since it was impossible to forecast how successfully the Bolsheviks would perform in the elections, they would have to be in power before the results were announced. This would provide them with the authority to undermine the results should they go against them.

Despite the intense conviction with which Lenin put his arguments to his colleagues, there were Bolsheviks on the **Central Committee** of the party who doubted the wisdom of striking against the Provisional Government at this point. To convince the doubters, Lenin slipped back into Petrograd on 7 October. His personal presence stiffened Bolshevik resolve, but did not produce total unity. During the next two weeks he spent exhausting hours at a series of Central Committee meetings trying to convince the waverers. On 10 October, the Central Committee committed itself to an armed insurrection, but failed to agree on a specific date. In the end, by another quirk of fate, it was Kerensky and the government, not the Bolsheviks, who initiated the actual rising.

Kerensky makes the first move

Rumours of an imminent Bolshevik coup had been circulating in Petrograd for some weeks, but it was not until an article, written by two members of the Bolshevik Central Committee, appeared in a journal, that the authorities felt they had sure proof. The writers of the article, **Grigor Zinoviev** and Lev Kamenev, argued that it would be a mistake to attempt to overthrow the government in the current circumstances. Kerensky interpreted this as a sure sign that a date had already been set. Rather than wait to be caught off-guard, he ordered a pre-emptive attack on the Bolsheviks. On 23 October, the offices of *Pravda* were occupied by government troops and a round-up of the leading Bolsheviks began. The Bolsheviks no longer had a choice; Lenin ordered the planned insurrection to begin.

Trotsky's role

That the Bolsheviks had a plan at all was the work not of Lenin but of Trotsky. While it was Lenin who was undoubtedly the great influence behind the October Revolution, it was Trotsky who actually organised it. The key to Trotsky's success in this was his chairmanship of the Petrograd soviet, to which he had been elected in September. On 9 October, the soviet set up the Military Revolutionary Committee (MRC) to organise the defence of Petrograd against a possible German attack or another Kornilov-type assault from within Russia. It proved a critical decision. Realising that if the Bolsheviks could control the MRC they would control Petrograd, Trotsky used his influence to have himself

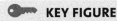

KEY TERMS

Troika A three-man team.

Red Guards Despite the Bolshevik legend that these were the crack forces of the revolution, the Red Guards, some 10,000 in number, were largely made up of elderly factory workers.

Cossacks The remnants of the élite cavalry regiment of the tsars.

Amazons A special corps of female soldiers recruited by Kerensky.

appointed as one of the **troika** to run the MRC. This meant he had at his disposal the only effective military force in Petrograd. He was now in a position to draft the plans for the overthrow of the Provisional Government. When Lenin gave the order for the uprising to begin, it was Trotsky who directed the **Red Guards** in their seizure of the key vantage points in Petrograd, such as the bridges and the telegraph offices.

The collapse of the Provisional Government

In the three days (25–27 October) that it took for the city to fall under Bolshevik control there was remarkably little fighting. There were only six deaths during the whole episode and these were all Red Guards, most probably accidentally shot by their own side. The simple fact was that the Provisional Government had hardly any military forces on which to call. The Petrograd garrison which had turned out to defend the government on previous occasions did not come to its aid now. The truth was that desertions had reduced the garrison to a few loyal officer-cadets, a small group of **Cossacks** and a unit known as the **Amazons**.

When the Red Guards approached the Winter Palace, which housed the Provisional Government, they expected stiff resistance, but there was none. The Bolshevik forces did not need to storm the gates; there was nobody defending them. The Winter Palace was a vast building, many times larger than London's Buckingham Palace. The Red Guards simply walked in through the back doors. This was enough to make the defenders give up. The Cossacks walked off when confronted by the Red Guards. After that, it did not take much pressure to persuade the cadets and the Amazons that it was better for them to lay down their arms and go home rather than die in a futile struggle.

The sounding of its guns in a pre-arranged signal by the pro-Soviet crew of the cruiser, *Aurora*, moored in the River Neva, convinced the remaining members of the government that their position was hopeless. As many as could, escaped unnoticed out of the building. Kerensky, having earlier left the city in a vain effort to raise loyal troops, fled to the US embassy. He later slipped out of Petrograd, disguised as a female nurse, and made his way to the USA, where he eventually became a professor of history.

The Bolsheviks take power

The Bolsheviks did not seize power; it fell into their hands. The speed and ease with which it had happened surprised even Lenin. In the early hours of 27 October, he said to Trotsky, 'from being on the run to supreme power makes one dizzy'. He then rolled himself up in a large fur coat, lay down on the floor, and went to sleep.

SOURCE H

A contingent of Amazons being trained in 1917. Kerensky had specifically recruited these female soldiers, also known as the 'Women's Battalion of Death', as an example of the fighting spirit of Russia's women.

From where would the Amazon recruits shown in Source H have most likely been drawn?

On the following evening, the All-Russian Congress of Soviets began its first session. The opening formalities had been barely completed when the chairman, who happened to be Lev Kamenev, informed the delegates that they were now the supreme authority in Russia; the Petrograd soviet had seized power in their name and had formed a new government. Kamenev then read out to the bewildered delegates the list of fourteen names of the new government they had supposedly just appointed. The fourteen were all Bolsheviks or their sympathisers. At the head of the list of **commissars** who made up the new *Sovnarkom* was the name of the chief minister: Vladimir Ilyich Lenin.

The SRs and the Mensheviks walked out, protesting that it was not a taking of power by the soviets but a Bolshevik coup. Trotsky jeered after them that they and their kind had 'consigned themselves to the garbage heap of history'. Lenin then announced to the Bolshevik and the Left SR delegates who had remained that they would now proceed 'to construct the towering edifice of socialist society'.

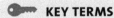 **KEY TERMS**

Commissars Russian for ministers: Lenin chose the word because he said it 'reeked of blood'.

Sovnarkom Russian for government or cabinet.

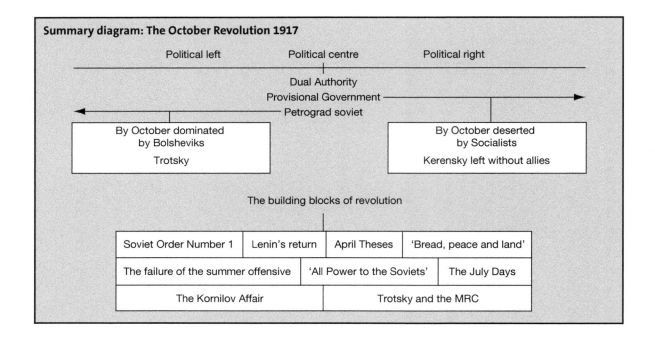

Summary diagram: The October Revolution 1917

The building blocks of revolution

Soviet Order Number 1	Lenin's return	April Theses	'Bread, peace and land'
The failure of the summer offensive		'All Power to the Soviets'	The July Days
The Kornilov Affair		Trotsky and the MRC	

Chapter summary

In February 1917, Tsar Nicholas II abdicated, a victim of scandal, desertion by his former supporters and his own incompetence. The February Revolution was followed by the establishment of a dual authority, which saw initial co-operation between the provisional committee and the Petrograd soviet. This harmony had broken down by the summer months and, prompted by Lenin, who had returned in April to demand the end of the Bolsheviks' co-operation with the Provisional Government, his party began to consider seizing power. An attempt to do so in July proved premature and brought the Bolsheviks close to destruction. They were saved only by the government's mishandling of the Kornilov affair, which enabled them to act as defenders of Petrograd against tsarist reaction.

Unable to deal with the major problems facing Russia – disastrous war losses, food shortages and a rebellious, land-seizing peasantry – Kerensky's government by the autumn had forfeited popular support. Although often absent from Petrograd, Lenin exerted such an influence that by late October he had persuaded his followers to strike against the government. Trotsky, in the name of the soviet, whose chairman and military chief he had become, organised the October Revolution, which overthrew a barely resistant government.

Refresher questions

Use these questions to remind yourself of the key material covered in this chapter.

1 How did Russia respond to the demands of war?

2 How was Russia's financial position damaged by the war?

3 How did the war disrupt the supply of food?

4 Why did the Russian transport system prove inadequate in wartime?

5 How well did the organisation of the Russian army adapt to the needs of war?

6 How did Nicholas respond to the war?

7 Why did Rasputin prove such an influential figure in the build-up to revolution?

8 Were the events of February 1917 a collapse at the top or a revolution from below?

9 Why was there so little initial political conflict between the Provisional Government and the Petrograd soviet?

10 What was the essential argument in Lenin's April Theses?

11 Why did the Provisional Government continue the war against Germany?

12 How were the Bolsheviks able to survive their failure in the July Days?

13 How real a threat was the Kornilov affair to the Provisional Government?

14 Why was the Provisional Government unable to cope with the problems it faced between March and October 1917?

15 What role did Lenin and Trotsky play in the October Revolution?

 Question practice

ESSAY QUESTIONS

1 'The main reason for dissatisfaction with the tsarist government in Russia by February 1917 was the suffering caused by defeats in the First World War.' Explain why you agree or disagree with this view.

2 How important was the return of Lenin to Petrograd in April 1917?

3 How far was the recovery of the Bolsheviks from their failure in the July Days due to the Kornilov affair?

4 To what extent was the success of the Bolshevik Rising in October 1917 due to the weakness of the Provisional Government?

SOURCE ANALYSIS QUESTIONS

1 With reference to Sources A and B and your understanding of the historical context, which of these two sources is more valuable in explaining why the February Revolution broke out?

2 With reference to Sources A, B and C, and your understanding of the historical context, assess the value of these sources to a historian studying the reasons for the collapse of the tsarist system in February 1917.

SOURCE A

From an extract of an *Okhrana* report, January 1917, quoted in Ronald Hingley, *The Russian Secret Police*, Hutchinson, 1970, p. 74.

There is a marked increase in hostile feelings among the peasants, not only against the government but also against all other social groups. The proletariat of the capital is on the verge of despair. The mass of

---

industrial workers are quite ready to let themselves go to the wildest excesses of a hunger riot. The prohibition of all labour meetings, the closing of trade unions, the prosecution of men taking an active part in the sick benefit funds, the suspension of labour newspapers, and so on, make the labour masses, led by the more advanced and already revolutionary-minded elements, assume an openly hostile attitude towards the Government and protest with all the means at their disposal against the continuation of the war.

SOURCE B

From a speech made by Paul Milyukov, leader of the liberal Kadet Party, to the *duma* on 1 November 1916.

Today we are aware that with this government we cannot legislate, and we cannot, with this government, lead Russia to victory. We are telling this government, as the declaration of the Progressive Bloc stated: We shall fight you, we shall fight you with all legitimate means until you go.

When the Duma declares again and again that the home front must be organised for a successful war and the government continues to insist that to organise the country means to organise a revolution, and consciously chooses chaos and disorganisation – is this stupidity or treason? We have many reasons for being discontented with the government. But all these reasons boil down to one general one: the incompetence and evil intentions of the present government. Cabinet members must agree unanimously as to the most urgent tasks. They must agree and be prepared to implement the programme of the Duma majority. They must rely on this majority, not just in the implementation of this programme, but in all their actions.

SOURCE C

From Nicolai Sukhanov, a Menshevik eyewitness, describing the situation in Petrograd in February 1917.

February 21st – I was sitting in my office. Behind a partition two typists were gossiping about food difficulties, arguments in the shopping queues, unrest among the women, an attempt to smash into a warehouse, 'Do you know,' declared one of these young ladies, 'if you ask me, it's the beginning of the Revolution.'

February 22nd and 23rd – the movements in the streets became clearly defined, going beyond the limits of the usual factory meetings.

February 24th – the movement swept over St Petersburg like a great flood. Many squares in the centre were crowded with workers. Fugitive meetings were held in the main streets and were dispersed by the Cossacks but without energy or zeal and after lengthy delays.

On 25th St Petersburg seethed in an atmosphere of extraordinary events from the morning on. The entire civil population felt itself to be in one camp against the enemy – the police and the military.

CHAPTER 2

The Bolshevik consolidation of power 1917–24

After October 1917 the Bolshevik Party sought to establish its control over Russia by a set of measures that aroused fierce opposition, leading to a two-year civil war and a series of foreign invasions. Triumphant in war, the Bolsheviks proceeded to impose their will by a reign of terror under Lenin that established Soviet Russia as a one-party authoritarian state. This process is covered in this chapter under the following headings:

★ The establishment of government and power

★ Peace with Germany

★ Civil war and foreign relations 1918–24

★ War Communism and New Economic Policy 1918–21

★ Lenin, government and the Communist Party

Key dates

1917		**1918 September**	Red Terror began
November	Bolshevik decrees issued	**1919**	Comintern established
December	*Cheka* created		Bolshevik Party renamed the Communist Party
1918–20	Russian civil war and foreign interventions	**1921**	Kronstadt Rising
	War Communism		Introduction of New Economic Policy
1918			Decree against factionalism
January	Dissolution of Constituent Assembly	**1922 December**	Soviet state became the USSR
March	Treaty of Brest-Litovsk	**1924 January**	Death of Lenin
July	Murder of Romanovs		

The establishment of government and power

▶ *How did the Bolsheviks tackle the problems confronting them in government?*

The traditional Soviet view was that after the Bolsheviks had taken power they transformed old Russia into a socialist society by following a set of measured, planned reforms that had been previously prepared. Few historians now accept that was what happened. Lenin's policy is now seen as having been a pragmatic adjustment to the harsh realities of the situation.

From the beginning, the Bolshevik regime was engaged in a desperate struggle for survival. Throughout 1917, it had spent its time preparing for revolution and had given little thought to the details of how affairs would be organised once this had been achieved. It had always been a Marxist belief that after the triumph of the proletariat, the state would 'wither away'. But circumstances were not to allow such a relaxed approach to government.

The distribution of power

Lenin claimed that the October Revolution had been a taking of power by the soviets. In fact, it had been a seizure of power by the Bolshevik Party. Nevertheless, Lenin persisted with the notion that *Sovnarkom* had been appointed by the Congress of Soviets. According to this view, the distribution of power in revolutionary Russia took the form of a pyramid, with *Sovnarkom* at the top, drawing its authority from the Russian people who expressed their will through the soviets at the base. The reality was altogether different. From the beginning, despite the pretence that the soviets held authority, it was in fact the Bolsheviks who were in power. The key body here was the Central Committee of the Bolshevik Party. It was this organisation under Lenin's direction that provided the members of the government. *Sovnarkom* was essentially a wing of the Bolshevik Party.

In theory, the Central Committee derived its authority from the All-Russian Congress of the Bolshevik Party, whose locally elected representatives voted on policy. In practice, the congress and the local parties did as they were told. This was in keeping with Lenin's insistence that the Bolshevik Party operate on the principle of **democratic centralism**, a formula which guaranteed that power was exercised from the top down, rather than the bottom up, and made Lenin unchallengeable.

The Bolsheviks' early measures

Before the October Revolution, Lenin had written powerfully against grasping landlords and oppressive capitalists, but he had not drawn up a specific plan

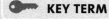 **KEY TERM**

Democratic centralism
Lenin's insistence that democracy in the Bolshevik Party lay in the obedience of its members to its leaders, who were the only ones who truly understood the science of revolution.

for their replacement. It is understandable, therefore, that his policy after taking power in 1917 was a pragmatic one. He argued that the change from a bourgeois to a proletarian economy could not be achieved overnight. The Bolshevik government would continue to use the existing structures and officials until the transition had been completed and a fully fledged socialist system could be adopted. This transitional stage was referred to as **state capitalism**.

Lenin was aware that there were many Bolsheviks who wanted the immediate introduction of a sweeping revolutionary policy, but he pointed out that the new regime simply did not possess the power to impose this. Its authority did not run much beyond Petrograd and Moscow. Until the Bolsheviks could exercise a truly national control, their policies would have to fit the prevailing circumstances. The government had inherited the demanding problems of food shortages, a crippled transport and communication system, and financial collapse. These necessarily restricted the choice of action. Lenin's government introduced three decrees that were meant to define its approach to national policy: decrees on peace, land and workers' control.

Decree on Peace, October 1917

Issued in October, this was not so much a decree as an appeal to the warring nations to enter into talks for 'a democratic peace without annexations'. Despite its apparent idealism, this was Lenin's hard-headed first step towards making peace with Germany, something which he knew the Bolshevik government had to do if it was to survive (see page 36).

Decree on Land, November 1917

The key part of this measure is quoted in Source A.

SOURCE A

From the Decree on Land, www.marxists.org/archive/lenin/works/1917/oct/ 25-26/26d.htm.

Private ownership of land shall be abolished forever; land shall not be sold, purchased, leased, mortgaged, or otherwise alienated. All land, whether state, crown, monastery, church, factory, private, public, peasant, etc., shall be confiscated without compensation and become the property of the whole people, and pass into the use of all those who cultivate it.

In truth, the decree simply gave Bolshevik approval to the reality of what had been happening in the countryside since the February Revolution: in many areas the peasants had overthrown their landlords and occupied their property.

Decree on Workers' Control, November 1917

This measure was also largely concerned with authorising what had already occurred. During 1917 a large number of factories had been taken over by the workers. However, the workers' committees that were then formed seldom

KEY TERM

State capitalism The system, during the first year of Bolshevik rule, by which the main pre-revolutionary economic and administrative structures were maintained.

To which section of Russian society did the decree in Source A aim to appeal?

ran the factories efficiently. The result was a serious fall in industrial output. The decree accepted the workers' takeover, but at the same time it instructed the workers' committees to maintain 'the strictest order and discipline' in the workplace.

Vesenkha

Although Lenin's government did not yet exercise full control over Russia, it pressed on with a scheme for establishing state direction of the economy. In December, **Vesenkha** was set up 'to take charge of all existing institutions for the regulation of economic life'.

Initially, *Vesenkha* was unable to exercise the full authority granted to it. However, it did preside over a number of important developments:

- Banks and railways were nationalised.
- Foreign debts were cancelled (see page 44).
- The transport system was improved.

These were important practical achievements, which suggested how effective centralised control might become should the Bolshevik regime be able to gain complete power.

The dissolution of the Constituent Assembly

As a revolutionary, Lenin had never worried much about how many people supported the Bolsheviks. Mere numbers did not concern him. He had no faith in democratic elections, which he dismissed as tricks by which the bourgeoisie kept itself in power. His primary objective was not to win mass support, but to create a party capable of seizing power when the opportune moment came.

After the successful October coup in 1917, Lenin was determined not to allow elections to undermine the Bolsheviks' newly gained power. However, there was an immediate problem. The October Revolution had come too late to prevent the elections to the **All-Russian Constituent Assembly** from going ahead in November as planned. When the results came through by the end of the year they did not make pleasant reading for the Bolsheviks:

Table 2.1 Results of the election for the Constituent Assembly, November 1917

Party	Votes	Number of seats
Social Revolutionaries (SRs)	17,490,000	370
Bolsheviks	9,844,000	175
National minority groups	8,257,000	99
Left SRs (pro-Bolshevik)	2,861,000	40
Kadets	1,986,000	17
Mensheviks	1,248,000	16
Total	41,686,000	717

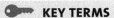

KEY TERMS

Vesenkha The Supreme Council of the National Economy.

All-Russian Constituent Assembly An elected parliament representing all the regions of Russia.

- They had been outvoted by nearly two to one by their major rival, the Social Revolutionary Party (SRs).
- They had won only 24 per cent of the total vote.
- They had gained barely a quarter of the seats in the assembly.

Lenin's motives for destroying the assembly

Lenin had originally supported the idea of a Constituent Assembly because it offered a way of further weakening the Provisional Government. Now, however, with his party in power, he had no need of an assembly. Furthermore, since it was overwhelmingly non-Bolshevik it would almost certainly make life difficult for his government. One possibility was that he could have tried to work with the new assembly, but that was not how Lenin operated. He was not a democrat; he did not deal in compromise. He was a revolutionary who believed that the only way to govern was by totally crushing all opposition.

Hence, Lenin's response to the Constituent Assembly when it gathered in January 1918, was simple and ruthless. After only one day's session, it was dissolved at gunpoint by the Red Guards. A few members tried to protest, but, with rifles trained at their heads, their resistance soon evaporated. It was a bitter end to the dreams of liberals and reformers. There would not be another democratic body in Russia until after the collapse of Soviet communism over 70 years later.

Lenin justified the Bolshevik action by arguing that the original reason for electing an assembly, the creation of an all-Russian representative body, had already been achieved by the formation of a Soviet government in October 1917. The will of the people had expressed itself in the October Revolution. The Constituent Assembly was, therefore, superfluous. More than that, it was corrupt. The elections, he asserted, had been rigged by the SRs and the Kadets; consequently, the results did not truly reflect the wishes of the Russian people. In such circumstances, Lenin declared: 'to hand over power to the Constituent Assembly would again be to compromise with the malignant bourgeoisie'.

Commenting on Lenin's attitude at this stage, Trotsky noted approvingly that Lenin was always ready to back his theories with force by using 'sharpshooters'. He recorded a remark Lenin had made to him in private: 'The dissolution of the Constituent Assembly by the Soviet government means a complete and frank liquidation of the idea of democracy by the idea of dictatorship.'

It was no surprise then that soon after the crushing of the assembly a measure was introduced outlawing all parties other than the Bolsheviks. Lenin's Russia was now a one-party state.

Summary diagram: The establishment of government and power

Bolshevik rule exercised through *Sovnarkom*	Lenin's personal hold over government and party based on principle of democratic centralism	Bolshevik measures to consolidate power
State capitalism adopted, to be run by *Vesenkha*	Decrees on: • land • peace • workers' control	Forcibly dissolved Constituent Assembly to prevent it being a brake on Bolshevik power

---

② Peace with Germany

▶ *Why were the Bolsheviks willing to make peace with Germany?*

At the time of his return to Russia in April 1917, Lenin had called for an anti-imperialist revolutionary war, but, after the Bolsheviks took power, he judged that the military exhaustion of Russia made it impossible for it to fight on successfully. He was, therefore, willing to consider making peace with Germany. Another reason was that Germany had continued to finance Lenin even after the October Revolution, an arrangement that Lenin was keen to maintain.

Trotsky, as commissar for war, shared Lenin's view that Bolshevik Russia had no realistic chance of successfully continuing the war. However, in the hope that within a short time the German armies would collapse on the western front and revolution would follow in Germany, Trotsky was determined to make the peace talks, which he attended as Russia's main spokesman, a protracted affair. He wanted to buy time for Bolshevik agitators to exploit the mutinies which the strain of war had produced in some units of the Austro-German armies.

Bolshevik tactics at Brest-Litovsk

This approach, for which Trotsky coined the slogan 'neither peace, nor war', was intended to confuse and infuriate the German delegation at Brest-Litovsk, the Polish town where the talks were held. Trotsky showed his contempt for what he called 'bourgeois propriety' by consistently flouting the traditional etiquette of European diplomacy. He invariably ignored the point under discussion and launched instead into revolutionary speeches calling on Germany to overthrow its bourgeois government.

Germany's chief negotiator, Field-Marshal **Paul von Hindenburg**, complained that Lenin and Trotsky 'behaved more like victors than vanquished'. What Hindenburg had not grasped was that the two Bolsheviks did, indeed, see

 **KEY FIGURE**

Paul von Hindenburg (1847–1934)

Prussian aristocrat and statesman, who led the German army 1914–18.

themselves as victors – potential if not actual. They were unperturbed by the thought of Russia's accepting defeat. Their conviction was that history was on their side and that a great international workers' rising was imminent. As **international revolutionaries**, Lenin and Trotsky had only a limited loyalty towards Russia as a nation. Their first concern was to spread the proletarian revolution worldwide.

This readiness to subordinate Russian national interests explains why the Russian delegation at Brest-Litovsk was eventually willing to sign a devastating peace treaty as soon as it became clear that the exasperated Germans were seriously considering marching on Petrograd to overthrow Lenin's government.

The terms of the Treaty of Brest-Litovsk 1918

The principal Russian losses were:

- A huge slice of territory – amounting to a third of European Russia, stretching from the Baltic to the Black Sea and including Ukraine, Russia's major grain-source – was ceded to Germany or its allies.
- The land lost by Russia – about a million square kilometres – contained a population of 45 million people.
- Russia was required to pay three billion roubles in war **reparations**.

Lenin acknowledged that there were Russians willing to fight on in a great cause. But they were, he said, 'romanticists' who did not understand that wars were not won by idealism alone; resources and technical skills were needed. The plain truth was that Bolshevik Russia did not yet have these in sufficient quantity to match Germany. Therefore, 'the Russian Revolution must sign the peace to obtain a breathing space to recuperate for the struggle'. Lenin's argument was a powerful one, yet he still experienced great difficulty in convincing his colleagues. A profound issue lay at the base of Bolshevik disagreements. To understand this, it has to be re-emphasised that Lenin and Trotsky were primarily international revolutionaries. They expected workers' risings, based on the Russian model, to sweep across Europe. Purely national conflicts would soon be superseded by the international class struggle of the workers. Lenin and Trotsky regarded the crippling terms of the Treaty of Brest-Litovsk as of small account when set against the great sweep of world revolution.

The 'Left Communists'

Not all Bolsheviks shared this vision. A number condemned the signing of the treaty. These were the 'Left Communists', those party members who were convinced that their first task was to consolidate the October Revolution by driving the German imperialist armies from Russia. The term was later used to describe party members who opposed the New Economic Policy (NEP, see page 55). In the end, after days of wrangling, it was only Lenin's insistence on the absolute need for party loyalty in a time of crisis that finally persuaded them

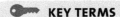

KEY TERMS

International revolutionaries Marxists who were willing to sacrifice national interests in the cause of a worldwide rising of workers.

Reparations Payment of the costs of war by the loser to the victor.

reluctantly to accept the treaty. What eventually destroyed the argument of the Left Communists and the Left SRs was the collapse of Germany's western front in August 1918, followed by the almost total withdrawal of German forces from Russia. Lenin's gamble that circumstances would soon make the Treaty of Brest-Litovsk meaningless had paid off and strengthened his hold over the party.

Summary diagram: Peace with Germany

> **Divergent attitudes among the Bolsheviks towards the war**
> Some wanted the continuation of a revolutionary war against Germany
> Others wanted an immediate peace to lessen strains on Russia

Lenin took a realistic stance:
- Russia could not win
- So best make peace to be able to fight another day

Trotsky took a compromise position:
- 'Neither peace, nor war'
- Russia could not win, but delay peace settlement as long as possible to encourage mutiny in Germany
- Used deliberately disruptive tactics at talks

The Treaty
Harsh terms imposed on Russia:
- Lost a third of its European lands
- Together with the 45 million people in these lands
- Russia was to pay 3 billion roubles in reparations

Consequence
Further conflict between Lenin and Left SRs

But defeat of Germany in November 1918 seemed to justify Lenin's policy

---

 # Civil war and foreign relations 1918–24

▶ *Why were the Bolsheviks able to win the civil war and repel the foreign interventions?*

▶ *In what ways were the Treaty of Rapallo (1922) and the Zinoviev Letter (1924) a consequence of Lenin's foreign policy?*

The Bolsheviks' crushing of the Constituent Assembly, followed by their outlawing of all other parties, showed that they had no intention of sharing power. This made civil war highly likely, given that the Bolsheviks had only a limited grip on Russia in the early years after the October Revolution. They were bound to face military opposition from their wide range of opponents who were unwilling to accept absolute rule by a minority party. Although civil war involved obvious dangers to the Bolsheviks, Lenin was convinced that his forces could win and in the process wipe out all their opponents, military and political. Better to have a short, brutal struggle than face many years of continual challenge from the anti-Bolsheviks, who were a large majority in Russia, as the Constituent Assembly election results had clearly shown (see page 34).

The conflict

The civil war that began in the summer of 1918 was not just a matter of the Bolsheviks (**Reds**) facing their political enemies (**Whites**) in a military struggle. It involved yet another colour: **Greens**.

The Bolsheviks presented the struggle as a class war, but it was never simply that. Local considerations often predominated over larger issues. Significantly, a number of Russia's national minorities, such as the Ukrainians and Georgians, fought in the war primarily to establish their independence from Russia. As in all civil wars, the disruption provided a cover for settling old scores and pursuing personal vendettas, and it was not uncommon for villages or families to be divided against each other.

On occasion, the fighting was simply a desperate struggle for food. The failure of the new regime to end hunger was an important factor in creating the initial military opposition to the Bolsheviks. In March 1918, the bread ration in Petrograd reached its lowest ever allocation of 50 grams a day. Hunger forced many workers out of the major industrial cities. By June 1918, the workforce in Petrograd had shrunk by 60 per cent and the overall population had declined

KEY TERMS

Reds Bolsheviks and their supporters.

Whites The Bolsheviks' opponents, including tsarists and those parties that had been suppressed by the new regime.

Greens Largely made up of groups from the national minorities, struggling for independence.

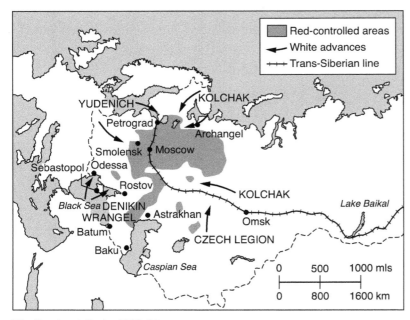

The Russian civil war 1918–20.

from 3 million to 2 million. The Bolshevik boast that October 1917 had established worker-control of Russian industry meant little now that the workers were deserting the factories in great numbers.

All this encouraged the Whites, and all the revolutionary and liberal groups who had been outlawed by the Bolsheviks, to come out openly against Lenin's regime.

- The SRs organised a number of uprisings in central Russia and established an anti-Bolshevik Volga 'republic' at Samara.
- A White 'volunteer army', led by General Denikin, had already been formed in the Caucasus region of southern Russia from tsarist loyalists and outlawed Kadets.
- In Siberia, a White army was formed under Admiral Kolchak, the self-proclaimed 'supreme ruler of Russia'.
- In Estonia, another ex-tsarist general, Yudenich, began to form a White army of resistance.
- In Ukraine, Baron Wrangle led a 'Caucasus Volunteer Army' against the Bolsheviks.
- White units appeared in many regions elsewhere. The speed with which they arose indicated just how limited Bolshevik control was outside the cities of western Russia.
- 40,000 Czechoslovak troops, who had fought for tsarist Russia in the First World War, found themselves isolated after the Treaty of Brest-Litovsk. They formed themselves into the Czech Legion and took the long journey eastwards to Vladivostok with the aim of eventually rejoining the Allies on the western front in the hope of winning their support for the formation of an independent Czechoslovakia. Local soviets began to challenge the Czech Legion and fierce fighting accompanied its progress along the trans-Siberian railway.

The terror

As in many civil wars, the Reds and Whites continually accused each other of committing atrocities. Both sides did undoubtedly use terror to crush opposition in the areas they seized. The actual fighting was not unduly bloody; it was in the aftermath, when the civilian population was forced to submit, that the savagery usually occurred. The Reds gained recruits by offering defeated enemy troops and neutral civilians the stark choice of enlistment or execution. Although the Reds imposed a reign of terror, the Whites' own record in ill-treating local populations was equally notorious.

Bolshevik victory

The civil war was a war of movement, largely dictated by the layout of Russia's railway system. It was because the Bolsheviks were largely successful in their desperate fight to maintain control of the railways that they were able to keep themselves supplied, while denying this advantage to the Whites.

White and Green weaknesses

The reasons for the final victory of the Reds over their White and Green opponents in the civil war are not difficult to determine:

- The various White armies fought as separate detachments.
- Apart from their obvious desire to overthrow the Bolsheviks, they were not bound together by a single aim.
- They were unwilling to sacrifice their individual interests in order to form a united anti-Bolshevik front. This allowed the Reds to pick off the White armies separately.
- In the rare cases in which the Whites did consider combining, they were too widely scattered geographically to be able to mount a sustained attack on the Reds.
- The Whites became too reliant on supplies from abroad, which seldom arrived in sufficient quantity, in the right places, or at the right time.
- The Whites lacked leaders of the quality of Trotsky.
- The Greens' limited aims of national independence for particular regions meant that they never formed a common front to challenge the Reds.

Red strengths

The Reds, in contrast, had a number of overwhelming advantages:

- They remained in control of a concentrated central area of western Russia that they were able to defend by maintaining their inner communication and supply lines.
- The two major cities, Petrograd and Moscow, the administrative centres of Russia, remained in their hands throughout the war.
- The Reds kept control of the railway network.
- The Reds' strongest hold was over the industrial centres of Russia. This was a key advantage since it gave them access to munitions and resources unavailable to the Whites.
- The Whites' dependence on supplies from abroad appeared to prove the Red accusation that they were in league with the foreign interventionists (see page 44). The civil war had produced a paradoxical situation in which the Reds were able to stand as champions of the Russian nation as well as proletarian revolutionaries.
- The Red Army was brilliantly organised and led by Trotsky.

Trotsky and the Red Army

Of all the factors explaining Red success, arguably the role of Trotsky, Russia's war commissar, was the most significant. Sensing that Trotsky was as essentially ruthless as himself, Lenin appointed him war commissar and left him entirely free to act on his own initiative. As commissar, Trotsky used his powers to end the independence of the trade unions, which he dismissed as 'unnecessary chatterboxes'. Early in 1920, the workers were brought under military discipline on the same terms as soldiers.

The emasculating of the trade unions was part of Trotsky's programme for building the Red Army. From his heavily armed special train, which served as his military headquarters and in which he travelled vast distances, Trotsky supervised the development of a new fighting force in Russia. Within two years he had turned an unpromising collection of tired Red Guard veterans and raw recruits into a formidable army of 3 million men. He enlisted large numbers of ex-tsarist officers to train the rank and file into efficient soldiers. As a precaution, Trotsky attached **political commissars** to the army. These became an integral part of the Red Army structure and were so successful a mechanism of control that they were attached to all departments of government under Lenin.

Trotsky tolerated no opposition from officers or men. The death sentence was imposed for desertion or disloyalty. In the heady revolutionary days before Trotsky took over, the traditional forms of army discipline had been greatly relaxed. Graded ranks, special uniforms, saluting and deferential titles were dropped as belonging to the reactionary past. Trotsky, however, had no truck with such fanciful experiments. He insisted that the demands of war meant that discipline had to be tighter, not looser. Although the term 'officer' was replaced by 'commander', in all other key respects the Red Army returned to the customary forms of rank and address, with the word 'Comrade' usually prefixing the standard terms, as in 'Comrade Captain'. The practice of electing officers, which had come into favour in the democratic atmosphere of the February Revolution, was abandoned, as were soldiers' committees.

To wage a successful war, Trotsky believed in the importance of morale and dedication, in addition to the more basic demands of resources and firepower. Throughout the struggle, the Reds were sustained by a driving sense of purpose instilled in them by Trotsky. His unrelenting approach helped to create an army which proved capable of fighting with an unshakeable belief in its own eventual victory.

Conscription

Trotsky responded to the civil war's increasing demand for manpower by enforcing conscription in those areas under Bolshevik control. Under the slogan 'Everything for the Front', Trotsky justified the severity of the Red Army's methods by referring to the dangers that Russia faced on all sides. Those individuals whose social or political background made them suspect as fighting-men were nevertheless conscripted, being formed into labour battalions for back-breaking service behind the lines, digging trenches, loading ammunition and pulling heavy guns. Most of the peasants who were drafted into the Red Army proved reluctant warriors, and were not regarded as reliable in a crisis. Desertions were commonplace, in spite of the heavy penalties. Trotsky and Lenin judged that the only dependable units were those drawn predominantly

KEY TERM

Political commissars
Dedicated party workers whose function was to accompany the officers permanently and report on their political correctness and loyalty.

from among the workers. Such units became in practice the élite corps of the Red Army. Heroic stories of the workers as defenders of the revolution quickly became legends.

Red idealism

Not everything was achieved by coercion; there were idealists among the troops who believed sincerely in the Communist mission to create a new proletarian world. Theirs was a vital contribution to the relatively high morale of the Reds. Although, by the standards of the European armies of the time, the Red Army was short of equipment and expertise, within Russia it soon came to outstrip its White opponents in its efficiency and sense of purpose.

The effects of the civil war on the Bolsheviks

The intensity of the civil war had lasting effects on the character of Lenin's party and government.

Bolshevik strength

On the domestic front, the civil war proved to be one of the great formative influences on the Bolshevik Party (renamed the Communist Party in 1919). The revolution had been born in war, and the government had been formed in war. Of all the members of the Communist Party in 1927, a third had joined in the years 1917–20 and had fought in the Red Army. This had created a tradition of military obedience and loyalty. The Bolsheviks of this generation were hard men, forged in the fires of war.

Bolshevik authoritarianism

A number of modern analysts have emphasised the central place that the civil war had in shaping the character of Communist rule in Soviet Russia. Robert Tucker, writing in the early 1990s, stressed that it was the military aspect of early Bolshevik government that left it with a 'readiness to resort to coercion, rule by administrative fiat [commands], centralised administration [and] summary justice'. No regime placed in the Bolshevik predicament between 1917 and 1921 could have survived without resort to authoritarian measures.

Centralisation of Bolshevik control

The move towards centralism in government increased as the civil war dragged on. The emergencies of war required immediate day-to-day decisions to be made. This led to effective power moving away from the Central Committee of the Communist (Bolshevik) Party, which was too cumbersome, into the hands of the two key subcommittees, the **Politburo** and the **Orgburo**, set up in 1919, which could act with the necessary speed. In practice, the authority of *Sovnarkom*, the official government of Soviet Russia, became indistinguishable from the rule of these party committees, which was served by the **Secretariat**.

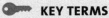 **KEY TERMS**

Politburo The political bureau, responsible for major policy decisions.

Orgburo The organisation bureau, which turned policies into practice.

Secretariat The civil service that carried out the administration of policies.

The foreign interventions 1918–20

When tsardom collapsed in 1917 the immediate worry for the Western Allies was that if the new Russian regime made a separate peace, Germany would be free to divert huge military resources from the eastern to the western front. To prevent this, the Allies offered large amounts of capital to Russia to keep it in the war, an offer which the Provisional Government had accepted in order to sustain itself. However, the Treaty of Brest-Litovsk in March 1918 ended all hope of Lenin's Russia renewing the war against Germany. The Allies' view was that in making a separate peace with Germany the Bolsheviks had betrayed the Allied cause. The result was a fierce determination among the Allies to prevent their vital war-supplies, previously loaned to Russia and still stockpiled there, from falling into German hands.

Soon after the signing of the treaty, British, French and US troops occupied the ports of Murmansk in the Arctic and Archangel in the White Sea (see the map on page 45). This was the beginning of a two-year period during which armed forces from a large number of countries occupied key areas of European, central and far-eastern Russia. Once the First World War had ended in November 1918, the attention of the major powers turned to the possibility of a major offensive against the Bolsheviks. The French and British in particular were alarmed by the creation of the **Comintern** and by the spread of revolution in Germany and central Europe.

The interventions spread

One of the first acts of the Bolshevik regime had been to announce that it would not pay back any of the foreign debts incurred by its predecessors. In addition, it froze all foreign assets in Russia. The bitter reaction to what was regarded as international theft was especially strong in France, where many financiers had invested heavily in tsarist Russia. It was the French who now took the lead in proposing an international campaign against the Reds. There followed a series of foreign invasions, of which the following were the most significant:

- In 1918, British land forces entered southern Russia and British warships entered Russian Baltic waters and the Black Sea, where they were joined by French naval vessels.
- The French also established a major land base around the Black Sea port of Odessa.
- In April 1918, Japanese troops occupied Russia's far-eastern port of Vladivostok. Four months later, they were joined by units from France, Britain, the USA and Italy.
- Czech, Finnish, Lithuanian, Polish and Romanian forces crossed into Russia.
- In 1919, troops from Japan and the USA occupied parts of Siberia.

 **KEY TERM**

Comintern Communist International, a body set up in Moscow in March 1919 to organise worldwide revolution.

The foreign interventions 1918–21.

An important point to stress is that these were not co-ordinated attacks and there was little co-operation between the interventionists. The declared motive of Britain, France, Germany, Italy, Japan and the USA was the legitimate protection of their individual interests. The objective of Czechoslovakia, Finland, Lithuania, Poland and Romania was to gain independence from Russia.

The failure of the interventions

Despite the fierce anti-Bolshevism expressed in many Western countries, no concerted attempt was ever made to unseat the Bolshevik regime. After the separate national forces had arrived in Russia, there was seldom effective liaison between them. Furthermore, such efforts as the foreign forces made to co-operate with the White armies came to nothing. The one major exception to this was in the Baltic states, where the national forces, backed by British warships and troops, crushed a Bolshevik invasion and forced Lenin's government to recognise the independence of Estonia, Latvia and Lithuania. Such interventionist success was not repeated elsewhere. After a token display of aggression, the foreign troops began to withdraw. By the end of 1919, all French and US troops had been recalled, and by the end of 1920, all other Western forces had left. It was only the Japanese who remained in Russia for the duration of the civil war, not finally leaving until 1922.

Propaganda success for the Bolsheviks

In no real sense were the withdrawals a military victory for the Bolsheviks, but that was exactly how they were portrayed in Soviet propaganda, which depicted Lenin's government as the saviour of the nation from foreign conquest. All the interventions had been imperialist invasions of Russia intent on overthrowing the Revolution. This apparent success over Russia's enemies helped the Bolshevik regime to recover the esteem it had lost over its 1918 capitulation to Germany.

War against Poland 1920

The failure of the foreign interventions encouraged the Bolsheviks to undertake what proved to be a disastrous attempt to expand their authority outside Russia. In 1920 the Red Army marched into neighbouring Poland, expecting the Polish workers to rise in rebellion against their own government. However, the Poles saw the invasion as traditional Russian aggression and drove the Red Army back across the border. Soviet morale was seriously damaged, which forced Lenin and the Bolsheviks to rethink the whole question of international revolution.

Lenin's approach to foreign affairs

Lenin adopted an essentially realistic approach to foreign affairs. He judged that the Polish reverse, the foreign interventions in Russia and the failure of Communist revolutions in Germany and Hungary all showed that the time was not right for world revolution. The capitalist nations were still too strong. The Bolsheviks would, therefore, without abandoning their long-term revolutionary objectives, adjust their foreign policy to meet the new situation. The Comintern would continue to call for world revolution, but Soviet Russia would soften its international attitude.

Lenin's concerns were very much in the tradition of Russian foreign policy. Western encroachment into Russia had been a constant fear of the tsars. That long-standing Russian worry had been increased by the hostility of European governments to the October Revolution and by their support of the Whites during the civil war. Lenin's reading of the international situation led him to conclude that discretion was the better part of valour. Under him, Soviet foreign policy was activated not by thoughts of expansion but by the desire to avoid conflict.

Treaty of Rapallo, April 1922

An example of this was the agreement the USSR entered into with Germany in 1922. The two countries were drawn together by the fact that in the eyes of the European powers they were both pariah nations:

- Germany, under the terms of the 1919 Versailles peace treaty, had had heavy reparations imposed on it and had been denied the right to rearm.
- Soviet Russia, as a revolutionary nation, had earned the hostility of the capitalist countries by renouncing all Russia's debts and calling on the peoples in the capitalist countries to overthrow their governments.

The agreement followed the breakdown of a conference in Genoa, which Germany and Russia had both attended. The conference had been intended to improve financial dealings among the European states. However, in the face of French insistence that Russia repay tsarist debts and that Germany accept the obligation to pay reparations, the two countries walked out of the conference and then proceeded to negotiate the Treaty of Rapallo, in which they promised to 'co-operate in a spirit of mutual goodwill in meeting the economic needs of both countries'. The main terms were:

- Russia would provide German forces with military training grounds and resources.
- In return, Russia would be granted special trading rights in Germany.

Four years later, in 1926, a further Soviet–German agreement, the Treaty of Berlin, was signed. This non-aggression pact also confirmed the main terms of the Rapallo treaty.

The Zinoviev letter 1924

In 1924, Britain, under its first Labour government, had been one of the first countries to give diplomatic recognition to the Soviet Union. This was followed by the negotiating of a trade and diplomatic agreement. An Anglo-Soviet treaty was drawn up containing the following main terms:

- Britain agreed to advance a £30 million loan to the Soviet Union.
- In return, the Soviet Union would pay compensation for the British financial assets the Bolsheviks had seized after the October Revolution in 1917.

However, at this point the drama over the Zinoviev letter intervened. On 25 October 1924, four days before a general election was due to be held in Britain, the London-based newspaper the *Daily Mail* carried the following headline: 'Soviet Plot: Red Propaganda in Britain: Revolution Urged in Britain.' Beneath the headline was printed a letter purportedly from Grigor Zinoviev, chief of the Comintern. It was addressed to the **British Communist Party**, whose members were urged, under the cover of the Anglo-Soviet treaty, to infiltrate the Labour Party and use it to bring down the British state in an armed insurrection. Zinoviev immediately denied having written such a letter and claimed that it was a forgery, concocted by **White Russian émigrés**, an interpretation that historians now accept. Nevertheless, at the time the letter undoubtedly contributed to the Labour Party's election defeat. The letter provided ammunition for those in Britain who believed that relations between the Labour government and revolutionary Russia were far too close for Britain's good. The result was that with the Labour Party out of office and the succeeding Conservative government wholly unwilling to consider continued negotiation, the Anglo-Soviet treaty was never ratified.

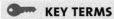 **KEY TERMS**

British Communist Party Set up in 1921, it was always subservient to the Comintern, which provided the bulk of its funds.

White Russian émigrés Anti-Bolsheviks who fled from Russia during the years following the 1917 October Revolution.

Summary diagram: Civil war and foreign relations 1918–24

Reasons for the war
- Reds – needed military victory to consolidate their hold on Russia
- Lenin welcomed it – looking for a showdown
- Whites – war the only way to challenge Bolshevik absolutism
- Greens – fighting for national independence

Why the Reds won
- Fighting a defensive war against disunited enemy
- Controlled the railway network
- Showed greater sense of purpose
- Higher morale
- Trotsky's Red Army proved invincible

Impact of the war on Bolsheviks
- It encouraged: toughness, authoritarianism and centralisation

Why the foreign interventions?
- Resentment at Russian withdrawal from war
- To recover supplies
- Fear of Bolshevism
- Anger at Bolshevik writing off of Russian debt
- To support the Whites

Who were the interventionists?
- Britain
- France
- Japan
- USA
- Italy
- Finland
- Lithuania
- Poland
- Romania

Where were the interventions?
- Black Sea
- Murmansk
- Vladivostok
- Siberia
- Caspian Sea

Why did the interventions fail?
- Lack of co-ordination and liaison
- Interventionists had no real stomach for a fight
- Very limited objectives
- Not a concerted effort to bring down the Bolsheviks

Postscript
- Bolsheviks over-extended themselves by invading Poland, only for the Red Army to be beaten back by the Poles
- Lenin realised revolution was not easily exported
- Treaty of Rapallo 1922
- Zinoviev letter 1924

War Communism and New Economic Policy 1918–21

▶ *Why was War Communism introduced in 1918 and replaced by NEP in 1921?*

War Communism is best understood as a series of harshly restrictive economic measures that Lenin began to introduce in the summer of 1918 to replace the system of state capitalism that the Bolsheviks had operated during their first nine months in power. The chief reason for adopting War Communism was the desperate situation created by the civil war. Lenin judged that the White menace could be met only by an intensification of authority in those regions which the Reds controlled (approximately 30 of the 50 provinces of European Russia). Every aspect of life, social, political and economic, had to be subordinated to the task of winning the civil war. Clerics were attacked as part of a campaign authorised by Lenin that promoted atheism as the new state belief system, prohibited public worship, and ordered the churches to be closed and their clergy arrested.

War Communism and industry

The first step towards War Communism as a formal policy was taken in June 1918 with the issuing of the **Decree on Nationalisation**, which, within two years, brought practically all the major industrial enterprises in Russia under central government control. However, nationalisation by itself did nothing to increase production. It was imposed at a time of severe industrial disruption, which had been caused initially by the strains of the war of 1914–17 but which worsened during the civil war. Military needs were given priority in the distribution of supplies, which resulted in many industries being starved of essential resources. The situation was made more serious by the factories being deprived of workers. This was a consequence both of conscription into the Red Army and of the flight from the urban areas of large numbers of inhabitants, who left either in search of food or to escape the fighting. The populations of Petrograd and Moscow dropped by a half between 1918 and 1921.

The problems for industry were deepened by hyperinflation. The scarcity of goods and the government's policy of continuing to print banknotes effectively destroyed the value of money. In desperation, the use of money was abolished altogether. All this meant that while War Communism tightened the Bolshevik grip on industry, it did not lead to economic growth. Table 2.2 (page 50) shows the failure of War Communism in economic terms.

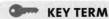 **KEY TERM**

Decree on Nationalisation The takeover by the state of the larger industrial concerns in Russia.

Table 2.2 Comparison of industrial output in 1913 and 1921

Output	1913	1921
Base index of gross industrial output	100	31
Base index of large-scale industrial output	100	21
Electricity (million kWh)	2039	520
Coal (millions of tonnes)	29.0	8.9
Oil (millions of tonnes)	9.2	3.8
Steel (millions of tonnes)	4.30	0.18
Imports (at 1913 rouble value, millions)	1374	208
Exports (at 1913 rouble value, millions)	1520	20

The impact of War Communism on agriculture

For Lenin, a major purpose of War Communism was to tighten government control over agriculture and force the peasants to provide more food. But the peasants proved difficult to bring into line. As a naturally conservative class, they were resistant to central government, whether tsarist or Bolshevik. The government blamed the resistance on the **kulaks** who, it was claimed, were hoarding their grain stocks in order to keep prices artificially high. This was untrue. There was little hoarding. The plain truth was that the peasants saw no point in producing more food until the government, which had become the main grain purchaser, was willing to pay a fair price for it.

Grain requisitioning

However, exasperated by the peasants' refusal to conform, the government condemned them as counter-revolutionaries and resorted to coercion. **Cheka** requisition units were sent into the countryside to take the grain by force. In August 1918, the people's commissar for food issued an order requiring that every requisition detachment should consist of 'not less than 75 men and two or three machine guns'. Between 1918 and 1921, the requisition squads systematically terrorised the countryside. Lenin gave instructions that 100 *kulaks* were to be hanged in public in order to terrify the population 'for hundreds of miles around'.

Yet the result was largely the reverse of the one intended. Even less food became available. Knowing that any surplus would simply be confiscated, the peasants produced only the barest minimum to feed themselves and their families. Nevertheless, throughout the period of War Communism, the Bolsheviks persisted in their belief that grain hoarding was the basic problem. Official reports continued to speak of 'concealment everywhere, in the hopes of selling grain to town speculators at fabulous prices'.

Famine

By 1921, a combination of requisitioning, drought and the general disruption of war had created a national famine. The grain harvests in 1920 and 1921

SOURCE B

In what ways do Source B and the map on this page indicate the severity of the 1921 famine?

A pile of unburied bodies in a cemetery in Buzuluk, grim testimony to the famine that struck the region in 1921. Similar tragedies were common across Russia, reducing some areas to cannibalism.

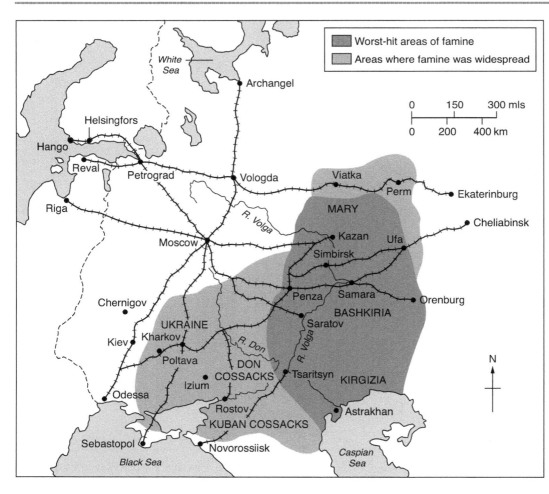

Areas of Russia worst hit by famine. © Sir Martin Gilbert, 2007

Worst-hit areas of famine

Areas where famine was widespread

produced less than half that gathered in 1913. Even *Pravda* admitted in 1921 that one in five of the population was starving. Matters became so desperate that the Bolsheviks, while careful to blame the *kulaks* and the Whites, were prepared to admit there was a famine and to accept foreign assistance. A number of countries supplied Russia with aid. The outstanding contribution came from the USA, whose **American Relief Association** provided food for some 10 million Russians. Despite such efforts, foreign help came too late to prevent mass starvation. Of the 10 million fatalities of the civil war period, over half had starved to death.

Bolshevik attitudes towards War Communism

It was clear that the grim economic situation had undermined the original justification for War Communism. During its operation, industrial and agricultural production had fallen alarmingly. Yet, this did not mean the policy necessarily became unpopular among the Bolsheviks themselves. Indeed, there were many in the party who, far from regarding it as a temporary measure to meet an extreme situation, believed that it represented true revolutionary communism. A representative figure was the party's leading economist, **Nicolai Bukharin**, who urged that War Communism should be retained as the permanent economic policy of the Bolshevik government. He saw it as true socialism in action since it involved:

- centralisation of industry
- ending of private ownership
- persecution of the peasants.

Lenin himself clung to War Communism as long as he could. However, the failure of the economy to recover and the scale of the famine led him to consider possible alternatives. He was finally convinced of the need for change by widespread anti-Bolshevik risings in 1920–1. These were a direct reaction against the brutality of requisitioning. One in particular, the Kronstadt Rising of 1921, was the most serious challenge to Bolshevik control since the October Revolution.

The Kronstadt Rising 1921

As long as unrest was confined to the peasants and to the Bolsheviks' political enemies, it was a containable problem. What became deeply worrying to Lenin in 1921 was the development of opposition to War Communism within the party and among the workers. Two prominent Bolsheviks, **Alexander Shlyapnikov** and **Alexandra Kollontai**, led a 'workers' opposition' group to protest against the excesses of War Communism; they accused the party leaders of losing touch with the proletariat.

Taking their cue from the workers' opposition, thousands of Petrograd workers crossed to the naval base on Kronstadt, an island a few miles offshore in the Gulf of Finland, whose sailors had played an important role in defending the

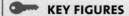

KEY TERM

American Relief Association Formed in 1921 by future US President Herbert Hoover to provide food and medical supplies for post-war Europe.

KEY FIGURES

Nikolai Bukharin (1888–1938)

At this stage, a supporter of Lenin's harsh treatment of the peasants; later he modified his approach, only to become a purge victim under Stalin.

Alexander Shlyapnikov (1885–1937)

The labour commissar, equivalent to a minister of labour, responsible for industry and its workers.

Alexandra Kollontai (1872–1952)

An outstanding intellectual and agitator in the Bolshevik Party.

Petrograd Bolsheviks in 1917. There, by February 1921, the workers had linked up with the sailors and dockers to demonstrate for greater freedom. They demanded that in a workers' state, which the Bolshevik government claimed Soviet Russia to be, the workers should be better, not worse, off than in tsarist times. They published a programme, headed 'What are we fighting for?' in which they itemised their disillusionment with the government (see Source C).

SOURCE C

From 'What are we fighting for?' February 1921, quoted in Richard Pipes, *Russia Under the Bolshevik Regime 1919–24*, Collins Harvill, 1994, pp. 384–5.

It has become ever more clear, and is now self-evident, that the Russian Communist Party is not the protector of the working people that it claims to be, that the interests of the working people are foreign to it, and that having gained power, its only fear is of losing it, and hence that all means are permissible to that end: slander, violence, deception, murder, revenge on the families of those who have revolted. The long suffering of the toilers has drawn to an end. The current revolt finally offers the toilers a chance to have their freely elected, functioning soviets, free of violent Party pressures, to refashion the state-run trade unions into free associations of workers, peasants, and the working intelligentsia. At last the police baton of the Communist autocracy is smashed.

According to Source C, why have the workers become disillusioned with the Soviet central government?

The Kronstadt Manifesto

In an attempt to pacify the strikers, Lenin sent a team of political commissars to Kronstadt. They were greeted with loud jeers and had to beat a humiliating retreat. Early in March, the sailors and workers of Kronstadt set up a fifteen-man revolutionary committee, which forwarded their grievances in a manifesto to the government, which included the following demands:

1. New elections to the soviets, to be held by secret ballot.
2. Freedom of speech and of the press.
3. Freedom of assembly.
4. Rights for trade unions and release of imprisoned trade unionists.
5. Ending of the right of Communists to be the only permitted socialist political party.
6. The release of left-wing political prisoners.
7. Ending of special food rations for Communist Party members.
8. Freedom for individuals to bring food from the country into the towns without confiscation.
9. Withdrawal of political commissars from the factories.
10. Ending of the Communist Party monopoly of the press.

The importance of the Kronstadt Rising

It was not the demands themselves that frightened the Bolsheviks; it was the people who had drafted them: the workers and sailors of Kronstadt. They had been the great supporters of the Bolsheviks in 1917. Trotsky had referred to them as the 'heroes of the revolution'. It was these same heroes who were now insisting that the Bolshevik government return to the promises that had inspired the revolution. For all the efforts of the Bolshevik press to brand the Kronstadt protesters as White agents, the truth was that they were genuine socialists who had previously been wholly loyal to Lenin's government, but who had become appalled by the regime's betrayal of the workers' cause.

The rising crushed

Angered by the growing number of strikers and their increasing demands, Trotsky ordered the Red Army under **General Tukhachevsky** to cross the late winter ice linking Kronstadt to Petrograd and crush 'the tools of former tsarist generals and agents of the interventionists'. An ultimatum was issued to the demonstrators. When this was rejected, Tukhachevsky gave the signal for his force, made up of Red Army units and *Cheka* detachments, to attack. After an artillery bombardment, 60,000 Red troops stormed the Kronstadt base. The sailors and workers resisted fiercely. Savage fighting occurred before they were finally overcome.

Aftermath of the rising

Immediately after the rising had been suppressed, the ringleaders who had survived were condemned as White reactionaries and shot. In the succeeding months the *Cheka* hunted down and executed those rebels who had escaped from Kronstadt. Lenin justified the severity on the grounds that the rising had been the work of the bourgeois enemies of the October Revolution. However, he took the lessons of Kronstadt to heart. To avoid the scandal and embarrassment of another open challenge to his party and government, he decided it was time to soften the severity of War Communism.

At the tenth conference of the Communist Party, which opened in March 1921, Lenin declared that the Kronstadt Rising had 'lit up reality like a lightning flash'. This was the prelude to his introduction of NEP, a move intended to tackle the famine and, in doing so, to lessen the opposition to Bolshevism. However, this was to be a purely economic adjustment. Lenin was not prepared to make political concessions: Communist control was to be made even tighter.

Lenin's great turn: the New Economic Policy

As with the policy of War Communism which it replaced, NEP was intended by Lenin primarily to meet Russia's urgent need for food. Whatever the purity of the revolutionary theory behind War Communism, it had clearly failed to deliver the goods. State terror had not forced the peasants into producing larger grain stocks. Pragmatic as ever, Lenin judged that if the peasants could not be forced, they must be persuaded (see Source D).

SOURCE D

**From Lenin's speech to the party congress, April 1921, quoted in V.I. Lenin,
Collected Works of Lenin, volume XXXII, Lawrence & Wishart, 1959, p. 341.**

*We must try to satisfy the demands of the peasants who are dissatisfied,
discontented, and cannot be otherwise. In essence the small farmer can be
satisfied with two things. First of all, there must be a certain amount of freedom
for the small private proprietor; and, secondly, commodities and products must
be provided … The effect will be the revival of the petty bourgeoisie and of
capitalism [but] the proletarian regime is in no danger as long as the proletariat
firmly holds power in its hands.*

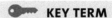

According to Lenin in
Source D, what measures
are necessary to preserve
his regime from danger?

Despite the deep disagreements that were soon to emerge within the Bolshevik
Party over NEP, the grim economic situation in Russia led the delegates to give
unanimous support to Lenin's proposals when they were first introduced. The
decree making NEP official government policy was published in the spring of
1921. Its essential features were:

- Central economic control to be relaxed by allowing more decisions to be
  taken at a local level.
- The requisitioning of grain to be abandoned and replaced by a **tax in kind**.
- The peasants to be allowed to keep their food surpluses and sell them for a
  profit.
- Public markets to be restored.
- Money, which had been abolished under War Communism, to be
  reintroduced as a means of trading, replacing the inefficient practice of
  bartering of goods which the peasants had been reduced to using.

KEY TERM

Tax in kind The
surrendering by the peasant
of a certain amount of his
produce, equivalent to a fixed
sum of money. This replaced
requisitioning, the seizure of
all the peasant's stocks.

Lenin was aware that the new policy marked a retreat from the principle of
state control of the economy. Knowing how uneasy this made some Bolsheviks,
Lenin stressed that NEP was only a temporary concession to capitalism. He
emphasised that the party still retained control of 'the commanding heights
of the economy', by which he meant large-scale industry, banking and foreign
trade. He added: 'we are prepared to let the peasants have their little bit of
capitalism as long as we keep the power'.

Bolshevik divisions over NEP

The adoption of NEP showed that the Bolshevik government since 1917 had
been unable to create a successful economy along purely ideological lines. Lenin
admitted as much. He told party members that it made no sense for Bolsheviks
to pretend that they could pursue an economic policy which took no account of
the circumstances. Lenin's realism demanded that political theory take second
place to economic necessity. It was this that troubled the members of the party,
such as Trotsky, who had regarded the repressive measures of War Communism
as the proper revolutionary strategy for the Bolsheviks to follow. Trotsky
described NEP as 'the first sign of the degeneration of Bolshevism'. A main

complaint of Trotsky and other objectors was that the reintroduction of money and private trading was creating a new class of profiteers whom they derisively dubbed **Nepmen**.

NEP became such a contentious issue among the Bolsheviks that Lenin took firm steps to prevent the party being torn apart over it. At the same party congress in 1921, at which NEP had been formally announced, he introduced a resolution 'On Party Unity', which forbade members from engaging in **factionalism**, Lenin's term for those disloyal Bolsheviks who opposed central party policy. The object of this proposal was to stifle objections to NEP by preventing so-called 'factions' within the party from criticising government or central committee decisions. By making acceptance of NEP a matter of basic loyalty to the government and party, Lenin made it impossible for doubting members to come out and openly challenge the policy, since this would appear tantamount to challenging the revolution itself.

Economic results of NEP

In the end, the most powerful reason for the party to accept NEP proved to be a statistical one. The production figures suggested that the policy worked. By the time of Lenin's death in 1924, the Soviet economy had begun to make a marked recovery. Table 2.3 indicates the scale of this.

Table 2.3 Growth under NEP 1921–4

Output	1921	1922	1923	1924
Grain harvest (millions of tonnes)	37.6	50.3	56.6	51.4
Value of factory output (roubles, millions)	2004	2619	4005	4660
Electricity (millions of kWh)	520	775	1146	1562
Average monthly wage of urban workers (roubles)	10.2	12.2	15.9	20.8

Lenin's claim that under the NEP the Bolsheviks would still control 'the commanding heights of the economy' was shown to be substantially correct by the census of 1923. Table 2.4 and Figure 2.1 indicate that, in broad terms, NEP had produced an economic balance between private traders, the state and **co-operatives**: while agriculture and trade were largely in private hands, the state dominated Russian industry.

Table 2.4 Balance between main types of enterprise

Enterprise	Proportion of industrial workforce (%)	Average number of workers in each factory
Private enterprises	12	2
State enterprises	85	155
Co-operatives	3	15

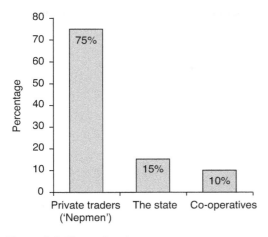

Figure 2.1 Share of trade.

The NEP was not a total success. Its opponents criticised it on the grounds that the balance it appeared to have achieved was notional rather than real. The fact was that industry failed to expand as rapidly as agriculture. The Nepmen may have done well, but there was high unemployment in the urban areas. NEP would continue to be a matter of dispute and division among the Bolsheviks long after Lenin's death. Yet despite the rows over it, it remained official Soviet policy until it was finally jettisoned by Stalin in 1928 when introducing his collectivisation schemes (see page 87).

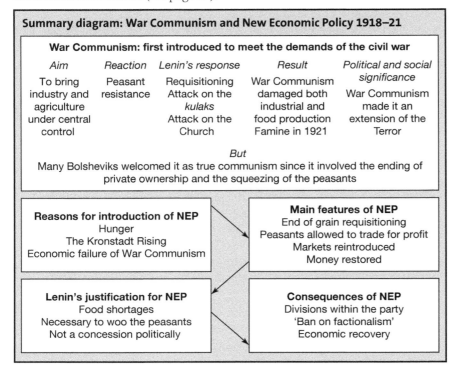

Summary diagram: War Communism and New Economic Policy 1918–21

War Communism: first introduced to meet the demands of the civil war

Aim	Reaction	Lenin's response	Result	Political and social significance
To bring industry and agriculture under central control	Peasant resistance	Requisitioning Attack on the *kulaks* Attack on the Church	War Communism damaged both industrial and food production Famine in 1921	War Communism made it an extension of the Terror

But
Many Bolsheviks welcomed it as true communism since it involved the ending of private ownership and the squeezing of the peasants

Reasons for introduction of NEP
Hunger
The Kronstadt Rising
Economic failure of War Communism

Main features of NEP
End of grain requisitioning
Peasants allowed to trade for profit
Markets reintroduced
Money restored

Lenin's justification for NEP
Food shortages
Necessary to woo the peasants
Not a concession politically

Consequences of NEP
Divisions within the party
'Ban on factionalism'
Economic recovery

5 Lenin, government and the Communist Party

▶ *How did Lenin approach the problem of governing Russia?*

▶ *What legacy did Lenin leave Soviet Russia?*

Lenin's methods of government

Such was the scale of the problems Lenin and the Bolsheviks faced after taking power that they were obliged to become increasingly authoritarian and oppressive in order to retain control. So severe was the suppression by the Bolsheviks of their internal enemies that it could be said that Lenin ruled through terror. Indeed, his methods of control earned the description the Red Terror. The chief instruments by which this terror was imposed were the *Cheka* and the Red Army.

The *Cheka*

Essentially the *Cheka* was a better organised and more efficient form of the tsarist secret police, at whose hands nearly every Bolshevik activist had suffered. Its express purpose was to destroy '**counter-revolution** and sabotage', terms that could be stretched to cover anything of which the Bolsheviks disapproved. This state police force had been created in December 1917 under the direction of **Felix Dzerzhinsky**. Lenin found him the ideal choice to lead the fight against the enemies of the revolution. Dzerzhinsky never allowed finer feelings or compassion to deter him from the task of destroying the enemies of Bolshevism. His remorseless attitude was shown in the various directives that issued from the *Cheka* headquarters in Moscow (see Source E).

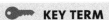

KEY TERM

Counter-revolution
A term used by the Bolsheviks to cover actions or ideas they regarded as reactionary and opposed to progress.

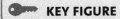

KEY FIGURE

Felix Dzerzhinsky (1877–1927)

An intellectual of Polish aristocratic background who sought to atone for his privileged origins by total dedication to the Bolshevik cause.

? According to Source E, what does Dzerzhinsky understand by the term 'revolutionary justice'?

SOURCE E

From a directive issued by Felix Dzerzhinsky, December 1917, quoted in G. Legett, *The Cheka: Lenin's Political Police*, Oxford University Press, 1981, p. 17.

Our Revolution is in danger. Do not concern yourselves with the forms of revolutionary justice. We have no need for justice now. Now we have need of a battle to the death! It is war now – face to face. I propose, I demand the use of the revolutionary sword which will put an end to all counter-revolutionaries. Do not demand incriminating evidence to prove that the prisoner has opposed the Soviet government by force or words. Your first duty is to ask him to which class he belongs, what are his origins, his education, his occupation. These questions should decide the fate of the prisoner.

The *Cheka*, which was to change its name several times over the years, but never its essential character, remains the outstanding expression of Bolshevik ruthlessness. Operating as a law unto itself, and answerable only to Lenin, it

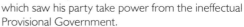

Profile: V.I. Lenin

1870	Lenin born Vladimir Ilyich Ulyanov to a family of Jewish ancestry
1897	Exiled to Siberia, took the alias Lenin
1900	Joined the Marxist Social Democratic (SD) Party
1903	Led the Bolshevik breakaway movement in the SD Party
1917	Led the Bolsheviks in the October Revolution
1917–22	Led the Bolsheviks in consolidating their hold on Russia
1924	Died after being incapacitated for two years by strokes

Background

A natural contrarian, Lenin was confirmed in his hatred of tsardom by the execution of his brother in 1887 for an attempted assassination of the tsar. On the authorities' list of 'dangerous persons' from the age of seventeen, Lenin became a powerful revolutionary writer. In 1903, he led the Bolsheviks in a breakaway movement from the Marxist Social Democratic (SD) Party, which he had joined five years earlier.

The October Revolution

In exile for most the period 1906–17, Lenin returned to Petrograd in April 1917 following the February Revolution. After a desperate six months of preparation, during which the Bolsheviks were almost destroyed, Lenin was the inspiration behind the successful coup in October which saw his party take power from the ineffectual Provisional Government.

Creator of the Soviet state

Over the next five years, Lenin, against great odds, proceeded to create a new Soviet state, imposing Bolshevik rule by severe authoritarian means, overcoming his internal opponents in a savage civil war and resisting the attempts of a number of foreign powers to crush Bolshevism. Thwarted in his plans to develop a socialist economy, Lenin was forced to return to capitalist methods in his New Economic Policy, introduced in 1921, though he accompanied this by still sterner prohibitions on political freedom.

Already weakened by an attempt on his life in 1918, Lenin suffered a number of strokes which from 1922 left him increasingly incapable of direct government. Having given no clear indication as to who should follow him as leader, he left the way open for a power struggle over the succession. At his death in 1924, Lenin bequeathed the Soviet state a legacy of totalitarianism, economic experimentation and Soviet hostility towards the outside world.

was granted unlimited powers of arrest, detention and torture, which it used in the most arbitrary way. It was the main instrument by which Lenin and his successors terrorised the Russian people into subservience.

The murder of the Romanovs

It was the *Cheka* who were responsible for the murder of the fallen tsar. In July 1918, a group of SRs assassinated the German ambassador as a protest against the Treaty of Brest-Litovsk. A month later an attempt was made on Lenin's life, followed by the murder of the Petrograd chairman of the *Cheka*. These incidents were made the pretext for intensifying Bolshevik terror across Russia. It was in this atmosphere that a local *Cheka* detachment, on Lenin's personal order, executed the ex-tsar and his family in Ekaterinburg in July 1918.

Class war

The summary shooting of the Romanovs without trial was typical of the manner in which the *Cheka* went about its business throughout Russia. In accordance with Dzerzhinsky's instructions, all pretence of legality was abandoned; the basic rules relating to evidence and proof of guilt no longer applied. Persecution was directed not simply against individuals, but against whole classes.

Some Bolsheviks were uneasy about the relentless savagery of the *Cheka* but there were no serious attempts to restrict its powers. The majority of party members accepted that the hazardous situation justified the severity of the repression. The foreign interventions and the civil war, fought out against the background of famine and social disorder, threatened the existence of the Communist Party and the government. This had the effect of quashing criticism of the *Cheka*'s methods. Dzerzhinsky declared that the proletarian revolution could not be saved except by 'exterminating the enemies of the working class'.

Labour camps

One of the most sinister developments was Dzerzhinsky's setting up of forced labour camps in which 'enemies of the revolution', a blanket term for all those the Bolsheviks considered to be actual or potential enemies, were incarcerated. By the time of Lenin's death there were 315 such camps. Developed as part of the Red Terror, they held White prisoners of war, uncooperative peasants, and political prisoners, such as SRs, who were considered a threat to Soviet authority. The regime in the camps was deliberately harsh; acute hunger and beatings were the everyday lot of the prisoners.

Show trials

The *Cheka* was also involved in the arrest of those subsequently prosecuted in a series of show trials. On Lenin's instruction, between April and August 1922, leading members of Russia's outlawed parties and of the Moscow clergy were put on humiliating public trial, before being sentenced to imprisonment. Lenin's authority was also behind an accompanying campaign to politicise the law. Under the new regime, the law was operated not as a means of protecting society and the individual but as an extension of political control. Lenin declared that the task of the courts was to apply revolutionary justice. 'The court is not to eliminate terror but to legitimise it.'

The Red Army

The work of Dzerzhinsky and the *Cheka* was complemented by that of Trotsky and the Red Army. More than any other factor, Trotsky's creation of the Red Army explains the survival of Lenin's government after 1917. This has obvious reference to the Reds' triumph in the civil war (see page 40), but the Red Army also became the means by which Lenin's Communists imposed their authority on the population at large. There was a sense in which Lenin's Russia was a militarised society. The insistence on obedience to authority, the punitive treatment of dissidents and doubters, and a constant call for citizens to be prepared to sacrifice themselves for the common good; these were the features of Lenin's Russia.

Lenin had always accepted the necessity of terror as an instrument of political control. Before 1917 he had often made it clear that a Marxist revolution could not survive if it was not prepared to smash its enemies: 'Coercion is necessary for the transition from capitalism to socialism. There is absolutely no contradiction between Soviet democracy and the exercise of dictatorial powers.'

Party authority

The critical consideration is that, whatever the form of government after 1917 might have appeared to be (see page 32), the reality was that Lenin governed Russia through the Communist Party, which became increasingly subservient to him. Having no clear plan before they came to power as to how they would govern in practice, the Bolsheviks resorted by default to government by a series of committees, each one responsible for a particular activity. But, since all the government committees were composed of, and dominated, by Lenin's nominees, the party under him became the sole source of authority. In Lenin's thinking, the role of the government he led was not to win large-scale public backing, but to direct the revolution from above, regardless of the scale of popular support. Moreover, in keeping with his notion of democratic centralism, it was the role of the leaders to lead, the duty of the party members to follow. Lenin defined it in the terms expressed in Source F.

SOURCE F

From Lenin's article 'What is to be done?', 1902, quoted in V.I. Lenin, *Collected Works of Lenin*, volume XXI, Lawrence & Wishart, 1959, p. 243.

Classes are led by parties, and parties are led by individuals who are called leaders. This is the ABC. The will of a class is sometimes fulfilled by a dictator. Soviet socialist democracy is not in the least incompatible with individual rule and dictatorship. What is necessary is individual rule, the recognition of the dictatorial powers of one man. All phrases about equal rights are nonsense.

According to Lenin's statement in Source F, what is the relationship between the Communist Party and its leader?

Lenin's legacy as government and party leader

Between 1922 and 1924 Lenin suffered a series of strokes which left him paralysed and unable to speak. Because he was so unwell during what proved to be the final two years of his life, he was unable to prepare for his succession. He gave no clear indication of what form of government should follow him. There were suggestions that he favoured a collective leadership of the **USSR**, but this cannot be known for sure since he left no precise instructions.

Possibly aware of the difficulties he was leaving, Lenin in his last writings in 1923 warned the party and government against losing their revolutionary character by becoming mired in routine and bureaucracy: 'Our state apparatus is so deplorable, so wretched.' It was a sign of his failing grasp that he did not realise that he more than anyone was responsible for the growth of the bureaucracy which he now condemned. An essential aspect of Lenin's leadership of Russia was that he regarded himself primarily as an international revolutionary.

KEY TERM

USSR Union of Soviet Socialist Republics (often shortened to Soviet Union), the official title for Communist Russia, adopted in 1922.

Originally, he had expected that the successful Bolshevik seizure of power in October 1917 would be the first stage in a worldwide proletarian uprising. When this proved mistaken, he had to adapt to a situation in which Bolshevik Russia became an isolated revolutionary state, beset by internal and external enemies.

Lenin responded by making another major adjustment to Marxist theory. Marx had taught that proletarian revolution would be an international class movement. Yet the 1917 revolution had been the work not of a class but of a party and had been restricted to one nation. Lenin explained this in terms of a **delayed revolution**; the international rising would occur at some point in the future. In the interim, Soviet Russia must consolidate its own individual revolution. This placed the Bolshevik government and its international agency, the Comintern, in an ambiguous position. What was their essential role to be? At Lenin's death in 1924, this question – whether Soviet Russia's primary aim was world revolution or national survival – was still unresolved.

Lenin's legacy

At his death in 1924 Lenin left Russia the following legacy:

- The one-party state – all parties other than the Bolsheviks had been outlawed by 1922.
- The bureaucratic state – despite the Bolsheviks' original belief in the withering away of the state, central power increased under Lenin and the number of government institutions and officials grew.
- The police state – the *Cheka* was the first of a series of secret police organisations in Soviet Russia whose task was imposing government control over the people.
- Democratic centralism – the requirement that party members obey and act on orders handed down by the party leaders.
- The ban on factionalism – prevented criticism of leadership within the party, in effect a prohibition of free speech.
- The destruction of the trade unions – with Lenin's encouragement, Trotsky had destroyed the independence of the trade unions with the result that the Russian workers were entirely at the mercy of the state.
- The politicising of the law – under Lenin the law was operated not as a means of protecting society and the individual, but as an extension of political control.
- The system of purges and show trials which were to become a notorious feature of Stalinism (see page 112) were created under Lenin.
- Labour camps – at the time of Lenin's death there were 315 such camps.
- Prohibition of public worship.
- The USSR's attitude towards the outside world based on the notion of delayed revolution.

Essentially, the basic apparatus of Stalin's later oppression (see page 108) was in place at Lenin's death.

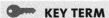

KEY TERM

Delayed revolution
According to Lenin, the gap between the workers' gaining consciousness of their latent power and their organised overthrow of their bourgeois oppressors.

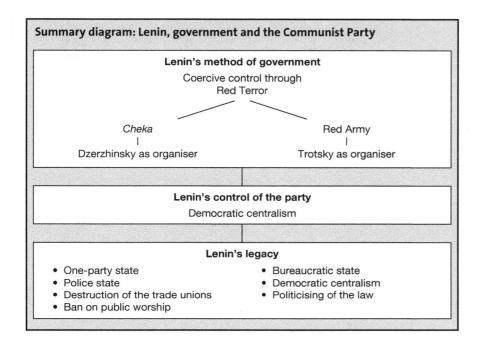

Summary diagram: Lenin, government and the Communist Party

Lenin's method of government
Coercive control through
Red Terror

Cheka
|
Dzerzhinsky as organiser

Red Army
|
Trotsky as organiser

Lenin's control of the party
Democratic centralism

Lenin's legacy
- One-party state
- Police state
- Destruction of the trade unions
- Ban on public worship
- Bureaucratic state
- Democratic centralism
- Politicising of the law

Chapter summary

After taking power in 1917, Lenin's Bolsheviks issued a number of decrees aimed at consolidating their tenuous hold. Appreciating that they were a minority party, they silenced opposition by dissolving the Constituent Assembly and outlawing all other parties. Lenin was also prepared to accept a humiliating peace with Germany since he judged that the Bolshevik regime could not survive if the war with Germany continued. Lenin's relentlessness at home led to a bitter civil war with the Whites and Greens, which the Reds eventually won through superior organisation and morale. Their victory, which owed much to Trotsky's military brilliance, was repeated in the repelling of a series of foreign interventions.

Having tried to tackle Russia's persistent food shortage by subjecting the peasants to the confiscatory policy of War Communism, Lenin changed course and introduced the New Economic Policy (NEP), a return to a market economy, in an attempt to incentivise them into producing more food. Such concessions to the peasantry angered some Bolsheviks, but the strength of Lenin's control over party and government meant that he was never seriously challenged. At his death in 1924, Lenin, by means of coercion, of which the *Cheka* was the principal instrument, had established a one-party, authoritarian Soviet state.

Refresher questions

Use these questions to remind yourself of the key material covered in this chapter.

1 What methods did Lenin use to consolidate Bolshevik control after 1917?

2 Why was Lenin prepared to accept the German terms in the Treaty of Brest-Litovsk?

3 Was the Bolshevik victory a result of Red strength or White weakness?

4 How big a factor was morale in the Reds' victory?

5 How much did the victory of the Reds in the civil war owe to Trotsky?

6 What influence did the civil war have on the character of Bolshevism?

7 Why did the foreign interventions fail?

8 What was Lenin's attitude towards international revolution?

9 What role did Trotsky play in the Red Terror?

10 What was the impact of War Communism on Soviet industry and agriculture?

11 In what ways was War Communism an extension of the Red Terror?

12 Why was the Kronstadt Rising so disturbing for Lenin and the Bolsheviks?

13 What was NEP meant to achieve?

14 How did Lenin preserve party unity over NEP?

15 What were the main features of Lenin's legacy?

 Question practice

ESSAY QUESTIONS

1 'The main reason why the Reds were able to overcome their opponents in the civil war of 1918–20 was the military leadership of Trotsky.' Explain why you agree or disagree with this view.

2 To what extent did their repelling of the foreign interventions help to consolidate the Bolsheviks' hold on power?

3 How far was the Kronstadt Rising in 1921 a sign that War Communism had failed?

4 How successful was NEP in solving the problems faced by Lenin's government?

SOURCE ANALYSIS QUESTIONS

1 With reference to Sources C (**page 53**) and D (**page 55**) and your understanding of the historical context, which of these two sources is more valuable in explaining why Lenin replaced War Communism with NEP in 1921?

2 With reference to Sources C (**page 53**), D (**page 55**) and E (**page 58**) and your understanding of the historical context, assess the value of these sources to a historian studying the methods by which Lenin exerted control of Russia between 1917 and 1921.

CHAPTER 3

Stalin's rise to power 1924–9

When Lenin, the Bolshevik leader, died he left many problems but no obvious successor. Few Russian Communists gave thought to Stalin as a likely leader. Yet five years later, after a bitter power struggle, it was Stalin who had outmanoeuvred his rivals and established his authority over the party and the nation. How he achieved this is the subject of this chapter, whose main themes are:

★ Stalin's record as a revolutionary before 1924

★ The power struggle within the Communist Party

★ 'Permanent revolution' versus 'socialism in one country'

★ Stalin's defeat of Trotsky and the Left

★ Stalin's defeat of the Right

Key dates

1924	Death of Lenin	**1926**	Trotsky joined Kamenev and Zinoviev in bloc
	Politburo opted for collective leadership	**1927**	Trotsky expelled from CPSU
1925	Trotsky lost his position as war commissar	**1928**	Stalin attacked the Right
	Kamenev and Zinoviev headed United Opposition	**1929**	Right finally defeated by Stalin
			Trotsky exiled from the USSR

1 Stalin's record as a revolutionary before 1924

▶ *How significant a role as a revolutionary had Stalin played before 1924?*

Stalin's background and character

Stalin, meaning 'man of steel', was not his real name. It was simply the alias he adopted in 1912, the last in a series of 40 that Joseph Vissarionovich Djugashvili had used to avoid detection as a revolutionary. He was born a **Georgian**, in

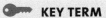

KEY TERM

Georgian People who inhabit the rugged land of Georgia. Strictly speaking, Stalin was Ossetian, a separate ethnic group living in northern Georgia. However, he always described himself as Georgian.

a poverty-stricken province in the south of the Russian Empire. His drunken father eked out a miserable existence as a cobbler. There have been suggestions that both Stalin's admiration of all things Russian and his contempt for middle-class intellectuals derived from a sense of resentment over his humble non-Russian origins.

Stalin's mother was a particularly devout woman and it was largely through her influence that her son was enrolled as a student in a Georgian Orthodox seminary in Tiflis (Tbilisi) the capital of Georgia. This did not show religious fervour on Stalin's part. The fact was that at this time in imperial Russia attendance at a church academy was the only way to obtain a Russian-style education, an essential requirement for anyone from the provinces who had ambition. Stalin was attracted less by theology than by the revolutionary ideas with which he came into contact.

Stalin's involvement in the Georgian resistance movement, agitating against tsarist control, led to his expulsion from the seminary in 1899. His anti-government activities drew him into the Social Democratic Workers' Party. From the time he left the seminary to the revolution of 1917 Stalin was a committed follower of Lenin. He threw himself into the task of raising funds for the Bolsheviks; his specialities were bank hold-ups and train robberies. With Lenin's backing, Stalin had risen by 1912 to become one of the six members of the Central Committee. He had also helped to found the party's newspaper, *Pravda*. By 1917, Stalin had been arrested eight times and had been sentenced to various periods of imprisonment and exile. Afterwards he tended to despise those revolutionaries who had escaped such experiences by fleeing to the relative comfort of self-imposed exile abroad.

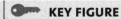
There was once a common view among historians that Stalin's pre-1924 career was unimportant. They tended to accepted **Nicolai Sukhanov**'s 1922 description of him as a 'dull, grey blank'. But research into the Soviet archives over the past 25 years has indicated that the notion of Stalin as a nonentity before 1924 is the opposite of the truth. A leading British authority, Robert Service, has shown that Stalin was very highly regarded by Lenin and played a central role in the Bolshevik Party. Another British scholar, Simon Sebag Montefiore, has stressed that far from being a grey blank, Stalin was an indispensable Bolshevik activist before 1917. Lenin had been impressed by Stalin's organising ability, insensitivity to suffering and willingness to obey orders. He once described him as 'that wonderful Georgian', a reference to his work as an agitator among the non-Russian peoples.

The October Revolution and civil war

Having spent the war years, 1914–17, in exile in Siberia, Stalin returned to Petrograd in March 1917. His role in the October Revolution is not wholly clear. Official accounts, written after he had taken power, were a mixture of distortion and invention, with any unflattering episodes totally omitted. What is reasonably certain is that Stalin was loyal to Lenin after the latter had returned to Petrograd in April 1917 and instructed the Bolsheviks to abandon all co-operation with other parties and devote themselves to preparing for a seizure of power. As a Leninist, Stalin was opposed to the **October deserters**, such as Kamenev and Zinoviev (see page 25).

During the period of crisis and civil war that accompanied the efforts of the Bolsheviks to consolidate their authority after 1917, Stalin's non-Russian background proved invaluable. His knowledge of the minority peoples of the old Russian Empire led to his being appointed **Commissar for Nationalities**. Lenin believed that Stalin's toughness qualified him for this role. As commissar, Stalin became the ruthless Bolshevik organiser for the whole of the Caucasus region (see the map on page 145) during the civil war from 1918 to 1920. This led to a number of disputes with Trotsky, the commissar for war. Superficially the quarrels were about strategy and tactics, but at a deeper level they were a clash of personalities and proved to be the beginning of a deep rivalry between the two men.

Lenin's testament

Although Stalin had been totally loyal to Lenin, there were two particular occasions when he had aroused Lenin's anger. After the civil war had ended, Stalin had been off-hand in discussions with the representatives from Georgia. Lenin, anxious to gain the support of the national minorities for the Bolshevik regime, had to intervene personally to prevent the Georgians leaving in a pique. On another occasion, in a more directly personal matter, Lenin learned from his wife, Krupskaya, that in a row over the Georgian question Stalin had subjected her to 'a storm of the coarsest abuse', telling her to keep her nose out of state affairs, and calling her 'a whore'. The very day that Lenin was informed of this, 22 December 1922, he dictated his **'testament'**, as a direct response.

Lenin's main criticism of Stalin read: 'Comrade Stalin, since becoming General Secretary of the Party in 1922, has concentrated enormous power in his hands; and I am not sure he always knows how to exercise that power with sufficient caution.' In a later postscript, Lenin urged the comrades to think about ways of removing Stalin from the position of general secretary (see Source A).

SOURCE A

From the postscript to Lenin's testament, January 1923, quoted in Robert Service, *Stalin: A Biography*, Macmillan, 2004, p. 209.

Stalin is too crude; and this defect, which is wholly bearable in relations among ourselves becomes intolerable in the post of General Secretary. I therefore make a proposal for comrades to think of a way to remove Stalin and in his place appoint someone else who is distinguished from comrade Stalin in all other respects through having the single superior feature of being more patient, more loyal, more courteous and more attentive to comrades, less capricious, etc.

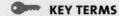

KEY TERMS

October deserters Those Bolsheviks who, in October 1917, believing that the party was not yet strong enough, had advised against an uprising.

Commissar for Nationalities Minister responsible for liaising with the non-Russian national minorities.

Testament A set of reflections and comments Lenin made on his fellow Communist leaders.

On what grounds does Lenin in Source A urge that Stalin be replaced as general secretary?

Despite this warning, nothing was done. Lenin was too ill during the final year of his life to be politically active. At his death in January 1924, he had still not taken any formal steps to remove Stalin, and the testament had not been made public.

Stalin's position in 1924

In the uncertain atmosphere that followed Lenin's death, a number of pieces of luck helped Stalin to promote his own claims, but it would be wrong to ascribe his success wholly to good fortune. The luck had to be used. Stalin may have lacked brilliance, but he had great ability. His particular qualities of perseverance and willingness to undertake laborious administrative work were ideally suited to the times. The government of Soviet Russia, as it had developed by 1924, had two main features: the **Council of People's Commissars** and the Secretariat. Both these bodies were staffed and controlled by the Bolshevik Party. The vital characteristic of this governmental system was that it was the party that ruled. By 1922, Soviet Russia was a one-party state. Membership of that one party was essential for all who held government posts at whatever level.

As government grew in scope, certain posts, which initially had not been considered especially significant, began to provide their holders with the levers of power. This had not been the intention, but was the unforeseen result of the emerging pattern of Bolshevik rule. It was in this context that Stalin's previous appointments to key posts in both government and party proved essential. These had been:

- *People's Commissar for Nationalities* (appointed 1917). In this post Stalin was in charge of the officials in the many regions and republics that made up the USSR (the official title of the Soviet state after 1922).
- *Liaison Officer between Politburo and Orgburo* (appointed 1919). This post placed Stalin in a unique position to monitor both the party's policy and the party's personnel.
- *Head of the Workers' and Peasants' Inspectorate* (appointed 1919). This position entitled Stalin to oversee the work of all government departments.
- *General Secretary of the Communist Party* (appointed 1922). In this position, Stalin recorded and conveyed party policy. This enabled him to build up personal files on all the members of the party. Nothing of note happened that Stalin did not know about.

Stalin became the indispensable link in the chain of command in the Communist Party and the Soviet government. What these posts gave him above all was the power of **patronage**. He used this authority to place his own supporters in top positions. Since they then owed their place to him, Stalin could count on their support in the voting in the various committees which made up the organisation of the party and the government. Such were the levers in Stalin's possession during the party infighting over the succession to Lenin. No

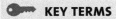

KEY TERMS

Council of People's Commissars A cabinet of ministers, responsible for creating government policies.

Patronage The right to appoint individuals to official posts in the party and government.

other contender came anywhere near matching Stalin in his hold on the party machine. Whatever the ability of the individuals or groups who opposed him, he could always outvote and outmanoeuvre them.

The Lenin enrolment

Stalin had also benefited politically from recent changes in the structure of the Communist Party. Between 1923 and 1925, the party had set out to increase the number of true proletarians in its ranks. This was known as the 'Lenin enrolment'. It resulted in the membership of the **CPSU** rising from 340,000 in 1922 to 600,000 by 1925. The new members were predominantly poorly educated and politically unsophisticated, but they were fully aware that the many privileges which came with party membership depended on their being loyal to those who had first invited them into the Bolshevik ranks. The task of vetting the 'Lenin enrolment' had fallen largely to the officials in the Secretariat who worked directly under Stalin as general secretary. In this way, the expansion of the party added to his growing power of patronage. It provided him with a reliable body of votes in the various party committees at local and central level.

KEY TERM

CPSU The Communist Party of the Soviet Union, the new name for the Bolshevik Party from 1918 onwards.

The attack on factionalism

Another lasting feature of Lenin's period in government that proved of great value to Stalin was what had become known as the 'attack on factionalism'. This referred to Lenin's condemnation in 1921 of divisions within the party (see page 56). The effect of this rejection of 'factionalism' was to frustrate any serious attempt to criticise party decisions or policies. It became extremely difficult to mount any form of legitimate opposition within the CPSU. Stalin gained directly from the ban on criticism of the party line. The charge of 'factionalism' provided him with a ready weapon for resisting challenges to the authority he had begun to exercise.

The Lenin legacy

There was an accompanying factor that legitimised Stalin's position. Stalin became heir to the 'Lenin legacy', the tradition of authority and leadership that Lenin had established during his lifetime, and the veneration in which he was held after his death. It is barely an exaggeration to say that in the eyes of the Communist Party, Lenin became a god. His actions and decisions became unchallengeable, and all arguments and disputes within the party were settled by reference to his statements and writings. Lenin became the measure of the correctness of Soviet theory and practice. Soviet communism became Leninism. After 1924, if a party member could assume the mantle of Lenin and appear to carry on Lenin's work, he would establish a formidable claim to power. This is exactly what Stalin began to do.

Summary diagram: Stalin's record as a revolutionary before 1924	
Background	**Key posts taken by Stalin during Lenin's time**
• Stalin had worked closely and loyally with Lenin • Stalin had been a major worker for the Bolsheviks • Lenin regarded him as 'that wonderful Georgian'	• People's Commissar for Nationalities • Liaison Officer between Politburo and Orgburo • Head of the Workers' and Peasants' Inspectorate • Secretary of the Communist Party
Key moment, January 1923	**Key benefits to Stalin from developments during Lenin's final years**
Lenin's death prevented his 'testament' from being published. This saved Stalin from being dismissed as General Secretary	• The 'Lenin enrolment' • The attack on factionalism • Lenin's legacy

 ## 2 The power struggle within the Communist Party

▶ *What were Stalin's advantages in the power struggle that followed Lenin's death?*

Following Lenin's death, a period of political manoeuvring began. This took the form of disputes between Left and Right Communists, terms which were not very precise but broadly referred to those in the party who wanted NEP to be modified or abandoned (Left) and those who wanted it to continue (Right). Although his position on NEP was not clear at this stage, Stalin came to be regarded as the dominant figure of the Right opposed to Trotsky on the Left. However, in this early period of manoeuvring the differences between the two rivals had as much to do with personality as policy.

Lenin's funeral

Immediately after Lenin's death, the Politburo, whose members were Stalin, Trotsky, **Rykov**, **Tomsky**, Kamenev and Zinoviev, publicly proclaimed their intention to continue as a collective leadership. However, behind the scenes the competition for individual authority had already begun. In the manoeuvring, Stalin gained an advantage by being the one to deliver the oration at Lenin's funeral. The sight of Stalin as leading mourner suggested a continuity between him and Lenin, an impression heightened by the contents of his speech in which, in the name of the party, he humbly dedicated himself to follow in the tradition of the departed leader (see Source B).

KEY FIGURES

Aleksei Rykov (1881–1938)

Chairman of the Central Committee of the CPSU.

Mikhail Tomsky (1880–1937)

Minister responsible for representing (in practice, controlling) the trade unions.

SOURCE B

From Stalin's address at Lenin's funeral, January 1924, quoted in *Stalin's Works*, volume 6, Lawrence & Wishart, 1955, p. 47.

In leaving us, Comrade Lenin commanded us to keep the unity of our Party. We swear to thee, Comrade Lenin, to honour thy command. In leaving us, Comrade Lenin ordered us to maintain and strengthen the dictatorship of the proletariat. We swear to thee, Comrade Lenin, to exert our full strength in honouring thy command. In leaving us, Comrade Lenin ordered us to strengthen with all our might the union of workers and peasants. We swear to thee, Comrade Lenin, to honour your command.

In Source B, what effect is Stalin trying to achieve by the constant repetition of his commitment to Lenin's commands?

Since Stalin's speech was the first crucial move to promote himself as Lenin's successor, it was to be expected that Trotsky, his chief rival, would try to counter it. Yet Trotsky was not even present at the funeral. It was a very conspicuous absence, and it is puzzling why Trotsky did not appreciate the importance of appearances following Lenin's death in January 1924. Initially he, not Stalin, had been offered the opportunity of making the major speech at the funeral. But not only did he decline this, he also failed to attend the ceremony itself. His excuse was that Stalin had given him the wrong date, but this simply was not true. Documents show that he learned the actual date early enough for him to have reached Moscow with time to spare. Instead he continued his planned journey and was on holiday on the day of the funeral. This was hardly the image of a dedicated Leninist.

What makes Trotsky's behaviour more inexplicable is that he was well aware of the danger that Stalin represented. In 1924 he prophesied that Stalin would become the 'dictator of the USSR'. He also gave a remarkable analysis of the basis of Stalin's power in the party (see Source C).

SOURCE C

From a comment made by Trotsky in 1924, quoted in Leon Trotsky, *Stalin: An Appraisal of the Man and His Influence*, Hollis & Carter, 1966, pp. 392–3.

The dialectics of history have already hooked him and will raise him up. He is needed by all of them; by the tired radicals, by the bureaucrats, by the Nepmen, the upstarts, by all the worms that are crawling out of the upturned soil of the manured revolution. He knows how to meet them on their own ground, he speaks their language and he knows how to lead them. He has the deserved reputation of an old revolutionary. He has will and daring. Right now he is organising around himself the sneaks of the Party, the artful dodgers.

In Source C, what political gifts does Trotsky grudgingly acknowledge that Stalin possesses?

Trotsky's description was a bitter but strikingly accurate assessment of how Stalin had made a large part of the party dependent on him. But logically, such awareness on Trotsky's part should have made him eager to prevent Stalin from stealing an advantage. His reluctance to act is a fascinating feature of Trotsky's enigmatic character.

Trotsky's character

Trotsky had a complex personality. He was one of those figures in history who may be described as having been their own worst enemy. Despite his many talents and intellectual brilliance, he had serious flaws that undermined his chances of success. At times, he was unreasonably self-assured; at other critical times, he suffered from diffidence and lack of judgement. An example of this had occurred earlier, at the time of Stalin's mishandling of the Georgian question (see page 67). Lenin's anger with Stalin had offered Trotsky a perfect opportunity to undermine Stalin's position, but for some reason he had declined to attack.

A possible clue to his reluctance is that he felt inhibited by his Jewishness. Trotsky knew that, in a nation such as Russia with its deeply ingrained **anti-Semitism**, his race made him an outsider. A remarkable example of his awareness of this occurred in 1917, when Lenin offered him the post of Deputy Chairman of the Soviet government. Trotsky rejected it on the grounds that his appointment would be an embarrassment to Lenin and the government. 'It would', he said, 'give enemies grounds for claiming that the country was ruled by a Jew.' It may have been similar reasoning that allowed Stalin to gain an advantage over him at the time of Lenin's funeral. It may have been, of course, that Trotsky simply did not want the responsibility of party leadership, but this does not accord with his worries over the dangers of Stalin taking the position or his own subsequent bid for power.

KEY TERM

Anti-Semitism Hatred of the Jewish race; for centuries Russia had been notorious for its vicious treatment of the Jews.

Suppression of Lenin's testament

A dangerous hurdle in Stalin's way was Lenin's testament. If it were to be published, Stalin would be gravely damaged by its contents. However, here, as so often during this period, fortune favoured him. Had the document been made public, not only Lenin's criticisms of Stalin, but also those concerning Trotsky, Zinoviev and Kamenev would have been revealed. Nearly all the members of the Politburo had reason for suppressing the testament. When the members of the Central Committee were presented with the document in May 1924, they realised that it was too damning broadly to be used exclusively against any one individual. They agreed to its being shelved indefinitely. Trotsky, for obvious personal reasons, went along with the decision, but in doing so he was declining yet another opportunity to challenge Stalin's right to power. In fact it was Trotsky, not Stalin, who the Politburo regarded as the greater danger.

Party members' attitudes towards Trotsky

The attitude of party members towards Trotsky was an important factor in the weakening of his position. Colleagues tended to regard Trotsky as dangerously ambitious and his rival Stalin as reliably self-effacing. This was because Trotsky was flamboyant and brilliant, while his rival was unspectacular and methodical. Trotsky was the type of person who attracted either admiration or distaste, but seldom loyalty. That was why he lacked a genuine following. It is true that he was highly regarded by the Red Army, whose creator he had been, but this was never matched by any comparable political support. Trotsky failed to build a power base within the party. This invariably gave him the appearance of an outsider.

Adding to his difficulties in this regard was the doubt about his commitment to Bolshevism. Until 1917, as Lenin had noted in his testament, Trotsky had belonged to the Mensheviks. This led to the suspicion that his conversion had been a matter of expediency rather than conviction. Many of the old-guard Bolsheviks regarded Trotsky as a Menshevik turncoat who could not be trusted. Kamenev and Zinoviev joined Stalin in an unofficial **triumvirate** within the Politburo. Their aim was to isolate Trotsky by exploiting his unpopularity with large sections of the party. The 'Lenin enrolment' helped them in this. The new proletarian members were hardly the type of men to be impressed by the cultured Trotsky. The seemingly down-to-earth Stalin was much more to their liking.

Bureaucratisation

Despite the attacks on him, Trotsky attempted to hold his ground. The issue he chose to fight on was **bureaucratisation**, which he linked with the abandonment of genuine discussion within the party. He had good reason to think he had selected a powerful cause. Lenin himself in his last writings had warned the party against the dangers of creeping bureaucracy. Accordingly, Trotsky pressed his views in the Central Committee, in the Politburo and at party congresses. His condemnation of the growth of bureaucracy was coupled with an appeal for a return to **party democracy**. He expanded his arguments in a series of essays, the most controversial of which was *Lessons of October*, in which he criticised Kamenev and Zinoviev for their past disagreements with Lenin. The assault was ill-judged, since it invited retaliation in kind. Trotsky's Menshevik past and his divergence from Leninism were highlighted in a number of books and pamphlets, most notably Kamenev's *Lenin or Trotsky?*

As a move in the power struggle, Trotsky's campaign for greater party democracy was misjudged. His censures on bureaucracy left Stalin largely unscathed. Moreover, Trotsky had overlooked the essential fact that Bolshevik rule since 1917 had always been bureaucratic. Indeed, it was because the Soviet state functioned as a bureaucracy that party members received privileges in political and public life. Trotsky's line was unlikely to gain significant support from party members who had a vested interest in maintaining the party's bureaucratic ways.

Disputes over NEP

Trotsky's reputation was further damaged by the issue of NEP. When introducing NEP, Lenin had admitted that it was a relaxing of strict socialism, but had emphasised that it was a temporary, stopgap measure. However, at the time of his death in 1924, the question was already being asked as to how long in practice NEP was meant to last. Was it not becoming a permanent

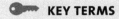

KEY TERMS

Triumvirate A ruling or influential bloc of three people.

Bureaucratisation The growth in power of the Secretariat, which was able to make decisions and operate policies without reference to ordinary party members.

Party democracy The right of all party members to express their opinion on policy.

Profile: Leon Trotsky

1879	Born into a Ukrainian Jewish family
1903	Sided with the Mensheviks in the SD split
1917	The principal organiser of the October Revolution
1918–20	Created the Red Army
1921	Destroyed the trade unions in Russia
1924–7	Outmanoeuvred in the power struggle with Stalin
1929	Banished from USSR
1940	Assassinated in Mexico on Stalin's orders

Early revolutionary achievements

Rebellious by nature, Trotsky felt sympathy for oppressed workers but, like Lenin, he rejected **economism**. As an active revolutionary, Trotsky initially sided with the Mensheviks after the SD split in 1903, and it was as a Menshevik that he led the St Petersburg soviet during the 1905 revolution. His activities led to his arrest and exile. Between 1906 and 1917 he lived abroad, developing his theory of 'permanent revolution'. Following the collapse of tsardom in February 1917, Trotsky returned to Petrograd and immediately joined the Bolshevik Party. He became chairman of the Petrograd soviet, a position from which he organised the Bolshevik Rising which overthrew the Provisional Government in October 1917.

Foreign and war commissar

Appointed foreign commissar by Lenin, he negotiated Russia's withdrawal from the war in the Treaty of Brest-Litovsk in 1918 before going on, as war commissar, to achieve his greatest success in leading the Red Amy to victory in the civil war of 1918–20. As a hardliner, Trotsky fully supported Lenin's repressive policy of War Communism. He planned the destruction of the Russian trade unions, and in 1921 ordered the suppression of the Kronstadt workers' rising. Unhappy with Lenin's introduction of NEP in 1921, he found himself becoming increasingly isolated in the party.

Exile

Despite his intellectual gifts, Trotsky was never fully accepted by his fellow Bolsheviks, which enabled Stalin to isolate him after 1924. In 1929, Trotsky was exiled from the USSR. In 1939, he founded the Fourth International, a movement of anti-Stalin international Marxists. Trotsky's end came in 1940 in Mexico City, when a Soviet agent, acting on Stalin's orders, smashed an ice-axe into his head.

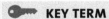

KEY TERM

Economism Putting the improvement of the workers' conditions before the need for revolution.

policy? The party members who were unhappy with it saw its continuation as a betrayal of revolutionary principles. They objected to a policy which, in effect, allowed the peasants to dictate the pace of Soviet Russia's advance towards full communism. A serious division had developed between Left Communists and Right Communists.

Stalin's exploitation of the NEP question

Although fierce disputes were to arise over the issue, initially the disagreement was simply about timing: how long should the NEP be allowed to run? However, in the power struggle of the 1920s these minor differences deepened into questions of political correctness and party loyalty. A rival's attitude towards NEP might be a weakness to be exploited; if it could be established that his views indicated deviant Marxist thinking it became possible to destroy his position in the party. Stalin did precisely this. He used Trotsky's attitude towards NEP as a way of undermining him. Trotsky had backed Lenin in 1921, but there were strong rumours that his support had been reluctant and that he regarded NEP as a deviation from true socialism. It was certainly the case that in 1923 Trotsky had led a group of party members in openly criticising *Gosplan* for its 'flagrant radical errors of economic policy'. Trotsky's charge was that the government had placed the interests of the Nepmen above those of the revolution and the Russian people. He urged a return to a much tighter state control of industry and warned that under NEP the revolutionary gains made under War Communism would be lost.

Stalin was quick to suggest to party members who already looked on Trotsky as a disruptive force that he was, indeed, suspect. The interesting point here is that Stalin's own view of NEP was far from clear at this stage. He had loyally supported Lenin's introduction of it in 1921, but had given little indication as to whether, or how long, it should be retained after Lenin's death. He preferred to keep his own views to himself and play on the differences between his colleagues.

The issue of modernisation

The NEP debate was one aspect of the question that remained unanswered at Lenin's death. How should the Soviet Union plan for the future? This would have been a demanding issue regardless of whether or not there had been a power struggle. What the rivalry for leadership did was to intensify the argument. The USSR was a poor country. To modernise and overcome its poverty, it would have to industrialise. Recent history had shown that a strong industrial base was an absolute essential for a modern state and there was common agreement among Soviet Communists about that. The quarrel was not over whether the USSR should industrialise, but over how and at what speed.

History had further shown that the industrial expansion which had taken place in the previous century, in such countries as Germany and Britain, had relied on a ready supply of resources and the availability of capital for investment. Russia was rich in natural resources, but these had yet to be effectively exploited, and it certainly did not possess large amounts of capital. Nor could it easily borrow any, since, after 1917, the Bolsheviks had rejected **capitalist methods of finance**. Moreover, even if the Bolsheviks had been willing to borrow, there were few countries after 1917 willing to risk the dangers of investing in revolutionary Russia.

The only usable resource, therefore, was the Russian people themselves, 80 per cent of whom were peasants. To achieve industrialisation, it was necessary that the peasants be persuaded or forced into producing a food surplus which could then be sold abroad to raise capital for industrial investment. Both Left and Right agreed that this was the only solution, but, whereas the Right were content to rely on persuasion, the Left demanded that the peasantry be forced into line. It was Trotsky who most clearly represented the view of the Left on this. He wanted the peasants to be coerced into co-operating. However, for him the industrialisation debate was secondary to the far more demanding question of Soviet Russia's role as the organiser of international revolution.

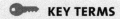

KEY TERMS

Gosplan The government body responsible for national economic planning.

Capitalist methods of finance The system in which the owners of private capital (money) increase their wealth by making loans on which interest has to be paid later by the borrower.

Summary diagram: The power struggle within the Communist Party

Stalin's advantages
- Held key posts in party and government
- Took initiative on Lenin's death

Trotsky's disadvantages
- Strange diffidence allowed Stalin to make the running
- Lacked a power base in the party

**Triumvirate (Stalin, Kamenev, Zinoviev)
versus Trotsky**

Issues on which Trotsky attempted to fight

Bureaucratisation   NEP   Modernisation of USSR

 # 'Permanent revolution' versus 'socialism in one country'

▶ *What were the main ideas dividing Trotsky and Stalin in their attitudes towards the role of the USSR as a revolutionary nation?*

The ideological divide between Trotsky and Stalin can be expressed as a clash between their opposing notions of 'permanent revolution' and 'socialism in one country'.

'Permanent revolution'

Trotsky's politics were inspired by his belief in 'permanent revolution', which was made up of a number of key ideas:

- Revolution was not a single event but a permanent (continuous) process in which risings took place from country to country.
- The events in Russia since 1917 were simply a first step towards a worldwide revolution of the proletariat.
- Individual nations did not matter. The interests of the international working class were paramount.
- True revolutionary socialism could be achieved in the USSR only if an international uprising took place.

Trotsky believed that the USSR could not survive alone in a hostile world. With its vast peasant population and undeveloped proletariat, it would prove 'incapable of holding its own against conservative Europe'. He contended that the immediate task of the USSR was 'to export revolution'. That was the only way to guarantee its survival. It should be stressed that at no point did Trotsky call for the Soviet Union to be sacrificed to some theoretical notion of world revolution. His argument was an opposite one; unless there was international revolution the Soviet Union would go under. Stalin, however, ignored the subtlety of his opponent's reasoning. He chose to portray Trotsky as someone intent on damaging the Soviet Union.

'Socialism in one country'

Stalin countered Trotsky's notion of 'permanent revolution' with his own concept of 'socialism in one country'. He meant by this that the nation's first task was to consolidate Lenin's revolution and the rule of the CPSU by turning the USSR into a modern state, capable of defending itself against its internal and external enemies. The Soviet Union, therefore, must work:

- To overcome its present agricultural and industrial problems by its own unaided efforts.
- To go on to build a modern state, the equal of any nation in the world.
- To make the survival of the Soviet Union an absolute priority, even if this meant suspending efforts to create international revolution.

Stalin used the contrast between this programme and Trotsky's to portray his rival as an enemy of the Soviet Union. Trotsky's ideas were condemned as an affront to Lenin and the Bolshevik revolution. An image was created of Trotsky as an isolated figure, a posturing Jewish intellectual, whose vague notions of international revolution threatened the security of the Soviet Union. Trotsky's position was further weakened by the fact that throughout the 1920s the Soviet Union went in fear of invasion by the combined capitalist nations. It was a constant theme in Soviet public propaganda. Although this fear was ill-founded, the tense atmosphere it created made Trotsky's notion of the USSR's engaging in foreign revolutionary wars appear even more irresponsible. A number of historians, including E.H. Carr and Isaac Deutscher, have remarked on Stalin's ability to rally support and silence opponents at critical moments by assuming the role of the great Russian patriot, concerned to save the nation from the grave dangers that threatened it.

Summary diagram: 'Permanent revolution' versus 'socialism in one country'	
'Permanent revolution'	**'Socialism in one country'**
Trotsky's ideas • Revolution a continuous process • Russian Revolution only a first step • Goal was international proletarian revolution • Individual nations did not matter • USSR safe only if international rising occurred	**Stalin's ideas** • Modernisation by USSR's own efforts • Survival of USSR an absolute priority • Suspension of efforts at international revolution

4 Stalin's defeat of Trotsky and the Left

▶ *What were the basic weaknesses of the Left in its challenge to Stalin?*

Trotsky's failure in the propaganda war of the 1920s meant that he was in no position to persuade either the Politburo or the Central Committee to vote for his proposals. Stalin's ability to **'deliver the votes'** in the crucial divisions was decisive. Following a vote against him in the 1925 party congress, Trotsky was relieved of his position as commissar for war. Lev Kamenev and Grigory Zinoviev, the respective chairmen of the Moscow and **Leningrad** soviets, played a key part in this. They used their influence over the local party organisations to ensure that it was a pro-Stalin, anti-Trotsky, congress that gathered.

Kamenev and Zinoviev

With Trotsky weakened, Stalin turned to the problem of how to deal with two key figures, who he now saw as potential rivals. Kamenev and Zinoviev had been motivated by a personal dislike of Trotsky, who at various times had tried to embarrass them by reminding the party of their failure to support Lenin in October 1917. Now it was their turn to be ousted. In the event, they created a trap for themselves. In 1925 Kamenev and Zinoviev, worried by the USSR's economic backwardness, publicly stated that it would require the victory of proletarian revolution in the capitalist nations in order for the Soviet Union to achieve socialism. Zinoviev wrote: 'When the time comes for the revolution in other countries and the proletariat comes to our aid, then we shall again go over to the offensive. For the time being we have only a little breathing space.'

Zinoviev called for NEP to be abandoned, for restrictions to be reimposed on the peasants, and for enforced industrialisation. It was understandable that Kamenev and Zinoviev, respective party bosses in the Soviet Union's only genuinely industrial areas, Moscow and Leningrad, should have thought in these terms. Their viewpoint formed the basis of what was termed the **United Opposition**, but it appeared to be indistinguishable from old Trotskyism. It was no surprise, therefore, when Trotsky joined his former opponents in 1926 to form a 'Trotskyite–Kamenevite–Zinovievite' opposition bloc.

Again, Stalin's control of the party machine proved critical. The party congress declined to be influenced by pressure from the United Opposition. Stalin's chief backers among the Right Communists were Rykov, Tomsky and Bukharin. They and their supporters combined to outvote the United Opposition. Kamenev and Zinoviev were dismissed from their posts as soviet chairmen, to be replaced by two of Stalin's staunchest allies, **Molotov** in Moscow and **Kirov** in Leningrad (see page 110). It was little surprise that soon afterwards, Trotsky was expelled from both the Politburo and the Central Committee.

KEY TERMS

'Deliver the votes' To use control of the party machine to gain majority support in key divisions.

Leningrad Petrograd had been renamed in Lenin's honour.

United Opposition The group led by Kamenev and Zinoviev, sometimes known as the New Opposition, which called for an end to NEP and the adoption of a rapid industrialisation programme.

KEY FIGURES

Vyacheslav Molotov (1890–1986)

A prominent Bolshevik agitator in 1917, he became a dedicated supporter of Stalin in home and foreign affairs. Winston Churchill, the British statesman, regarded him as an 'automaton'.

Sergei Kirov (1886–1934)

An able and popular individual who rose quickly in the party, holding a number of key posts; he was murdered in mysterious circumstances in 1934, possibly at Stalin's instigation.

Trotsky exiled

Trotsky still did not admit defeat. In 1927, on the tenth anniversary of the Bolshevik Rising, he tried to rally support in a direct challenge to Stalin's authority. Even fewer members of congress than before were prepared to side with him and he was again outvoted. His complete failure led to congress's accepting Stalin's proposal that Trotsky be expelled from the party altogether. An internal exile order against him in 1927 was followed two years later by total exile from the USSR.

Stalin's victory over Trotsky was not primarily a matter of ability or principle. Stalin won because Trotsky lacked a power base. Trotsky's superiority as a speaker and writer, and his greater intellectual gifts, counted for little when set against Stalin's grip on the party machine. It is difficult to see how, after 1924, Trotsky could have ever mounted a serious challenge to his rival. Even had his own particular failings not stopped him from acting at vital moments, Trotsky never had control of the political system as it operated in Soviet Russia. Politics is the art of the possible. After 1924 all the possibilities belonged to Stalin, and he used them.

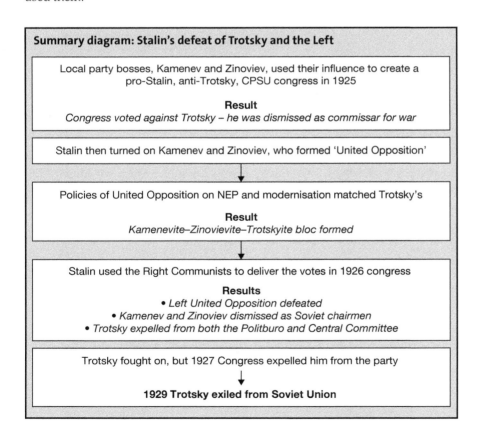

Summary diagram: Stalin's defeat of Trotsky and the Left

Local party bosses, Kamenev and Zinoviev, used their influence to create a pro-Stalin, anti-Trotsky, CPSU congress in 1925

Result
Congress voted against Trotsky – he was dismissed as commissar for war

Stalin then turned on Kamenev and Zinoviev, who formed 'United Opposition'

Policies of United Opposition on NEP and modernisation matched Trotsky's

Result
Kamenevite–Zinovievite–Trotskyite bloc formed

Stalin used the Right Communists to deliver the votes in 1926 congress

Results
• *Left United Opposition defeated*
• *Kamenev and Zinoviev dismissed as Soviet chairmen*
• *Trotsky expelled from both the Politburo and Central Committee*

Trotsky fought on, but 1927 Congress expelled him from the party

1929 Trotsky exiled from Soviet Union

Stalin's defeat of the Right

▶ *How did Stalin exploit the attitude of the Right towards NEP and industrialisation?*

Although a victory of Stalin over the Right opposition is best studied as a feature of his industrialisation programme (see page 95), it is important also to see it as the last stage in the consolidation of his authority over the party and over the USSR. The defeat of the Right marks the end of any serious attempt to limit his power. From the late 1920s to his death in 1953 he would become increasingly dictatorial.

The major representatives of the Right were Rykov, Tomsky and Bukharin, the three who had loyally served Stalin in his outflanking of Trotsky and the Left. Politically, the Right were by no means as challenging to Stalin as the Trotskyite bloc had been. What made Stalin move against them was that they stood in the way of the industrial and agricultural schemes that his growing strength by 1928 put him in a position to begin implementing.

Collectivisation and industrialisation

Historians are uncertain as to when Stalin finally decided that the answer to the Soviet Union's growth problem was to impose **collectivisation** and **industrialisation**. It is unlikely to have been an early decision; the probability is that it was another piece of opportunism. Having defeated the Left politically he may then have felt free to adopt their economic policies.

Some scholars have suggested that in 1928 Stalin became genuinely concerned about the serious grain shortage and decided that the only way to avoid a crisis was to resort to the drastic methods of collectivisation. It no longer mattered that this had been the very solution that the Left had advanced, since they were now scattered. For some time it had been the view of Bukharin and the Right that it was unnecessary to force the pace of industrialisation in the USSR. They argued that it would be less disruptive to let industry develop its own momentum. The state should assist, but it should not direct. Similarly, the peasants should not be controlled and oppressed; this would make them resentful and less productive. The Right agreed that it was from the land that the means of financing industrialisation would have to come, but they suggested that, by offering the peasants the chance to become prosperous, far more grain would be produced for sale abroad. Bukharin argued in the Politburo and at the party congress in 1928 that Stalin's aggressive policy of **state grain procurements** was counter-productive. He declared that there were alternatives to these repressive policies. Bukharin was prepared to state openly what everybody knew, but was afraid to admit: that Stalin's programme was no different from the one that Trotsky had previously advocated.

Weaknesses of the Right

The Right suffered from a number of weaknesses, which Stalin was able to exploit: these related to their ideas, their organisation and their support.

Ideas

- The Right's economic arguments were not unsound, but in the taut atmosphere of the late 1920s created by fear of invasion, they appeared timid and unrealistic.
- The Right's plea for a softer line with the peasants was unacceptable to the party hardliners around Stalin, who argued that the threatening times required a dedicated resistance to the enemies of revolution both within the USSR and outside it.
- Stalin was able to suggest that the Right was guilty of underestimating the crisis facing the party and the Soviet Union. He declared that it was a time for closing the ranks, in keeping with the tradition of 1917.

Stalin showed a shrewd understanding of the mentality of party members. The majority were far more likely to respond to the call for a return to a hard-line policy, such as had helped them to survive the desperate days of the civil war, than they were to risk the revolution itself by untimely concessions to a peasantry that had no real place in the proletarian future. The party of Marx and Lenin, they asserted, would not be well served by the policies of the Right.

Organisation

- The difficulty experienced by the Right Communists in advancing their views was the same as that which had confronted the Left. How could they impress their ideas on the party while Stalin remained master of the party's organisation?
- Bukharin and his colleagues wanted to remain good party men and it was this sense of loyalty that weakened them in their attempts to oppose Stalin. Fearful of creating 'factionalism', they hoped that they could win the party round to their way of thinking without causing deep divisions. On occasion they were sharply outspoken, Bukharin particularly so, but their basic approach was conciliatory.

All this played into Stalin's hands. Since it was largely his supporters who were responsible for drafting and distributing party information, it was not difficult for Stalin to belittle the Right as a weak and irresponsible clique.

Support

The Right's only substantial support lay in the trade unions, whose central council was chaired by Tomsky, and in the CPSU's Moscow branch where **Nicolai Uglanov** was the party secretary. When Stalin realised that these might be a source of opposition he acted quickly and decisively. He sent **Lazar Kaganovich** to undertake a purge of the suspect trade unionists. The Right

 KEY FIGURES

Nicolai Uglanov (1886–1940)

An admirer and supporter of Bukharin.

Lazar Kaganovich (1893–1991)

A ruthless and ambitious young Politburo member from Ukraine.

proved totally incapable of organising resistance to this political blitz. Molotov, Stalin's faithful henchman, was dispatched to Moscow, where he enlisted the support of the pro-Stalin members to achieve a similar purge of the local party officials.

By early 1929, the Right had been undermined beyond recovery:

- Tomsky was no longer the national trade union leader.
- Uglanov had been replaced in the Moscow party organisation.
- Rykov had been superseded as premier by Molotov.
- Bukharin had been voted out as chairman of the Comintern and had lost his place in the Politburo.
- Tomsky, Rykov and Bukharin, the main trio of the 'Right Opportunists' as they were termed by the Stalinist press, were allowed to remain in the party but only after they had publicly admitted the error of their ways.

Stalin's triumph over both Left and Right was complete. He was now in a position to exercise power as the new *vozhd*. The grey blank was about to become the Red tsar.

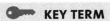

KEY TERM

Vozhd A supreme leader; equivalent to *Führer* in German.

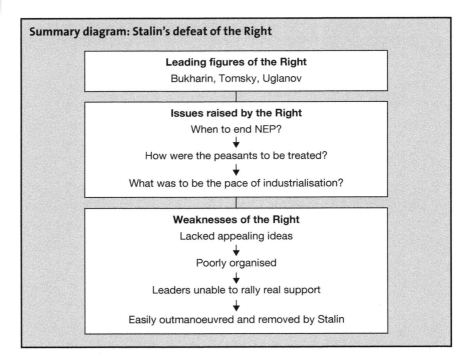

Summary diagram: Stalin's defeat of the Right

Leading figures of the Right
Bukharin, Tomsky, Uglanov

Issues raised by the Right
When to end NEP?
↓
How were the peasants to be treated?
↓
What was to be the pace of industrialisation?

Weaknesses of the Right
Lacked appealing ideas
↓
Poorly organised
↓
Leaders unable to rally real support
↓
Easily outmanoeuvred and removed by Stalin

Chapter summary

Having proved himself a loyal follower of Lenin and a highly active revolutionary terrorist before 1917, Stalin played a part in the October Revolution and went on to serve as a commissar in Lenin's government of Russia. Although criticised in Lenin's last testament, Stalin adroitly used the various positions he had gained within the Bolshevik Party to make himself indispensable as an administrator. As general secretary, his detailed knowledge of all the members left him ideally placed to outmanoeuvre his rivals in the power struggle after Lenin's death.

Stalin isolated Trotsky, his greatest challenger, by convincing the CPSU that if Trotsky's concept of permanent revolution was put into practice it would mean the overthrow of the Soviet Union. Stalin's alternative strategy was 'socialism in one country', which emphasised the necessity of the besieged Soviet Union making its own survival a priority over the pursuit of international revolution. Stalin also exploited the party dispute over NEP to crush Trotsky and the other Left Bolsheviks. Having rid himself of the Left opposition, Stalin then turned unscrupulously on the Rightists who had supported him against Trotsky and removed them from key positions in party and government, replacing them with his own appointees.

Refresher questions

Use these questions to remind yourself of the key material covered in this chapter.

1 How significant was Stalin's revolutionary career before 1924?

2 How had Stalin been able to rise up the Bolshevik ranks?

3 What was the significance for Stalin of the 'Lenin enrolment'?

4 How did Lenin's attack on factionalism assist Stalin?

5 What gains did Stalin derive from the Lenin legacy?

6 What were Stalin's advantages in his leadership struggle with Trotsky?

7 What were Trotsky's weaknesses in his leadership struggle with Stalin?

8 Why was there a Left–Right division over the question of how the USSR should modernise?

9 What were the essential features of Trotsky's concept of 'permanent revolution'?

10 What were the essential features of Stalin's concept of 'revolution in one country'?

11 What were the basic weaknesses of the Left in its challenge to Stalin?

12 Why was the Right unable to mount a successful challenge to Stalin?

Question practice

ESSAY QUESTIONS

1 'Following the death of Lenin in 1924, Stalin was well placed to become Soviet leader because he was general secretary of the party.' Explain why you agree or disagree with this view.

2 To what extent were Trotsky's own failings the reason for his defeat in the power struggle with Stalin between 1924 and 1929?

3 'It was not their ideas but their poor organisation that allowed Stalin to overcome the Left Communists after 1924.' Assess the validity of this view.

4 How important was Stalin's theory of 'socialism in one country' in his defeat of the Right Communists?

SOURCE ANALYSIS QUESTIONS

1 With reference to Sources B and C (**page 71**) and your understanding of the historical context, which of these two sources is more valuable in explaining why Trotsky was at a disadvantage in his dealings with Stalin after 1924?

2 With reference to Sources A (**page 67**), B (**page 71**) and C (**page 71**), and your understanding of the historical context, assess the value of these sources to a historian studying Stalin's ability to outmanoeuvre Trotsky in the power struggle of 1924–9.

CHAPTER 4

Stalin's rule: economy and society 1929–41

Stalin decided that the USSR could not survive unless it rapidly modernised its economy. To this end, he set about completely reshaping Soviet agriculture and industry. This had immense economic, social and political consequences. These are examined as three themes:

★ Stalin's economic aims after 1929: the great turn

★ Collectivisation and the war against the peasantry

★ Industrialisation: the first three Five-Year Plans

The key debate on *page 104* of this chapter asks the question: Were Stalin's economic policies justified by their results?

Key dates

1928	Collectivisation began	1933	Start of the second Five-Year Plan
	Start of the first Five-Year Plan	1938	Start of the third Five-Year Plan
1932–3	Widespread famine in the USSR	1941–5	The 'Great Patriotic War'

1 Stalin's economic aims after 1929: the great turn

▶ *What were Stalin's motives in revolutionising the Soviet economy?*

In the late 1920s Stalin decided to impose on the USSR a crash programme of reform of the economy. Agriculture and industry were to be revolutionised. This was to prove such a dramatic development that Stalin referred to it as the **'second revolution'**, a way of equating it in importance with that of the 1917 revolution itself. Historians often use the term the 'great turn' to suggest that what Stalin did was as significant as Lenin's introduction of NEP in 1921 (see page 54). The cue for the great change had been provided in 1926 by a critical resolution of the party congress 'to transform our country from an agrarian into an industrial one, capable by its own efforts of producing the necessary means of modernisation'. Stalin planned to turn that resolution into reality.

 KEY TERM

Second revolution The modernisation of the Soviet economy by means of state direction and central control.

Revolution from above

Stalin's economic policy had one essential aim, the modernisation of the Soviet economy, and two essential methods, collectivisation and industrialisation. From 1928 onwards, the attempt to modernise the USSR saw the Soviet state take over the running of the nation's economy. It is also frequently referred to as a 'revolution from above'.

In the Bolshevik interpretation of events, 1917 had been a **revolution from below**. The Bolshevik-led proletariat had begun the construction of a state in which the workers ruled. Bukharin and the Right had used this notion to argue that, since the USSR was now a proletarian society, the economy should be left to develop at its own pace, without interference from the government. But Stalin's economic programme ended such thinking. The state would now command and direct the economy from above.

A central planning agency, known as *Gosplan,* had been created earlier under Lenin (see page 75). However, what was different about Stalin's schemes was their scale and thoroughness. Under Stalin, state control was to be total. There was an important political aspect to this. He saw in a hard-line policy the best means of confirming his authority over party and government. When he introduced his radical economic changes, Stalin claimed that they marked as significant a stage in Soviet communism as had Lenin's fateful decision to sanction the October uprising in 1917. This comparison was obviously intended to enhance his own status as a revolutionary leader following in the footsteps of Lenin.

Modernisation

It would be wrong to regard Stalin's policy as wholly a matter of **political expediency**. Judging from his speeches and actions after 1928, he had become convinced that the needs of Soviet Russia could be met only by modernisation. By that, Stalin meant bringing his economically backward nation up to a level of industrial production that would enable it to catch up with and then overtake the advanced economies of Western Europe and the USA. He believed that the survival of the revolution and of Soviet Russia depended on the nation's ability to turn itself into a modern industrial society within the shortest possible time. That was the essence of his slogan 'socialism in one country' (see page 77). Asserting that the Soviet Union was 100 years behind the advanced countries, he claimed: 'We must make good this distance in ten years or we shall be crushed.'

KEY TERMS

Revolution from below
The CPSU consistently claimed that the 1917 revolution had been a genuine rising of the people rather than a power grab by the Bolsheviks.

Political expediency
Pursuing a course of action with the primary aim of gaining a political advantage.

```
┌────────────────────────────────────────────────────────────────────┐
│ Summary diagram: Stalin's economic aims after 1929: the great turn   │
│                                                                      │
│   ┌──────────────────────────────────────────────────────────────┐  │
│   │                            Aims                              │  │
│   ├──────────────────────────────────────────────────────────────┤  │
│   │ • 'Second revolution' to fulfil the first by modernising     │  │
│   │   Soviet economy through state direction and control         │  │
│   │ • Revolution from above                                      │  │
│   │ • Economic motive: to enable the USSR to catch up with the   │  │
│   │   Western economies                                          │  │
│   └──────────────────────────────────────────────────────────────┘  │
│                             ⇩                                        │
│   ┌──────────────────────────────────────────────────────────────┐  │
│   │                           Means                              │  │
│   ├──────────────────────────────────────────────────────────────┤  │
│   │ • Collectivisation and industrialisation under *Gosplan*     │  │
│   │   direction                                                  │  │
│   │ • Political motive: to confirm Stalin's authority as leader  │  │
│   └──────────────────────────────────────────────────────────────┘  │
└────────────────────────────────────────────────────────────────────┘
```

② Collectivisation and the war against the peasantry

▶ *What part was collectivisation intended to play in Stalin's plan for the modernisation of the USSR?*

Stalin was not a trained economist. He worked to a very simple formula which ran along these lines:

The USSR needed to industrialise.

↓

Industrialisation required large amounts of manpower and **capital**.

↓

The backward USSR did not have sufficient capital and could not borrow from abroad because of its strained relations with the capitalist world.

↓

Since Russia's natural resources, such as oil and gas, had yet to be effectively exploited, this left land as the only available resource.

↓

Therefore, the peasants must produce surplus food to be sold abroad to raise capital.

↓

Efficient farming under collectivisation would create a surplus of farm labourers who would thus become available as factory workers.

The necessary first step towards using the land to raise capital was the collectivisation of Russian agriculture. This involved the state taking the land

KEY TERM

Capital The finance for investing in the purchasing of industrial machinery, plants and factories.

from the peasants, who would no longer farm for their own individual profit. Instead they would pool their efforts and receive a wage. Stalin calculated that this change would allow the Soviet Union to use the collective profits from the land to finance a massive industrialisation programme. For him, the needs of the land were always subordinate to those of industry.

Collective and state farms

In introducing collectivisation, Stalin referred to 'the setting up of **collective farms** and **state farms** in order to squeeze out all capitalist elements from the land'. In practice, there was little difference between the two. Both types of farm were to be the means by which private peasant ownership would be ended and agriculture made to serve the interests of the state. The plan was to group between 50 and 100 holdings into one unit. It was believed that large farms would be more efficient and would encourage the effective use of agricultural machinery. Indeed, the motorised tractor became the outstanding symbol of this mechanising of Soviet farming.

Improved farming methods on the new farms, so ran the argument, would decrease the number of rural workers needed and so release workers for the new factories.

The *kulaks*

When introducing collectivisation in 1928, Stalin claimed that it was 'voluntary', the free and eager choice of the peasants. But in truth it was forced on a very reluctant peasantry. In a major propaganda offensive, he copied Lenin in identifying a class of *kulaks*, who were holding back the workers' revolution by monopolising the best land and employing cheap peasant labour to farm it (see page 50). By hoarding their farm produce, they kept food prices high, thus making themselves rich at the expense of the workers and poorer peasants. Unless they were broken as a class, they would prevent the modernisation of the USSR.

The concept of a *kulak* class is now known to have been a Stalinist myth. The so-called *kulaks* were really only those hard-working peasants who had proved more efficient farmers than their neighbours. In no sense did they constitute the class of exploiting landowners described in Stalinist propaganda. Nonetheless, given the tradition of landlord oppression going back to tsarist times, the notion of grasping *kulaks* proved a very powerful one and provided the grounds for the coercion of the peasantry as a whole – middling and poor peasants, as well as *kulaks*.

Surplus food, surplus peasants

As a revolutionary, Stalin followed Lenin in having little sympathy for the peasants. Communist theory taught that the days of the peasantry as a revolutionary social force had passed. The future belonged to the urban workers.

KEY TERMS

Collective farms (*Kolkhozy* in Russian.) Run as co-operatives in which the peasants pooled their resources and shared their labour and wages.

State farms (*Sovkhozy* in Russian.) Contained peasants working directly for the state, which paid them a wage.

It was held that October 1917 had been the first stage in the triumph of this proletarian class. Therefore, it was perfectly fitting that the peasantry should, in a time of national crisis, bow to the demands of industrialisation.

It was certainly true that for generations the Russian countryside had been overpopulated, creating a chronic land shortage. Even in the best years of NEP, food production had seldom matched needs. Yet Stalin insisted that the problem was not the lack of food but its poor distribution; food shortages were the result of grain-hoarding by the rich peasants. This argument was then used to explain the urgent need for collectivisation as a way of securing adequate food supplies. It also provided the moral grounds for the onslaught on the *kulaks*, who were condemned as enemies of the Soviet nation in its struggle to modernise itself in the face of international, capitalist hostility.

SOURCE A

What opportunities did searches such as that shown in this photo give for oppressing the *kulaks*?

Members of the Communist Youth League unearthing bags of grain hidden by peasants in a cemetery near Odessa.

De-kulakisation

In some regions the poorer peasants undertook 'de-kulakisation' with enthusiasm, since it provided them with an excuse to settle old scores and give vent to local jealousies. Land and property were seized from the minority of better-off peasants, and they and their families were physically attacked. Such treatment was often the prelude to arrest, and imprisonment or **deportation** by **OGPU** anti-*kulak* squads, authorised by Stalin and modelled on the gangs that had persecuted the peasants during the state-organised terror of the civil war period (see page 50).

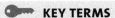 **KEY TERMS**

Deportation Removal to remote, barren areas.

OGPU Succeeded the *Cheka* as the state security force. In turn it became the NKVD, the MVD and then the KGB.

The renewal of terror also served as a warning to the peasantry of the likely consequences of resisting the state reorganisation of Soviet agriculture. The destruction of the *kulaks* was thus an integral part of the whole collectivisation process. As a Soviet official later admitted: 'most party officers thought that the whole point of de-Kulakisation was its value as an administrative measure, speeding up tempos of collectivisation'.

SOURCE B

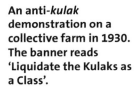
Who was likely to have organised a demonstration like the one shown here?

An anti-*kulak* demonstration on a collective farm in 1930. The banner reads 'Liquidate the Kulaks as a Class'.

Resistance to collectivisation

In the period between December 1929 and March 1930, nearly half the peasant farms in the USSR were collectivised. Yet millions of peasants resisted. What amounted to civil war broke out in the countryside. The following figures indicate the scale of the disturbances as recorded in official data for the period 1929–30:

- 30,000 arson attacks occurred.
- The number of organised rural mass disturbances increased from 172 for the first half of 1929 to 229 for the second half.

The role of women

A particularly striking feature of the disturbances was the prominent role women played in them. In Okhochaya, a village in Ukraine, women broke into the barns and seized the bags of grain dumped there by the requisition squads after they had taken it from the peasants. Women, as mothers and organisers of the household, were invariably the first to suffer the harsh consequences of the new agricultural system, and so it was they who were often the first to take action. One peasant explained in illuminatingly simple terms why his spouse was so opposed to collectivisation: 'My wife does not want to socialise our cow.' There were cases of mothers with their children lying down in front of the tractors and trucks sent to break up the private farms and impose collectivisation. One male peasant admitted that the men preferred women to lead the demonstrations since they would be less likely to suffer reprisals from the authorities who certainly, judging by court records, appeared reluctant initially to prosecute female demonstrators.

Peasant resistance, however, no matter how valiant or desperate, stood no chance of stopping collectivisation. The officials and their requisition squads pressed on with their disruptive enforcement policies. Such was the turmoil in the countryside that Stalin called a halt, blaming the troubles on overzealous officials who had become 'dizzy with success'. Many of the peasants were allowed to return to their original holdings. However, the delay was only temporary. Having cleared his name by blaming the difficulties on local officials, Stalin restarted collectivisation in a more determined, if somewhat slower, manner. By the end of the 1930s virtually the whole of the peasantry had been collectivised (see Figure 4.1).

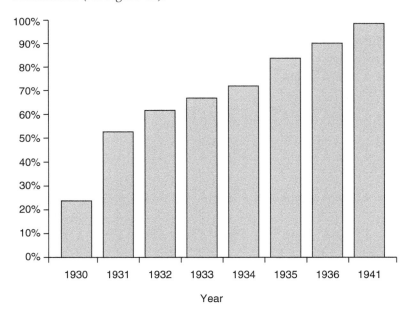

Figure 4.1 Cumulative percentage of peasant holdings collectivised in the USSR 1930–41.

Upheaval and distress

Behind these remarkable figures lay the story of a massive social upheaval. Bewildered and confused, the peasants either would not or could not co-operate in the deliberate destruction of their traditional way of life. The consequences were increasingly tragic. The majority of peasants ate their seed corn and slaughtered their livestock. There were no crops left to harvest or animals to rear.

The Soviet authorities responded with still fiercer coercion, but this simply made matters worse: imprisonment, deportation and execution could not replenish the barns or restock the herds. Special contingents of party workers were sent from the towns to restore food production levels by working on the land themselves. But their ignorance of farming only added to the disruption. By a bitter irony, even as starvation set in, the little grain that was available was being exported as 'surplus' to obtain the foreign capital that industry demanded. By 1932 the situation on the land was catastrophic.

In what ways do the data in Figure 4.1 and Tables 4.1 and 4.2 illustrate the impact of collectivisation in the countryside?

Table 4.1 The fall in food consumption (in kilograms per head)

Year	Bread	Potatoes	Meat and lard	Butter
1928	250.4	141.1	24.8	1.35
1932	214.6	125.0	11.2	0.70

Table 4.2 The fall in livestock (in millions)

Year	Horses	Cattle	Pigs	Sheep and goats
1928	33	70	26	146
1932	15	34	9	42

The data in Figure 4.1 and Tables 4.1 and 4.2 refer to the USSR as a whole. In the urban areas there was more food available. Indeed, a major purpose of the grain requisition squads was to maintain adequate supplies to the industrial regions. This meant that the misery in the countryside was proportionally greater, with areas such as Ukraine and Kazakhstan suffering particularly severely. The devastation experienced by the Kazakhs can be gauged from the fact that in this period they lost nearly 90 per cent of their livestock.

Nationwide famine

Starvation, which in many parts of the Soviet Union persisted throughout the 1930s, was at its worst in the years 1932–3, when a national famine occurred. Collectivisation led to despair among the peasants. In many areas they simply stopped producing, either as an act of desperate resistance or through sheer inability to adapt to the violently enforced land system. Hungry and embittered, they made for the towns in growing numbers. It had, of course, been part of Stalin's collectivisation plan to move the peasants into the industrial regions. However, so great was the migration that a system of internal passports had to be introduced in an effort to control the flow. Some idea of the horrors can be obtained from the eyewitness account given in Source C.

What image of peasant suffering and the official Soviet response to it is depicted in Source C?

SOURCE C

From Victor Serge, *Memoirs of a Revolutionary, 1901–1941*, Oxford University Press, 1963, p. 246.

Trainloads of deported peasants left for the icy North, the forests, the steppes, the deserts. These were whole populations, denuded [stripped] of everything;

the old folk starved to death in mid-journey, new-born babes were buried on the banks of the roadside, and each wilderness had its little cross of boughs or white wood. Other populations dragging all their mean possessions on wagons, rushed towards the frontiers of Poland, Rumania, and China and crossed them – by no means intact, to be sure – in spite of the machine guns … Agricultural technicians and experts were brave in denouncing the blunders and excesses; they were arrested in thousands and made to appear in huge sabotage trials so that responsibility might be unloaded on somebody.

Official silence

Despite overwhelming evidence of the tragedy that had overtaken the USSR, the official Stalinist line was that there was no famine. In the whole of the contemporary Soviet press there were only two oblique references to it. This conspiracy of silence was of more than political significance. As well as protecting the reputation of Stalin the great planner, it effectively prevented the introduction of measures to remedy the distress. Since the famine did not officially exist, Soviet Russia could not publicly take steps to relieve it. For the same reason, it could not appeal, as had been done during an earlier Russian famine in 1921, for aid from the outside world (see page 52).

Thus, what Isaac Deutscher, historian and former Trotskyist, called 'the first purely man-made famine in history' went unacknowledged in order to avoid discrediting Stalin. Not for the last time, large numbers of the Soviet people were sacrificed on the altar of Stalin's reputation. There was a strong rumour that Stalin's wife, **Nadezdha Alliluyeva**, had been driven to suicide by the knowledge that it was her husband's brutal policies that had caused the famine. Shortly before her death she had railed at Stalin as an uncaring monster. 'You torment your wife. You torment the whole Russian people.'

The truth of Nadezdha Alliluyeva's charge has now been put beyond doubt by the findings of scholars who have examined the Soviet archives that were opened up after the fall of the USSR in the early 1990s. Historian Lynne Viola in 2007 confirmed the horrific character of Stalin's treatment of the peasantry. She described how, between 1930 and 1932, Stalin drove 2 million peasants into internal exile as slave labourers, a quarter of that number dying of hunger and exposure. Her work, which built on the pioneering studies of Robert Conquest, the first major Western historian to chart Stalin's brutalities, serves as a belated and devastating corrective to the view advanced at the time by pro-Soviet sympathisers in the West that their hero Stalin was creating a paradise on earth.

Even allowing for the occasional progressive aspect of collectivisation, such as the building and distributing of mechanised tractors, the overall picture remained bleak. The mass of the peasantry had been uprooted and left bewildered. Despite severe reprisals and coercion, the peasants were unable to produce the surplus food that Stalin demanded. By 1939 Soviet agricultural

 KEY FIGURE

Nadezdha Alliluyeva (1902–32)

Stalin's second wife. His grief at her suicide may help to explain why Stalin became increasingly embittered and unfeeling towards people in general.

productivity had barely returned to the level recorded for tsarist Russia in 1913. But the most damning consideration still remains the man-made famine, which in the 1930s killed between 10 million and 15 million peasants.

Positive aspects of collectivisation

So widespread was the misery produced by collectivisation that it can lead to the overlooking of another important consideration. The hard fact is that Stalin's policies did force a large number of peasants to leave the land. This was a process that Russia needed. Economic historians have often stressed that the land crisis in Russia long pre-dated Stalinism. Since the nineteenth century, land in Russia had been growing ever more incapable of supporting the increasing numbers of people who lived unproductively on it. Unless a major shift occurred in the imbalance between urban and rural dwellers Russia would be in sustained difficulties. The nation needed to change from an agricultural and rural society to an urban and industrial one.

There is a case for arguing, therefore, that Stalin's collectivisation programme, brutally applied though it was, did answer one of the USSR's great needs. Leaving aside questions of human suffering, the enforced migration under Stalin made economic sense. It relieved the pressure on the land and provided the workforce that enabled the industrialisation programme to be started. Perhaps all this could be summed up by saying that Stalin's aims were understandable but his methods unacceptable.

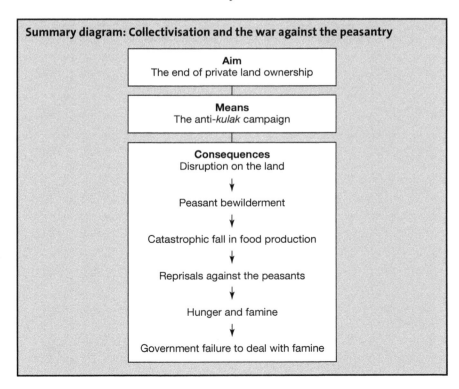

Summary diagram: Collectivisation and the war against the peasantry

Aim
The end of private land ownership

Means
The anti-*kulak* campaign

Consequences
Disruption on the land
↓
Peasant bewilderment
↓
Catastrophic fall in food production
↓
Reprisals against the peasants
↓
Hunger and famine
↓
Government failure to deal with famine

Industrialisation: the first three Five-Year Plans

▶ *What were Stalin's aims for Soviet industry in the 1930s and what methods did he use to achieve them?*

Stalin described his industrialisation plans for the USSR as an attempt to establish a war economy. He declared that he was making war on the failings of Russia's past and on the class enemies within the nation. He also claimed that he was preparing the USSR for war against its capitalist foes abroad. This was not simply martial imagery. Stalin regarded iron, steel and oil as the sinews of war. Their successful production would guarantee the strength and readiness of the nation to face its enemies. For Stalin, industry meant heavy industry. He believed that the industrial revolutions which had made Western Europe and North America so strong had been based on iron and steel production. It followed that the USSR must adopt a similar industrial pattern in its drive towards modernisation. The difference would be that, whereas the West had taken the capitalist road, the USSR would follow the path of socialism.

Stalin had grounds for his optimism. It so happened that the Soviet industrialisation drive in the 1930s coincided with the **Great Depression** in the Western world. Stalin claimed that the USSR was introducing into its own economy the technical successes of Western industrialisation but was rejecting the destructive capitalist system that went with them. Socialist planning would enable the USSR to avoid the errors that had begun to undermine the Western economies.

Soviet industrialisation under Stalin took the form of a series of Five-Year Plans (FYPs). *Gosplan* was required by Stalin to draw up a list of quotas of production ranging across the whole of Soviet industry. The process began in 1928 and, except for the war years 1941–5, lasted until Stalin's death in 1953. In all, there were five separate plans:

- first FYP: October 1928 to December 1932
- second FYP: January 1933 to December 1937
- third FYP: January 1938 to June 1941
- fourth FYP: January 1946 to December 1950
- fifth FYP: January 1951 to December 1955.

The first Five-Year Plan: 1928–32

The word 'plan' is misleading. The first FYP laid down what was to be achieved, but did not say how it was to be done. It simply assumed that the quotas would be met. What the first FYP represented, therefore, was a set of targets rather than a plan. As had happened with collectivisation, local officials and managers falsified their production figures to give the impression that they had met their

KEY TERM

Great Depression
A period of severe economic stagnation which began in the USA in 1929 and lasted until the mid-1930s, affecting the whole of the industrial world. Marxists regarded it as a portent of the final collapse of capitalism.

targets when, in fact, they had fallen short. For this reason, precise statistics for the first FYP are difficult to determine. A further complication is that three quite distinct versions of the first FYP eventually appeared. Impressed by the apparent progress of the plan in its early stages, Stalin encouraged the formulation of an 'optimal' plan which reassessed targets upwards. These new quotas were hopelessly unrealistic and stood no chance of being reached. Nonetheless, on the basis of the supposed achievements of this 'optimal' plan the figures were amended still higher in 1932. Western analysts suggest the data in Table 4.3 as the closest approximation to the real figures.

Table 4.3 Industrial output in USSR under the first FYPs

Product (in millions of tonnes)	1927–8: First plan	1932–3: 'Optimal'	1932: Amended	1932: Actual
Coal	35.0	75.0	95–105	64.0
Oil	11.7	21.7	40–55	21.4
Iron ore	6.7	20.2	24–32	12.1
Pig iron	3.2	10.0	15–16	6.2

Propaganda and collective effort

The importance of these figures should not be exaggerated. At the time it was the grand design that mattered, not the detail. The plan was a huge propaganda project aimed at convincing the Soviet people that they were personally engaged in a vast industrial enterprise. By their own efforts, they were changing the character of the society in which they lived and providing it with the means of achieving greatness. Nor was it all a matter of enforcement, fierce though that was. Among the young especially, there was an enthusiasm and a commitment that suggested that many Soviet citizens believed they were genuinely building a new and better world. The sense of the Soviet people as masters of their own fate was expressed in the slogan, 'There is no fortress that we Bolsheviks cannot storm'. John Scott, an American Communist and one of the many pro-Soviet Western industrial advisers who came to the USSR at this time, was impressed by the mixture of idealism and coercion that characterised the early stages of Stalinist industrialisation. He described how the city of Magnitogorsk in the Urals was built from scratch (see Source D).

SOURCE D

From John Scott, *Behind the Urals*, Secker & Warburg, 1942, p. 52.

Within several years, half a billion cubic feet of excavation was done, forty-two million cubic feet of reinforced concrete poured, five million cubic feet of fire bricks laid, a quarter of a million tons of structured steel erected. This was done without sufficient labour, without necessary quantities of the most elementary materials. Brigades of young enthusiasts from every corner of the Soviet Union arrived in the summer of 1930 and did the groundwork of railroad and dam construction necessary. Later, groups of local peasants and herdsmen came to Magnitogorsk because of bad conditions in the villages, due to collectivisation.

? How is the enthusiasm of the workers, as described in Source D, to be explained?

Many of the peasants were completely unfamiliar with industrial tools and processes. A colony of several hundred foreign engineers and specialists, some of whom made as high as one hundred dollars a day, arrived to advise and direct the work.

From 1928 until 1932 nearly a quarter of a million people came to Magnitogorsk. About three quarters of these new arrivals came of their own free will seeking work, bread-cards, better conditions. The rest came under compulsion.

SOURCE E

How does the poster attempt to achieve the effect of presenting Stalin as a hero?

'The Five-Year Plan' – a propaganda wall poster of the 1930s, depicting Stalin as the heroic creator of a powerful, industrialising Soviet Union. He is overcoming the forces of religion, international capitalism, and Russian conservatism and backwardness.

Successes of the first FYP

No matter how much the figures may have been rigged at the time, the first FYP was an extraordinary achievement overall. Coal, iron and the generation of electricity all increased in huge proportions. The production of steel and chemicals was less impressive, while the output of finished textiles actually declined. A striking feature of the plan was the low priority it gave to improving the material lives of the Soviet people. No effort was made to reward the workers by providing them with affordable consumer goods. Living conditions actually deteriorated in this period. Accommodation in the towns and cities remained substandard.

The Soviet authorities' neglect of basic social needs was not accidental. The plan had never been intended to raise living standards. Its purpose was collective, not individual. It called for sacrifice on the part of the workers in the construction of a socialist state, which would be able to sustain itself economically and militarily against the enmity of the outside world. It was the idea of sacrifice that Stalin used as a justification for demanding that, whatever the social disruption it caused, the relentless industrialisation drive could not be relaxed (see Source F).

? Why is Stalin so insistent in Source F on emphasising Russia's past humiliations?

SOURCE F

From Stalin's speech in February 1931, quoted in *Works of Josef Stalin*, volume 13, Lawrence & Wishart, 1955, p. 40.

It is sometimes asked whether it is not possible to slow down the tempo somewhat, to put a check on the movement. No, comrades, it is not possible! The tempo must not be reduced! To slacken the tempo would mean falling behind. And those who fall behind get beaten. But we do not want to be beaten. No, we refuse to be beaten! One feature of old Russia was the continual beatings she suffered because of her backwardness. She was beaten by the Mongols. She was beaten by the Turks. She was beaten by the Polish and Lithuanian gentry. She was beaten by the British and French capitalists. She was beaten by the Japanese barons. All beat her – because of her backwardness, military backwardness, cultural backwardness, political backwardness, industrial backwardness, agricultural backwardness. They beat her because to do so was profitable and could be done with impunity.

Resistance and sabotage

Stalin's passionate appeal to Russian history subordinated everything to the driving need for national survival, a need which justified the severity that accompanied his enforced transformation of the Soviet economy. He presented the FYP as a defence of the USSR against international hostility. This enabled him to brand resistance to the plan as 'sabotage'. A series of public trials of industrial 'wreckers', including a number of foreign workers, were staged to impress on the party and the masses, the futility of protesting against the industrialisation programme. In 1928, in a prelude to the first FYP, Stalin claimed to have discovered an anti-Soviet conspiracy among the mining engineers of Shakhty in the Donbass region of Ukraine. Their subsequent public trial was intended to frighten the workers into line. It also showed that the privileged position of the skilled workers, the **bourgeois experts**, was to be tolerated no longer.

This attack on the experts was part of a pattern in the first FYP that stressed quantity at the expense of quality. The push towards sheer volume of output was intended to prove the correctness of Stalin's grand economic schemes. Modern historian Sheila Fitzpatrick has described this as being an aspect of Stalin's **gigantomania**, his love of mighty building projects, such as canals, bridges and docks, which he regarded as proof that the USSR was advancing to greatness. Stalin's emphasis on gross output may also be interpreted as shrewdness on his part. He knew that the untrained peasants who now filled the factories would not turn immediately into skilled workers. It made sense, therefore, in the short term, to ignore the question of quality and to stress quantity.

Passing the blame

Stalin was seemingly untroubled by the low quality of production. His notions of industrial 'saboteurs' and 'wreckers' allowed him to place the blame for poor

🔑 KEY TERMS

Bourgeois experts
A mocking reference to those workers whose skills had enabled them to earn higher wages and thus be less committed to building the new Russia.

Gigantomania The worship of size for its own sake.

quality and underproduction on managers and workers who were not prepared to play their proper part in rebuilding the nation. He used OGPU agents and party *cadres* to terrorise the workforce. 'Sabotage' became a blanket term used to denounce anyone considered not to be pulling his weight. The simplest errors, such as being late for work or mislaying tools, could lead to such a charge.

At a higher level, those factory managers or foremen who did not meet their production quotas might find themselves on public trial as enemies of the Soviet state. In such an atmosphere of fear and recrimination, doctoring official returns and inflating output figures became normal practice. Everybody at every level engaged in a game of pretence. This was why Soviet statistics for industrial growth were so unreliable and why it was possible for Stalin to claim in mid-course that, since the first FYP had already met its initial targets, it would be shortened to a four-year plan. In Stalin's industrial revolution appearances were everything. This was where the logic of gigantomania had led.

Stalin: the master planner?

The industrial policies of this time have been described as the 'Stalinist blueprint' or 'Stalin's economic model'. Modern scholars are, however, wary of using such terms. Historian Norman Stone, for example, interprets Stalin's policies not as far-sighted strategy but as 'simply putting one foot in front of the other as he went along'. Despite the growing tendency in all official Soviet documents of the 1930s to include a fulsome reference to Stalin, the master-planner, there was in fact very little planning from the top.

It is true that Stalin's government exhorted, cajoled and bullied the workers into ever greater efforts towards ever greater production. But such planning as there was occurred not at national but at local level. It was the regional and site managers who, struggling desperately to make sense of the instructions they were given from on high, formulated the actual schemes for reaching their given production quotas. This was why, when things went wrong, it was easy for Stalin and his Kremlin colleagues to accuse lesser officials of sabotage while themselves avoiding any taint of incompetence.

The second and third Five-Year Plans

Although the second and third FYPs were modelled on the pattern of the first, the targets set for them were more realistic. Nevertheless, they still revealed the same lack of co-ordination that had characterised the first FYP. Overproduction occurred in some parts of the economy, underproduction in others, which frequently led to whole branches of industry being held up for lack of essential supplies. For example, some projects had too little timber at times, while at other times enough timber but insufficient steel. Spare parts were hard to come by, which often meant broken machines standing unrepaired and idle for long periods.

KEY TERM

Cadres Party members who were sent into factories and construction sites to spy and report back on managers and workers.

The hardest struggle was to maintain a proper supply of materials; this often led to fierce competition between regions and sectors of industry, all of them anxious to escape the charge of failing to achieve their targets. As a result there was hoarding of resources and a lack of co-operation between the various parts of the industrial system. Complaints about poor standards, carefully veiled so as not to appear critical of Stalin and the plan, were frequent. What successes there were occurred again in heavy industry, where the second FYP began to reap the benefit of the creation of large-scale plants under the first plan.

Scapegoats

The reluctance to tell the full truth hindered genuine industrial growth. Since no one was willing to admit that there was an error in the planning, faults went unchecked until serious breakdowns occurred. There then followed the familiar search for scapegoats. It was during the period of the second and third FYPs that Stalin's political purges were at their fiercest (see pages 108–17). In such an all-pervading atmosphere of terror the mere accusation of 'sabotage' was taken as a proof of guilt. Productivity suffered as a result. As Russian-born British historian Alec Nove observed: 'Everywhere there were said to be spies, wreckers, diversionists. There was a grave shortage of qualified personnel, so the deportation of many thousands of engineers and technologists to distant concentration camps represented a severe loss'.

The Stakhanovite movement 1935

Despite Stalin's claims to the contrary, the living standards of the workers failed to rise. However, the party's control of newspapers, cinema and radio meant that only a favourable view of the plans was ever presented. The official line was that all was well and the workers were happy. Support for this claim was dramatically provided by the Stakhanovite movement: in August 1935, it was officially claimed that **Alexei Stakhanov**, a miner in the Donbass region, had, on his own, cut over 100 tonnes of coal in one five-hour shift, which was more than over fourteen times his required quota. His achievement was seized on by the authorities as a glorious example of what was possible in a Soviet Union guided by Joseph Stalin.

Miners and workers everywhere were urged to match Stakhanov's dedication by similar **storming**. But, despite the excitement this aroused, storming proved more loss than gain. While some Stakhanovite groups boasted higher output, this was achieved only by giving them privileged access to tools and supplies and by changing work plans to accommodate them. The resulting disruption led to an overall loss of production in those areas where the Stakhanovite movement was at its most enthusiastic.

Workers' rights

After 1917, the Russian trade unions had become powerless. In Bolshevik theory, in a truly socialist state such as Russia now was, there was no distinction

KEY FIGURE

Alexei Stakhanov (1906–77)

As was admitted by the Soviet authorities in 1988, his achievement was a gross exaggeration. He had not worked on his own but as part of a team, which had been supplied with the best coal-cutting machines available.

KEY TERM

Storming An intensive period of work to meet a high set target. Despite the propaganda with which it was introduced, storming proved a very inefficient form of industrial labour and was soon abandoned.

between the interests of government and those of the workers. Therefore, there was no longer any need for a separate trade union movement. In 1920, Trotsky had taken violent steps to destroy the independence of the unions and bring them directly under Bolshevik control. The result was that after 1920 the unions were simply the means by which the Bolshevik government enforced its requirements on the workers.

Under Stalin's industrialisation programme, any vestige of workers' rights disappeared. Strikes were prohibited and the traditional demands for better pay and conditions were regarded as selfish in a time of national crisis. A code of 'labour discipline' was drawn up, demanding maximum effort and output; failure to conform was punishable by a range of penalties from loss of wages to imprisonment in forced labour camps. On paper, wages improved during the second FYP, but in real terms, since there was food rationing and high prices, living standards were lower in 1937 than they had been in 1928.

Living and working conditions

Throughout the period of the FYPs, Stalin's Soviet government asserted that the nation was under siege. It claimed that, unless priority was given to defence needs, the very existence of the USSR was in jeopardy. Set against such a threat, workers' material interests were of little significance. For workers to demand improved conditions at a time when the Soviet Union was fighting for survival was unthinkable; they would be betraying the nation. It was small wonder, then, that food remained scarce and expensive and severe overcrowding persisted.

Nearly all workers lived in cramped apartments. Public housing policy did produce a large number of tenement blocks in towns and cities – usually five-storey structures with no lifts. Quite apart from their architectural ugliness they were a hazard to health. So great was the overcrowding that it was common for young families to live with their in-laws and equally common for four or five families to share a single lavatory and a single kitchen, which was often no more than an alcove with a gas-ring. There were rotas for the use of these facilities. Queuing to relieve oneself or to cook was part of the daily routine.

There was money available, but the government spent it not on improving social conditions but on armaments. Between 1933 and 1937, defence expenditure rose from four to seventeen per cent of the overall industrial budget. By 1940, under the terms of the third FYP, which renewed the commitment to heavy industrial development, a third of the USSR's government spending was on arms.

Strengths of the first three Five-Year Plans

In judging the scale of Stalin's achievement, it is helpful to cite such statistics relating to industrial output during the period of the first three FYPs as are reliable. The data in Table 4.4 (page 102) are drawn from the work of economic historian E. Zaleski, whose findings are based on careful analysis of Soviet and Western sources.

Table 4.4 Industrial output during the first three FYPs

Output	1927	1930	1932	1935	1937	1940
Coal (millions of tonnes)	35	60	64	100	128	150
Steel (millions of tonnes)	3	5	6	13	18	18
Oil (millions of tonnes)	12	17	21	24	26	26
Electricity (millions of kWh)	18	22	20	45	80	90

The data indicate a remarkable increase in production overall. In a little over twelve years, coal production had grown five times, steel six and oil output had more than doubled. Perhaps the most impressive statistic is the one showing that electricity generation quintupled. These four key products provided the basis for the military economy that enabled the USSR not only to survive four years of German occupation but eventually to amass sufficient resources to drive the German army out of Soviet territory. The climax of this was the Soviet invasion and defeat of Germany in 1945 (see page 146).

Weaknesses of the Five-Year Plans

However, Stalin's economic reforms succeeded only in the traditional areas of heavy industry. In those sectors where unskilled and forced labour could be easily used, as in large building projects such as factories, bridges, refineries and canals, the results were impressive. But the Soviet economy itself remained unbalanced. Stalin gave little thought to developing an overall economic strategy. Nor were modern industrial methods adopted. Old, wasteful techniques, such as relying on mass labour rather than efficient machines, continued to be used. Vital financial and material resources were squandered.

Stalin's love of what he called 'the grand projects of communism' meant that no real attention was paid to producing quality goods that could then be profitably sold abroad to raise the money the USSR so badly needed. He loved to show off to foreign visitors the great projects that were either completed or under construction. Two enterprises of which he was especially proud were the city of Magnitogorsk (see page 96) and the **White Sea Canal**. Yet, it was all vainglorious. Despite Stalin's boasts and the adulation with which he was regarded by foreign sympathisers, the simple fact remained that his policies had deprived the Soviet Union of any chance of genuinely competing with the modernising economies of Europe and the USA.

A serious failing of the FYPs was their neglect of agriculture, which continued to be deprived of funds since it was regarded as wholly secondary to the needs of industry. This neglect proved very damaging. The lack of agricultural growth resulted in constant food shortages which could be met only by buying foreign supplies. This drained the USSR's limited financial resources.

Despite the official adulation of Stalin for his great diplomatic triumph in achieving the non-aggression pact with Nazi Germany in August 1939 (see page 136), there was no relaxation within the Soviet Union of the war

KEY TERM

White Sea Canal In fact three canals linking Leningrad with the White Sea; built predominantly by forced labourers, who died in their thousands, the canal proved practically worthless since it was hardly used after construction.

atmosphere. Indeed, the conditions of the ordinary people continued to deteriorate. An official decree of 1940 empowered Stalin's government to encroach even further on workers' liberties by imposing such measures as:

- direction of labour
- enforced settlement of undeveloped areas
- severe penalties for slacking and absenteeism.

In 1941, when the German invasion effectively destroyed the third FYP, the conditions of the Soviet industrial workers were marginally lower than in 1928. Yet whatever the hardship of the workers, the fact was that in 1941 the USSR was economically strong enough to engage in an ultimately successful military struggle of unprecedented duration and intensity. In Soviet propaganda, this was what mattered, not minor questions of living standards. The USSR's triumph over Nazism would later be claimed as the ultimate proof of the wisdom of Stalin's enforced industrialisation programme.

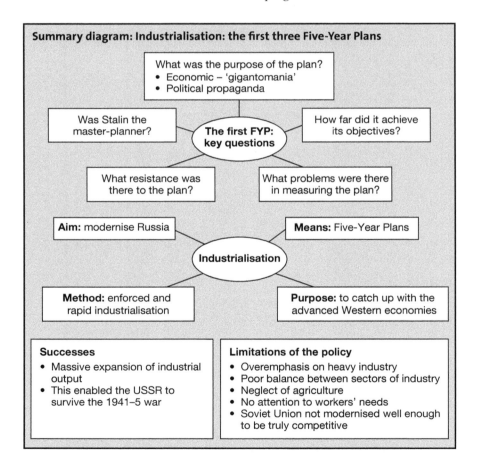

Summary diagram: Industrialisation: the first three Five-Year Plans

What was the purpose of the plan?
- Economic – 'gigantomania'
- Political propaganda

Was Stalin the master-planner?

The first FYP: key questions

How far did it achieve its objectives?

What resistance was there to the plan?

What problems were there in measuring the plan?

Aim: modernise Russia

Means: Five-Year Plans

Industrialisation

Method: enforced and rapid industrialisation

Purpose: to catch up with the advanced Western economies

Successes
- Massive expansion of industrial output
- This enabled the USSR to survive the 1941–5 war

Limitations of the policy
- Overemphasis on heavy industry
- Poor balance between sectors of industry
- Neglect of agriculture
- No attention to workers' needs
- Soviet Union not modernised well enough to be truly competitive

Key debate

▶ *Were Stalin's economic policies justified by their results?*

Many historians have contributed to the analysis of Stalin's economic policies and their impact on the Soviet Union and its people. Some argue that whatever the economic gains resulting from the policies, the methods used to implement them went beyond what was acceptable in human terms. Others suggest that, questions of human suffering aside, the policies did not meet their economic objectives. Another viewpoint is that the problems facing the Soviet Union justified the harsh measures Stalin used. The following survey introduces the views of some of the main contributors to the debate.

Alec Nove, a Russian-born scholar, who produced his major works in the 1960s and 1970s, argued strongly from a liberal viewpoint that 'Stalin's collectivisation and industrialisation programmes were bad economics' since they caused upheaval on the land and misery to the peasants without producing the industrial growth that the USSR needed. Furthermore, the condition of the industrial workers deteriorated under Stalin's policies.

Nove's approach was shared by British historian Robert Conquest, who initially supported the Soviet experiment, but became disillusioned by Stalin's policies. In the 1960s, he produced a major study of Stalin's economic programme in which he condemned the coercive methods that had been used, remarking: 'Stalinism is one way of attaining industrialisation, just as cannibalism is one way of attaining a high protein diet.'

Sheila Fitzpatrick, a scholar with left-wing leanings, broadly agrees with the criticisms made by Nove and Conquest, adding that Stalin's gigantomania, his obsession with large-scale projects, distorted the economy at a critical time when what was needed was proper investment and planning. Fitzpatrick lays emphasis on Stalin's failure to improve Soviet living standards.

EXTRACT 1

From Sheila Fitzpatrick, *The Russian Revolution*, Oxford University Press, 2008, p. 146.

The decline in living standards and quality of life affected almost all classes of the population, urban and rural. Peasants suffered most as a result of collectivization. But life in the towns was made miserable by food rationing, queues, constant shortages of consumer goods including shoes and clothing, acute overcrowding of housing, the endless inconveniences associated with the elimination of private trade, and deterioration of urban services of all kinds.

Significantly, however, she modifies her criticism by pointing out that Stalin's policies need to be seen in a broad social and political context. Harsh though Stalin was, he was trying to bring stability to a Soviet Russia that had known only turmoil and division since 1917.

This line of reasoning was shared by British historian Peter Gattrell, who, while acknowledging that Stalin was certainly coercive in his methods, stressed that the outcome of collectivisation and industrialisation was an economy strong enough by 1941 to sustain the USSR through four years of the most demanding of modern wars. Gattrell suggested that, hard though it is for the Western liberal mind to accept, it may be that Russia could not have been modernised by any other methods except those used by Stalin.

David Hoffman, an American analyst, offers a strongly contrary view by arguing that Stalin's use of coercion in seeking economic and social change proved both inhumane and ineffective.

EXTRACT 2

From David L. Hoffman, *Stalinist Values: The Cultural Norms of Soviet Modernity*, Cornell University Press, 2003, p. 111.

Social change must be gradual and consensual if it is to succeed. Even if violence achieves superficial change, it does not permanently transform the way people think and act. Moreover in the Soviet case the means and ends were themselves in contradiction. State coercion by its very nature could not create social harmony. The arrest and execution of millions of people only sowed hatred, mistrust and disharmony in Soviet society.

Robert Service, Stalin's outstanding British biographer, makes the following succinct assessment of the effects of his subject's collectivisation and industrialisation programme by 1940.

EXTRACT 3

From Robert Service, *Stalin: A Biography*, Macmillan, 2004, p. 274.

Disruption was everywhere in the economy. Ukraine, south Russia, and Kazakhstan were starving. The Gulag [Russia's labour camp system] heaved with prisoners. Nevertheless the economic transformation was no fiction. The USSR under Stalin's rule had been pointed decisively in the direction of becoming an industrial, urban society. This had been his great objective. His gamble was paying off for him, albeit not for millions of victims. Magnitogorsk and the White Sea Canal were constructed at the expense of the lives of Gulag convicts, Ukrainian peasants and even undernourished, overworked factory labourers.

Chapter summary

Judging that economic growth was essential to the very survival of the Soviet Union, Stalin embarked on a massive programme of agricultural and industrial reform. He brushed aside doubters within the CPSU who were disturbed by the pace of change. Subordinating the land and its peasants to the needs of industry and the workers, he used coercion and terror to enforce his will. Collectivisation created such social and economic disruption that famine followed in its wake. While blaming local officials for their excess of zeal, Stalin declined to relax the pressure. By the mid-1930s the great majority of the peasants had lost their private property and were living in collectives.

The same relentless drive was maintained in the industrialisation programme. In a series of Five-Year Plans, Stalin sought to create a modern economy based on heavy-industrial production. There were successes, magnified in Stalinist propaganda, but the pre-set targets were not universally met. Nevertheless, enough was achieved for the level of success to become a matter of historical debate, some analysts claiming that the level of progress justified the harsh methods used to achieve it, others arguing that Stalin's policies were based on a false understanding of modernisation and were therefore essentially destructive.

 Refresher questions

Use these questions to remind yourself of the key material covered in this chapter.

1 In what way was collectivisation intended to serve the interests of industrialisation?

2 What were the effects of collectivisation on the peasantry?

3 Why could the famine of the early 1930s not be dealt with effectively?

4 How successful had collectivisation proved to be by 1939?

5 What were Stalin's aims for Soviet industry in the 1930s?

6 What was the purpose of the first FYP?

7 How far did the first FYP achieve its objectives?

8 Why was there so little resistance to the first FYP?

9 How far was the first FYP planned from the top?

10 What were the strengths and weaknesses of the second and third FYPs?

Question practice

ESSAY QUESTIONS

1 'The main reason why Stalin undertook the transformation of Soviet agriculture between 1929 and 1941 was to improve food supplies in the USSR.' Assess the validity of this view.
2 How far did collectivisation prepare the path for industrialisation in the Soviet Union in the years 1929–41?
3 To what extent was the Russian economy transformed in the years 1929–41?
4 'The lives of Russian peasants were hugely disrupted in the years 1929–41.' Assess the validity of this view.

INTERPRETATION QUESTION

1 Using your understanding of the historical context, assess how convincing the arguments in Extracts 1, 2 and 3 (**pages 104–5**) are in relation to their evaluation of Stalin's economic policies.

SOURCE ANALYSIS QUESTION

1 With reference to Sources C (**page 92**), D (**page 96**) and F (**page 98**) and your understanding of the historical context, assess the value of these sources to a historian studying the impact of Stalin's collectivisation and industrialisation programmes on the Soviet people.

CHAPTER 5

Stalin's dictatorship, power and society 1929–41

With victory over his rivals achieved by 1929, Stalin then spent the next decade following two interlocking policies: the modernisation of the Soviet economy and the establishment of total political control. This chapter deals with the manner in which the Soviet Union moved towards totalitarianism under Stalin and examines the impact of this on Soviet culture and the lives of the people. The key features covered are:

★ The purges and the mechanisms of control

★ Soviet totalitarianism and its impact on culture and society

★ Stalin's cult of personality

★ Stalin's foreign policy 1933–41

Key dates

1929	Stalin established as *vozhd*	1936	Zinoviev and Kamenev tried and executed
1931–4	The 'Stalin enrolment'		
1932	Start of the purges	1937	Purge of the armed forces began
1933–4	Stalin's instruments of control created	1938–41	Spread of purges across USSR
1934–6	Post-Kirov purges	1939	Nazi–Soviet Pact
1936–9	The 'Great Terror'	1939–41	Seizure of Poland and Baltic states

1 The purges and the mechanisms of control

▶ *What means did Stalin use to consolidate his control over the USSR?*

Having become the *vozhd* of the Soviet Union by 1929, Stalin spent the rest of his life consolidating and extending his authority. The purges were his principal weapon for achieving this. They became the chief mechanism for removing anyone he regarded as a threat to his authority. The Stalinist purges, which began in 1932, were not unprecedented. Public show trials had been held during the early stages of the first Five-Year Plan as a way of exposing 'saboteurs' who were accused of damaging the USSR's industrial programme (see page 98).

However, prosecutions were not restricted to industrial enemies. In 1932 the trial took place of M.N. Ryutin, a Right Communist, who had published an attack on Stalin, describing him as 'the evil genius who has brought the revolution to the verge of destruction' and calling for his removal from office. Ryutin and his supporters were publicly tried and expelled from the party. This was the prelude to the first major purge of the CPSU by Stalin. Between 1933 and 1934 nearly a million members, over a third of the total membership, were excluded from the party on the grounds that they were Ryutinites. The purge was organised by **Nikolai Yezhov**, the chief of the control commission, the branch of the Central Committee responsible for party discipline.

At the beginning, party purges were not as violent as they later became. The usual procedure was to oblige members to hand in their **party card** for checking, at which point any suspect individuals would not have their cards returned to them. This was tantamount to expulsion since, without cards, members were denied access to all party activities. Under such a system, it became progressively difficult to mount effective opposition.

Stalin's motivation

Despite Stalin's increasing control, attempts were made in the early 1930s to criticise him, as the Ryutin affair illustrates. These efforts were ineffectual, but they led Stalin to believe that organised resistance to him was still possible. It was such a belief that led Stalin to develop the purges into a systematic terrorising, not of obvious political opponents, but of colleagues and party members. It is difficult to explain precisely why Stalin initiated such a terror. Historians accept that they are dealing with behaviour that sometimes went beyond reason and logic. Stalin was deeply suspicious by nature and suffered from increasing paranoia as he grew older. Right up to his death in 1953, he continued to believe he was under threat from actual or potential enemies. Robert Service writes that Stalin had 'a gross personality disorder'.

SOURCE A

From Robert Service, *Stalin: A Biography*, Macmillan, 2004, p. 344.

[Stalin] had a Georgian sense of honour and revenge. Notions of getting even with adversaries never left him. He had a Bolshevik viewpoint on Revolution. Violence, dictatorship and terror were methods he and fellow Party veterans took to be normal. The physical extermination of enemies was entirely acceptable to them.

Stalin's daughter, Svetlana, said revealingly about him that once he took a dislike to someone, 'he translated that person into the ranks of enemies'. Such thinking on Stalin's part meant that everyone was suspect and consequently no one was safe. In Service's words, Stalin saw 'malevolent human agency in every personal or political problem he encountered'. Purges became not so much a series of episodes as a permanent condition of Soviet political life. Terror was all-pervading throughout the remainder of Stalin's rule.

KEY FIGURE

Nikolai Yezhov (1895–1940)
Known as the 'poisonous dwarf' because of his diminutive stature and vicious personality, he became head of the NKVD in 1937; he was himself tried and shot three years later.

KEY TERM

Party card The official CPSU warrant granting membership to the holder. It was a prized possession in Soviet Russia since it entitled the holder to a wide range of privileges, such as quality accommodation, higher food rations, access to health care and education for the member's children.

According to Source A, what explains Stalin's readiness to resort to violence?

Stalin's instruments of control

In the years 1933–4, as an accompaniment to the purges, Stalin centralised all the major law enforcement agencies:

- the civilian police
- labour camp commandants and guards (see page 116)
- border and security guards.

All these bodies were put under the authority of the NKVD, the state secret police, successor to the *Cheka* and forerunner of the KGB, a body which was directly answerable to Stalin.

The post-Kirov purges 1934–6

In Leningrad on 1 December 1934, Sergei Kirov, the secretary of the Leningrad soviet, was shot and killed in his own office. It is possible that Stalin was implicated. What is certain is that the murder worked directly to his advantage. Kirov had been a highly popular figure in the party and had been elected to the Politburo. He was known to be unhappy with the speed of Stalin's industrialisation drive and also with the growing number of purges. If organised opposition to Stalin were to form within the party, Kirov was the most likely individual around whom dissatisfied members might have rallied. That danger to Stalin had now been removed.

Stalin was quick to exploit the situation. Within two hours of learning of Kirov's murder he had signed a 'Decree against terrorist acts' – an order giving the NKVD limitless powers to pursue the enemies of the state and the party. On the pretext of hunting down the killers, a fresh purge of the party was begun. Led by Genrikh Yagoda, head of the NKVD, 3000 suspected conspirators were rounded up and then imprisoned or executed; tens of thousands of other people were deported from Leningrad. Stalin then filled the vacant positions with his own nominees. As a result of these replacements, there was no significant area of Soviet bureaucracy which Stalin did not control.

- In 1935 Kirov's key post as party boss in Leningrad was filled by **Andrei Zhdanov**.
- The equivalent post in Moscow was taken by Nikita Khrushchev, another ardent Stalin supporter (see page 179).
- In recognition of his successful courtroom bullying of 'oppositionists' in the earlier purge trials, **Andrei Vyshinsky** was appointed state prosecutor.
- Stalin's fellow Georgian, **Lavrenti Beria**, was entrusted with overseeing state security in the national-minority areas of the USSR.
- Stalin's personal secretary, **Alexander Poskrebyshev**, was put in charge of the Secretariat.

The outstanding feature of the post-Kirov purges was the status of many of the victims. Prominent among those arrested were Kamenev and Zinoviev. Their

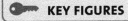

arrest sent out a clear message: whatever their status, no party members were safe. Arbitrary arrest and summary execution became the norm. An impression of this can be gained from noting the fate of the representatives at the party congress of 1934:

- Of the 1996 delegates who attended, 1108 were executed during the next three years.
- In addition, out of the 139 Central Committee members elected at that gathering, all but 41 were executed during the purges.

Historian Leonard Shapiro, in a celebrated study of the CPSU, described these events as 'Stalin's victory over the party'. From this point on, the CPSU was entirely under his control. It ceased, in effect, to have a separate existence. Stalin had become the party.

The 'Stalin enrolment' 1931–4

Stalin's successful purge was made easier by a shift in the make-up of the party, known as the 'Stalin enrolment'. Between 1931 and 1934, the CPSU had, under Stalin's direction, deliberately increased its membership. Unlike the old Bolsheviks, most of the new members had been uninvolved in the revolution of 1917 or in the struggle to consolidate the CPSU's hold on Russia in the 1920s. They joined the party primarily to advance their careers. Having made little contribution to the CPSU so far, they were fully aware that they owed the privileges that came with membership wholly to Stalin's patronage. As Stalin had calculated, this made them eager to support the elimination of the anti-Stalinist elements in the party. It improved their own chances of promotion. The competition for good jobs in Soviet Russia was invariably fierce. Purges always left positions to be filled. As the chief dispenser of positions, Stalin knew that the self-interest of these new party members would keep them loyal to him.

The 'Great Purge' 1936–9

It might be expected that, once Stalin's complete mastery over the party had been established, the purges would stop. But they did not; they increased in intensity. Repeating his constant assertion that the Soviet Union was in a state of siege, Stalin called for still greater vigilance against the enemies within, who were in league with the Soviet Union's foreign enemies. Between 1936 and 1939, a progressive terrorising of the USSR occurred, affecting the whole population. Its scale gained it the title of the 'Great Purge' (or the 'Great Terror'), which took its most dramatic form in the public show trials of Stalin's former Bolshevik colleagues. The one-time heroes of the 1917 revolution were imprisoned or executed as enemies of the state.

The descriptions applied to the accused during the purges bore little relation to political reality. 'Right', 'Left' and Centre' opposition blocs were identified and the groupings invariably had the catch-all term 'Trotskyite' tagged on to them, but such words were convenient prosecution labels rather than definitions of a genuine political opposition. They were intended to isolate those in the CPSU and the Soviet state whom Stalin wished to destroy.

Stalin's 'Great Terror' terror programme breaks down into three stages:

- the purge of the party
- the purge of the armed forces
- the purge of the people.

The purge of the party – show trials

Stalin's destruction of those in the party he regarded as a major threat was achieved by the holding of three major show trials:

- In 1936, Kamenev and Zinoviev and fourteen other leading Bolsheviks were accused of involvement in the Kirov murder and plotting to subvert the Soviet state. After a public trial they were condemned and executed.
- In 1937, seventeen Bolsheviks were denounced collectively as the 'Anti-Soviet Trotskyist Centre', and were charged with spying for Nazi Germany. All but three of them were executed.
- In 1938, Bukharin, Rykov, Tomsky and twenty others, branded 'Trotskyite-Rightists', were publicly tried on a variety of counts, including sabotage and spying; all were found guilty. Bukharin and Rykov were executed; Tomsky killed himself.

Remarkably, the great majority went to their death after confessing their guilt. An obvious question arises: why did they confess? After all, these men were tough Bolsheviks. Physical and mental tortures, including threats to their families, were used, but arguably more important was their sense of demoralisation at having been accused and disgraced by the party to which they had dedicated their lives. In a curious sense, their admission of guilt was a last act of loyalty to the party. In his final speech in court, Bukharin accepted the infallibility of the party and of Stalin, referring to him as 'the hope of the world'. The atmosphere of the trials was described by a British observer (Source B).

SOURCE B

From Fitzroy McClean, *Eastern Approaches*, Jonathan Cape, 1951, p. 82.

To the right of the judges, facing the accused, stood Vyshinsky, the Public Prosecutor. An officer of the court started to read out the indictment. The trial had begun. The prisoners were charged, collectively and individually, with every conceivable crime: high treason, murder, and sabotage. They had plotted to wreck industry and agriculture, to assassinate Stalin, to dismember the Soviet Union for the benefit of their capitalist allies. One after another, using the same words, they admitted their guilt: Bukharin, Rykov, Yagoda. Each prisoner incriminated his fellows and was in turn incriminated by them. There was no attempt to evade responsibility.

? Why in Source B does the writer stress that the accused were 'in full possession of their faculties'?

They were men in full possession of their faculties. And yet what they said seemed to bear no relation to reality. The fabric that was being built up was fantastic beyond belief. As the trial progressed it became clearer that the underlying purpose of every testimony was to blacken the leaders of the 'bloc' to represent them not as political prisoners but as common murderers, poisoners and spies.

SOURCE C

How does this montage illustrate the extent of the purges against leading members of the party?

This montage, composed by Trotsky's supporters, illustrates the remarkable fact that of the original 1917 Central Committee of the Bolshevik Party only Stalin was still in a position of power in 1938. The majority of the other 23 members had, of course, been destroyed in the purges.

Lack of resistance

Whatever their reasons for confessing, that the leading Bolsheviks did so made it extremely difficult for other victims to plead their own innocence. The psychological impact of the public confessions of such figures as Kamenev and Zinoviev was profound. It created an atmosphere in which innocent victims submitted in open court to false charges, and went to their death begging the party's forgiveness.

Stalin's insistence on a policy of show trials showed his astuteness. There is little doubt that he had the power to conduct the purges without using legal proceedings. However, by making the victims deliver humiliating confessions in open court, Stalin was able to reveal the scale of the conspiracy against him and to prove the need for the purging to continue. He was ably assisted in this by his chief prosecutor, Vyshinsky, who became notorious for the ferocity of his verbal assaults on the accused during the show trials (Source D).

? According to Vyshinsky in Source D, what is the main crime the accused have committed?

SOURCE D

Extract from Andrei Vyshinsky's prosecution speech at the People's Commissariat of Justice, 11 March 1938, quoted in F.W. Stacey, *Stalin and the Making of Modern Russia*, Edward Arnold, 1970, p. 33.

Comrade Judges, as the Court investigation of the present case proceeded, it brought to light ever more the horrors of the chain of unparalleled, monstrous crimes committed by the accused, the entire abominable chain of heinous deeds. In what other trial was it possible to uncover the real nature of these crimes with such force to tear the mask of perfidy from the faces of these scoundrels and to show the whole world the bestial countenance of the international brigands who cunningly direct the hands of miscreants against our peaceful Socialist labour that has set up the new, happy, flourishing Socialist society of workers and peasants? Our whole country from young to old is awaiting one thing: the traitors and spies who are selling our country to the enemy must be shot like dirty dogs. Our people are demanding one thing: crush the accursed reptiles!

The purge of the armed forces

A particularly significant development in the purges occurred in 1937 when the Soviet military came under threat. Stalin's control of the Soviet Union would not have been complete if the armed services had continued as an independent force. It was essential that they be kept subservient. Stalin also had a lingering fear that the army, which had been Trotsky's creation (see page 41), might still have sympathy for their old leader. In May 1937, Vyshinsky, Stalin's chief prosecutor, announced that 'a gigantic conspiracy' had been uncovered in the Red Army. Marshal **Mikhail Tukhachevsky** was arrested along with seven other generals. On the pretext that speed was essential to prevent a military coup, a trial was held immediately, this time in secret. Tukhachevsky was charged with having spied for Germany and Japan.

The outcome was predetermined. In June 1937, after their ritual confession and condemnation, Tukhachevsky and his fellow generals were shot. To prevent any chance of a military reaction, a wholesale destruction of the Red Army establishment was undertaken on the grounds that it was riddled with traitors. In the following eighteen months:

- all eleven **war commissars** were removed from office
- three of the five **marshals of the Soviet Union** were dismissed
- 91 of the 101-man Supreme Military Council were arrested, of whom 80 were executed
- fourteen of the sixteen army commanders and nearly two-thirds of the 280 divisional commanders were removed
- 35,000 commissioned officers were either imprisoned or shot
- the navy did not escape; between 1937 and 1939 all the serving admirals of the fleet were shot and thousands of naval officers were sent to labour camps

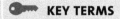

KEY FIGURE

Mikhail Tukhachevsky (1893–1937)

An outstanding military leader, a founder, with Trotsky, of the Red Army.

KEY TERMS

War commissars Ministers responsible for military organisation.

Marshals of the Soviet Union Equivalent to field marshals or five-star generals.

- the air force was similarly decimated during that period, only one of its senior commanders surviving the purge.

The result was that all three services were left seriously undermanned and staffed by inexperienced or incompetent replacements. Given the defence needs of the USSR, the deliberate crippling of the Soviet military is the aspect of the purges that appears most irrational.

The purge of the people

Stalin's gaining of total dominance over party, government and military did not mean the end of the purges. The apparatus of terror was retained and the search for enemies continued. Purges were used to force the pace of the FYPs; charges of industrial sabotage were made against managers and workers in the factories. Purges were also a way of forcing the regions and nationalities into total subordination to Stalin.

The show trials that had taken place in Moscow and Leningrad, with their catalogue of accusations, confessions and death sentences, were repeated in all the republics of the USSR. For example, between 1937 and 1939 in Stalin's home state of Georgia:

- two state prime ministers were removed
- four-fifths of the regional party secretaries were dismissed
- thousands of lesser officials lost their posts.

To accommodate the great numbers of prisoners created by the purges, a **gulag** was established across the USSR.

Mass repression: the *Yezhovshchina*

No area of Soviet life entirely escaped the purges. The constant fear that this created conditioned the way the Soviet people lived their lives. The greatest impact of the purges was on the middle and lower ranks of Soviet society:

- One person in every eight of the population was arrested during Stalin's purges.
- Almost every family in the USSR suffered the loss of at least one of its members as a victim of the terror.

In the years 1937–8, mass repression was imposed. Known as the *Yezhovshchina*, after its chief organiser, **Nikolai Yezhov**, this purge was typified by the practice in which NKVD squads entered selected localities and removed hundreds of inhabitants for execution. The number of victims to be arrested was specified in set quotas as if they were industrial production targets. There was no appeal against sentence and the death warrant invariably required that the execution 'be carried out immediately'. The shootings took place in specially designated zones. One notorious example of this was Butovo, a village outside Moscow, which became one of the NKVD's killing fields. Later excavations revealed mass graves containing over 20,000 bodies, dating back to the late 1930s and

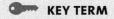 **KEY TERM**

Gulag An extensive network of prison and labour camps.

SOURCE E

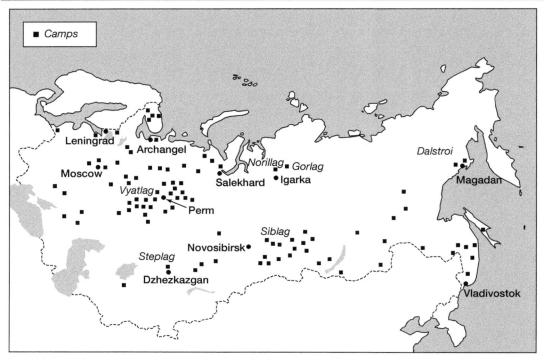

Map of the gulag, 1937–57. By 1941, as a result of the purges, there were an estimated 8 million prisoners in the gulag. The average sentence was ten years, which, given the conditions in the camps, was equivalent to a death sentence. As an example of state-organised repression, Stalin's gulag stands alongside Hitler's concentration camps and Mao Zedong's *laogai* (prison camps).

? What does Source E indicate about the scale of Stalin's repression?

indicating that nightly over many months victims had been taken to Butovo and shot in batches of 100.

In so far as the terrorising of ordinary people had any specific purpose, it was to frighten the USSR's national minorities into abandoning any remaining thoughts of challenging Moscow's control. It forced them into a full acceptance of Stalin's enforced industrialisation programme.

Responsibility for the purges

There is little doubt that Stalin himself initiated, and remained the driving force behind, the purges. He exploited the Russian autocratic tradition that he inherited to rid himself of real or imagined enemies. Yet leading scholars, such as Stalin's biographer, Robert Service, now stress that, while Stalin was undoubtedly the architect of the terror, the responsibility for implementing it goes beyond him.

SOURCE F

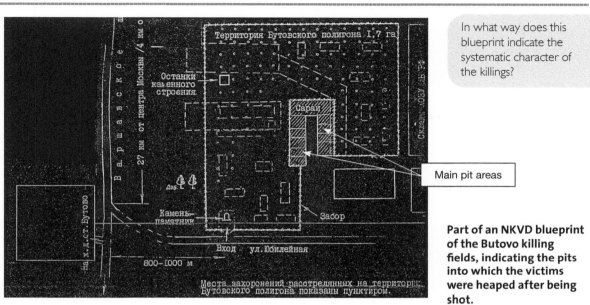

In what way does this blueprint indicate the systematic character of the killings?

Main pit areas

Part of an NKVD blueprint of the Butovo killing fields, indicating the pits into which the victims were heaped after being shot.

- Stalinism was not as all-embracing a system of government as has often been assumed. The disorganised state of much of Soviet bureaucracy, particularly at a local level, allowed officials to use their own initiative in applying the terror.
- How the purges were actually carried out largely depended on the local party organisation. Many welcomed them as an opportunity to settle old scores.
- Revolutionary idealism was mixed with self-interest as party members saw the purges as a way of advancing themselves by filling the jobs vacated by the victims. In this sense, the purges came from below as much as from above, their ferocity being sustained by the lower rank officials in government and party who wanted to replace their superiors, whom they regarded as a conservative élite.
- The purges were popular with those Russians who believed that their country could be prevented from slipping back into its historic backwardness only by being powerfully and ruthlessly led. They judged that Stalin's unrelenting methods were precisely what the nation needed.
- The disruption of Soviet society, caused by the upheavals of collectivisation and industrialisation, destroyed social cohesion and so encouraged party and government officials to resort to the most extreme measures.
- The notion of civil rights was not strong enough in Russia to offer an alternative to what was being done in the name of the Communist revolution.

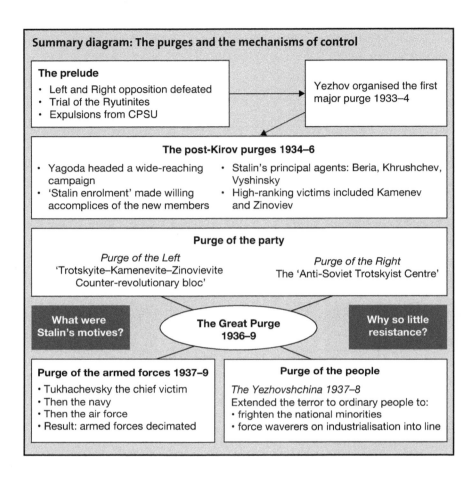

Summary diagram: The purges and the mechanisms of control

The prelude
- Left and Right opposition defeated
- Trial of the Ryutinites
- Expulsions from CPSU

Yezhov organised the first major purge 1933–4

The post-Kirov purges 1934–6
- Yagoda headed a wide-reaching campaign
- 'Stalin enrolment' made willing accomplices of the new members
- Stalin's principal agents: Beria, Khrushchev, Vyshinsky
- High-ranking victims included Kamenev and Zinoviev

Purge of the party

Purge of the Left
'Trotskyite–Kamenevite–Zinovievite Counter-revolutionary bloc'

Purge of the Right
The 'Anti-Soviet Trotskyist Centre'

What were Stalin's motives?

The Great Purge 1936–9

Why so little resistance?

Purge of the armed forces 1937–9
- Tukhachevsky the chief victim
- Then the navy
- Then the air force
- Result: armed forces decimated

Purge of the people
The Yezhovshchina 1937–8
Extended the terror to ordinary people to:
- frighten the national minorities
- force waverers on industrialisation into line

 # Soviet totalitarianism and its impact on culture and society

▶ *What were the main characteristics of Stalin's totalitarian state?*
▶ *What impact did Stalinism have on the lives of the Soviet people?*

Totalitarianism is a governmental system under which individuals become subordinate to the state and lose all personal autonomy. Such a regime seeks to control not simply political life, but society in all its various features, cultural, economic, communal and personal. The Soviet Union under Stalin became one of the twentieth century's outstanding examples of such a system.

Bureaucracy, terror and economic transformation

By 1941, the basic features of Stalin's totalitarian state had been established. Stalin ran the USSR by a bureaucratic system of government. In doing this, he fulfilled the work begun by Lenin of turning revolutionary Russia into a one-party state. Political and social control was maintained by a terror system whose main instruments were regular purges and show trials directed against the party, the armed services and the people. It was Stalin's political control that had enabled him to create a **command economy** (see page 85).

Absolutism

Despite the power he wielded, Stalin's anxiety over the vulnerability of the Soviet Union in a capitalist world led him to create a siege mentality in the country. He insisted that even in peacetime the Soviet people had to be on permanent guard from enemies within and hostile nations outside. This was an extension of his concept of 'Revolution in One Country', a policy which subordinated everything to the interests of the Soviet Union as a nation.

Stalin's absolutism meant the suppression of any form of genuine democracy, since he operated on the principle, laid down by Lenin, of democratic centralism, which obliged members of the CPSU to accept uncritically and obey all orders and instructions handed down by the party leaders. Under Stalin, the Soviet Union recognised only one correct and acceptable ideology, **Marxism–Leninism–Stalinism**. All other belief systems were prohibited. Strict censorship was imposed as a means of enforcing political and cultural conformity. Little of importance took place in the USSR of which Stalin did not approve.

Character of the Soviet state

Despite his control, Stalin was not all-powerful – no one individual in a nation can be. His authority depended ultimately on the willingness of thousands of underlings to carry out his orders and policies. That he could rely on this is explained by some historians by the character of Soviet communism itself. Richard Pipes and Robert Service, for example, draw attention to the violence that was intrinsic to Soviet communism. Stalin once asserted that violence was an 'inevitable law of the revolutionary movement', a restatement of Lenin's declaration that the task of Bolshevism was 'the ruthless destruction of the enemy'. The Stalinist purges, therefore, were a logical historical progression.

The concepts of individual or civil rights were undeveloped in Russia. Tsardom had been an autocracy in which the first duty of the people had been to obey. The Communists had not changed that. Indeed, Lenin and Stalin had re-emphasised the necessity of obedience to central authority.

The *nomenklatura*

Among the main beneficiaries of this tradition of obedience were the *nomenklatura*. The common characteristic of those who led Stalin's purges was their unswerving personal loyalty to him, a loyalty that overcame any doubts they might have had regarding the nature of their work. Stalin had no difficulty in finding eager subordinates to organise the terror campaign. They formed the

KEY TERMS

Command economy
A system in which all the main areas of economic activity are under central government control and direction.

Marxism–Leninism–Stalinism The concept of an ideological continuity between the founder of Marxism and its great interpreters, Lenin and Stalin.

Nomenklatura The Soviet establishment, an élite set of privileged officials who ran the party and government.

new class of officials that he created to replace the old Bolsheviks decimated in the purges. Dedicated to Stalin, on whom their positions depended, the *nomenklatura* enjoyed rights and privileges denied to the rest of the population. Including their families, they numbered around 600,000 (in a population of 180 million) by the late 1930s. Such people were unlikely to question Stalin's orders. The more potential rivals they exterminated, the safer their jobs were.

Significantly, the willingness to be totally obedient was not exclusive to minor officials. Of equal note was the eagerness with which Stalin's top ministers carried out his campaigns of terror and persecution. Although they were terrified of him, they did not simply obey him out of fear. People like Beria and Molotov derived the same vindictive satisfaction from their work as their master. Like him, they appeared to have no moral scruples.

Stalinism and Soviet culture

In Marxist theory, culture was not a detached form of activity, separate from politics and economics. Rather, it was the expression of the political and economic system operating in society. It followed that in a proletarian society, such as the Soviet Union claimed to be, culture had to be proletarian. It was this conviction that informed Stalin's attitude to the arts.

Literature

In 1932, Stalin declared to a gathering of Soviet writers that they were 'engineers of the human soul'. Their task was essentially a social, not an artistic one. They had to reshape the thinking and behaviour of the Soviet people. The goal of the artist had to be socialist realism. It is not surprising, therefore, that when the **Soviet Union of Writers** was formed in 1934 it declared that its first objective was to convince all its members of the need to struggle for **socialist realism** in their works. This could be best achieved by conforming to a set of guidelines. Writers were to ensure that their work:

- was acceptable to the party in theme and presentation
- was written in a style immediately understandable to the workers who would read it
- contained characters whom the readers could recognise as socialist role models or examples of class enemies.

These rules applied to creative writing in all its forms: novels, plays, poems and film scripts. It was not easy for genuine writers to continue working within these restrictions, but conformity was the price of acceptance, even of survival. Surveillance, scrutiny and denunciations intensified throughout the 1930s. Suicides among writers denied self-expression became common in such an intimidating atmosphere. Historian Robert Service notes in his biography of Stalin that 'More great intellectuals perished in the 1930s than survived.' In 1934, **Osip Mandelstam** was betrayed following a private gathering of writers at which he had recited a mocking poem about Stalin, which contained the lines

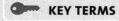

KEY TERMS

Soviet Union of Writers
The body which had authority over all published writers and had the right to ban any work of which it disapproved.

Socialist realism The notion that all creative works must be representational, relating directly to the people and easily understood by them.

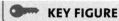

KEY FIGURE

Osip Mandelstam (1891–1938)
A leading literary figure, whose work emphasised the need to recognise the unique worth of human beings.

'Around him, fawning half-men for him to play with, as he prates and points a finger.' Mandelstam died four years later in the gulag. He once remarked, 'Only in Russia is poetry taken seriously, so seriously men are killed for it.'

Stalin took a close personal interest in new works. Criticism from him was enough to destroy a writer. The atmosphere of repression and the restrictions on genuine creativity had the effect of elevating conformist mediocrities to positions of influence and power, a common characteristic of totalitarian regimes in the twentieth century.

Theatre and film

The Soviet Union of Writers set the tone for all other organisations in the arts. Film-making, opera and ballet all had to respond to the Stalinist demand for socialist realism. Abstract forms were frowned on because they broke the rule that works should be immediately accessible to the public. An idea of the repression that operated can be gained from the following figures:

- In the years 1936–7, 68 films out of 150 had to be withdrawn in mid-production and another thirty taken out of circulation.
- In the years 1936–7, ten out of nineteen plays and ballets were ordered to be withdrawn.
- In the 1937–8 theatre season, 60 plays were banned from performance, ten theatres closed in Moscow and another ten in Leningrad.

A prominent victim was the director **Vsevolod Meyerhold**, whose appeal for artistic liberty – 'The theatre is a living creative thing. We must have freedom, yes, freedom' – led to a campaign being mounted against him by Stalin's sycophantic supporters. He was arrested in 1938. After a two-year imprisonment during which he was regularly beaten until he fainted, he was shot. His name was one on a list of 346 death sentences that Stalin signed on one day, 16 January, in 1940.

Even **Sergei Eisenstein**, whose films *Battleship Potemkin* and *October*, celebrating the revolutionary Russian proletariat, had done so much to advance the Communist cause, was heavily censured. This was because a later work of his, *Ivan the Terrible*, was judged to be an unflattering portrait of a great Russian leader and, therefore, by implication, disrespectful of Stalin.

Painting and sculpture

Painters and sculptors were left in no doubt as to what was required of them. Their duty to conform to socialist realism in their style and at the same time honour their great leader was captured in an article in the art magazine *Iskusstvo* describing a prize painting of Stalin. 'The image of Comrade Stalin is the symbol of the Soviet people's glory, calling for new heroic exploits for the benefit of our great motherland.'

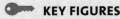 **KEY FIGURES**

Vsevolod Meyerhold (1874–1940)

A major influence on European theatre through his concept of 'total theatre', which sought to break down the barriers between actors and audience.

Sergei Eisenstein (1898–1948)

An internationally acclaimed film director, renowned for his pioneering cinematic technique.

In what ways do the posters in Source G illustrate the artistic notion of socialist realism?

SOURCE G

Posters from the 1930s, typical of the propaganda of the time showing Stalin as the leader of his adoring people. Poster art was a very effective way for the Stalinist authorities to put their message across.

'Under the leadership of the great Stalin, forward to Communism.'

'Thank you dear Stalin, for our happy childhood.'

Music

Since music is essentially abstract, it was more difficult to make composers respond to Stalin's notions of social realism. Nevertheless, it was the art form which most interested Stalin, who regarded himself as an expert in the field. He claimed to be able to recognise socialist music and to know what type of song would inspire the people. He tried to impose his judgement on the Soviet Union's leading composer, Dmitri Shostakovich, some of whose works were banned for being 'bourgeois and formalistic'. However, the Great Patriotic War (see pages 141–7) was to give Shostakovich the opportunity to express his deep patriotism. His powerful orchestral works depicted in sound the courageous struggle and final victory of the Soviet people. At the end of the war, in return for being reinstated, he promised to bring his music closer to 'the folk art of the people'.

Religion

Stalin shared Lenin's notion that religious faith had no place in a Communist society. Religion, with its other-worldly values, was seen as an affront to the collective needs of the nation. In 1928, a campaign to close the churches was begun. The Orthodox Church was the main target but all religions and denominations were at risk. Clerics who refused to co-operate were arrested; thousands in Moscow and Leningrad were sent into exile.

The suppression of religion in the urban areas proved a fairly straightforward affair. It was a different story in the countryside. The destruction of the rural churches and the confiscation of the relics and **icons** that most peasants had in their homes led to revolts in many areas. The authorities had failed to understand that what to their secular minds were merely superstitions, were to the peasants a precious part of their traditions. The result was widespread resistance across the rural provinces of the USSR. The response of the authorities was to declare that those who opposed the restrictions on religion were really doing so in order to resist collectivisation. This allowed the requisition squads to brand the religious protesters as *kulaks* and to seize their property.

Such was the bitterness these methods created that Stalin instructed his officials to call a halt. But this was only temporary. In the late 1930s, as part of the Great Terror, the assault on religion was renewed:

- 800 higher clergy and 4000 ordinary priests were imprisoned, along with many thousands of ordinary worshippers.
- By 1940, only 500 churches were open for worship in the Soviet Union – one per cent of the figure in 1917.

Education

Stalin believed that a first step in modernising the USSR was to spread literacy. To this end, formal education was made a priority, with the following key features:

- ten years of compulsory schooling for all children aged five to fifteen
- core curriculum specified: reading and writing, mathematics, science, history, geography, Russian language, Marxist theory
- state-prescribed textbooks to be used

KEY TERM

Icons Paintings of Christ and Christian saints whose artistic beauty was one of the great glories of the Orthodox Church.

- homework to be a regular requirement
- state-organised tests and examinations
- school uniforms made compulsory.

The emphasis on regulation was not accidental. The intention was to create a disciplined generation of young people ready to join the workforce that was engaged through the Five-Year Plans in constructing the new Communist society. At school, pupils were taught continually and in all subjects that Stalin was their guide and protector. It was an interesting aspect of the prescribed school curriculum that history was to be taught not as 'an abstract sociological scheme' but as a chronological story full of stirring tales of the great Russian heroes of the past such as **Ivan the Terrible** and **Peter the Great**, leading up to the triumph of Lenin and the Bolsheviks in 1917.

A striking feature of the school structure was that fees were charged for the final three years (for fifteen to eighteen year olds) of non-compulsory secondary schooling, a requirement that appeared to challenge the notion of an egalitarian education system. The official justification for this was that the Soviet Union needed a specially trained section of the community to serve the people in expert ways; doctors and scientists were obvious examples. Those who stayed on at school after the age of fifteen were obviously young people of marked ability who would eventually enter university to become the specialists of the future. This was undeniably a selection process, but the argument was that it was selection by ability, not by class.

That was the official line. However, although there was an undoubted rise in overall standards, the system also created an educated élite. Those who continued after the age of fifteen were mainly the children of government officials and party members who could afford the fees. Private tuition and private education became normal for them. As a consequence, as university education expanded, it was party members or their children who had the first claim on the best places. As graduates, they then had access to the three key areas of Soviet administration: industry, the civil service and the armed services. Osip Mandelstam described how 'a thin layer of privileged people gradually came into being with **packets**, country villas, and cars. Those who had been granted a share of the cake eagerly did everything asked of them.'

Universities

In intellectual terms, the Soviet Union's most prestigious institution was the Academy of Sciences, which incorporated all major research organisations, some 250 in number with over 50,000 individual members. The term 'sciences' translates broadly to cover all the main intellectual and practical streams: the arts, science, medicine, management. All leading scholars were members of the Academy. In 1935, the Academy was brought under direct government control. In return for increased academic and social privileges, it pledged itself totally to Stalin in his building of the new Communist society. What this meant in

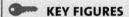

KEY FIGURES

Ivan the Terrible (reigned 1547–84)

A powerful tsar who considerably extended Russian territory through conquest.

Peter the Great (reigned 1689–1725)

A reforming tsar who attempted to modernise Russia by incorporating Western European ways.

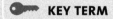

KEY TERM

Packets Special benefits and privileges.

practice was that all the academicians would henceforth produce work wholly in keeping with Stalinist values.

One particularly distressing aspect of this was that Soviet historians no longer engaged in genuine historical research and analysis. Their reputation as scholars depended on their presenting history shaped and interpreted as Stalin wished. They ceased to be historians in any meaningful sense and became, instead, intellectual lackeys of the regime.

The Lysenko affair

Where academic subservience could lead was evident in an infamous case which damaged Soviet science and agriculture for decades. In the 1930s, **Trofim Lysenko**, a quack geneticist, claimed to have discovered ways of developing 'super-crops', which would grow in any season and produce a yield anything up to sixteen times greater than the harvests produced by traditional methods. Stalin, who had convinced himself that there was such a thing as 'socialist science', superior to that practised in the bourgeois West, was convinced by Lysenko's claims and gave him his full support. This meant that, although the claims were in fact wholly false, based on rigged experiments, Lysenko was unchallengeable by his colleagues. Those who dared protest that his methods were faulty were removed from their posts and dispatched to the gulag.

Women's roles

The equality of women was one of the basic principles that Soviet communism espoused, yet the attempt to achieve this goal ran into many difficulties in Stalinist Russia, one of which was Stalin's own conservative social views.

Marriage and the family

In keeping with their Marxist rejection of marriage as a bourgeois institution, Lenin's Bolsheviks had made divorce easier and had attempted to liberate women from what they saw as the bondage of children and family. However, after only a brief period of experiment, Lenin's government had come to question its earlier enthusiasm for sweeping change in this area. Stalin shared their doubts. Indeed, he was convinced that the earlier Bolshevik social experiment had failed. By the end of the 1930s, the Soviet divorce rate was the highest in Europe, one divorce for every two marriages. This led him to embark on what has been called the 'great retreat'. Stalin began to stress the value of the family as a stabilising influence in society. He let it be known that he did not approve of the sexual freedoms that had followed the 1917 revolution. He argued that a good Communist was a socially responsible one: 'a poor husband and father, a poor wife and mother, cannot be good citizens'.

Aware of the social upheavals that collectivisation and industrialisation were causing, Stalin tried to create some form of balance by emphasising the traditional social values attaching to the role of women as home-makers and

 KEY FIGURE

Trofim Lysenko (1898–1976)
Appointed head of the Soviet Academy of Agricultural sciences, he hounded those biologists who dared point out the flaws in his theories. It was not until 1965 that Lysenko's fraudulent ideas were finally exposed in the USSR.

child raisers. He was also greatly exercised by the number of orphaned children living on the streets of the urban areas. Left to fend for themselves, the children had formed themselves into feral gangs of scavengers and violent thieves. Disorder of this kind further convinced Stalin of the need to re-establish family structures.

Changes in social policy

Stalin's first major move came in June 1936, with a decree that reversed much of earlier Bolshevik social policy:

- unregistered marriages were no longer recognised.
- Divorce was made more difficult.
- The right to abortion was severely restricted.
- The family was declared to be the basis of Soviet society.
- Homosexuality was outlawed.

The status of women

One group that felt adversely affected by the changes in social policy were the female members of the party and the **intelligentsia**, who had welcomed the Russian Revolution as the beginning of female liberation. However, the strictures on sexual freedom under Stalin, and the emphasis on family and motherhood allowed little room for the notion of the independent female.

Soviet propaganda spoke of the equality of women, but there was no great advance towards this in practical terms. A 'housewives' movement' was created in 1936 under Stalin's patronage. Composed largely of the wives of high-ranking industrialists and managers, it set itself the task of 'civilising' the tastes and improving the conditions of the workers. However, the reality was that few resources were allocated and little attention was paid to organisations such as this. Stalin spoke continually of the nation being under siege and of the need to build a war economy. This made any movement not directly concerned with industrial production or defence seem largely irrelevant, a category into which most of the women's organisations fell.

There were individual cases of women gaining in status and income in Stalin's time. However, these were a small minority and were invariably unmarried or childless women. Married women with children carried a double burden. The great demand for labour that accompanied Stalin's industrialisation drive required that women join the workforce. By 1936 there were 9 million women in the factories. They now had to fulfil two roles: as mothers raising the young and as workers contributing to the modernisation of the Soviet Union. This imposed great strains on them.

It is true that factories and plants were urged to provide crèches so that more mothers with young children could be employed, but this was done primarily to meet the needs of industry, not those of the mother. Childcare at the factories was regimented by such measures as the requirement that breastfeeding took place at a given time so as not to interfere with production. One positive result

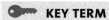

KEY TERM

Intelligentsia People of influence in the intellectual world, for example, academics and writers.

of Stalin's insistence that Soviet women see their primary role as mothers producing babies for the nation led to the setting up of clinics and a general improvement in the standards of midwifery and gynaecology.

Such gains as women made were undermined by Stalin's appeal for the nation to act selflessly in its hour of need. It is true that Soviet propaganda spoke of the true equality of women but there was a patronising air about much that went on. *Zhenotdel*, set up under Lenin as an organisation to represent the views of the party's female members, was allowed to lapse in 1930 on the grounds that its work was done. The clear conclusion is that for all the Soviet talk of women's progress under Stalinism, the evidence suggests that they were increasingly exploited. It is hard to dispute the conclusion of the distinguished scholar Geoffrey Hosking, that 'the fruits of female emancipation became building blocks of the Stalinist **neopatriarchal** social system'.

Health

In 1918, Lenin's Bolshevik government had set up the People's Commissariat of Health. Its aim was nothing less than to provide a free health service for all Russians. The commissariat continued to operate in Stalin's time with the same objective, but, from the beginning, the sad fact was that Soviet Russia never had the resources to match its intentions. The disruptions of the civil war period made it impossible to develop a structured health service on the lines originally envisaged. Things picked up in the better economic conditions produced by NEP. **Infant mortality** dropped and the spread of contagious diseases was checked. But famine remained a constant threat.

In the 1930s, the collectivisation policy enforced by Stalin created the largest famine in Russian history. This made the worst hit areas –Ukraine and Kazakhstan – places of death and disease. Such was the scale of the horror that the existing health services in those regions simply could not cope. Although some parts of the USSR were relatively unscathed, it proved impossible to transfer medical supplies from these areas on a big enough scale to provide real help to the stricken regions. There was also the chilling fact that, since Stalin refused to acknowledge that there was a famine, no real effort was made by the central government to deal with its consequences.

It is true that in the unaffected areas in the 1930s there was a genuine advance in health standards. The number of qualified doctors and nurses increased and while the benefits of this may not have reached the majority of the population there were spectacular successes, which were made much of in Stalinist propaganda. Sanatoria, for the treatment of **tuberculosis,** and rest and retirement homes for the workers were created. There were even holiday centres in such places as Yalta on the Black Sea where selected workers were sent as a reward for their efforts. However, the number who enjoyed such treatment was a tiny fraction of the workforce. The main beneficiaries of improved medical care were not ordinary Russians but party members and the *nomenklatura*. It was one of the privileges of belonging to the political establishment.

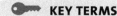 **KEY TERMS**

Zhenotdel The Women's Bureau of the Communist Party.

Neopatriarchal A new form of male domination.

Infant mortality The number of children who die per 100 or per 1000 of all those in a particular age group.

Tuberculosis A wasting disease often affecting the lungs, which was especially prevalent in Russia.

Summary diagram: Soviet totalitarianism and its impact on culture and society

Culture and education	Women's role	Health
Stalinist ideology imposed by the *nomenklatura* bureaucracy	Stalin reversed Bolshevik policy towards women and the family	The attempt to improve health standards
All the arts required to conform to socialist realism	Stalin's insistence on the importance of the family	The impact of the war
Religion suppressed as superstition	The treatment of *Zhenotdel*	How healthy were the Soviet people under Stalin?
Education aimed at instilling conformity	Double role of women in Soviet society	Soviet achievements in medical science
	Women in the workplace	
	How liberated were women in Stalin's time?	

Stalin created a totalitarian state

3 Stalin's cult of personality

▶ *How did Stalin establish a cult of personality?*

Adolf Hitler once wrote that 'the personality cult is the best form of government'. It is not certain whether Stalin ever read this, but it would be a fitting commentary on his leadership of the Soviet Union. One of the strongest charges made by Nikita Khrushchev in his later attack on Stalin's record was that he had indulged in the cult of personality (see page 182). He was referring to the way Stalin dominated every aspect of Soviet life, so that he became not simply a leader, but the embodiment of the nation itself. Similarly, the Communist Party became indistinguishable from Stalin himself as a person. Communism was no longer a set of theories; it was no longer Leninism. It was whatever Stalin said and did. Soviet communism was Stalinism.

Stalin's image

From the early 1930s onwards, Stalin's picture began to appear everywhere. Every newspaper, book and film, no matter what its theme, carried a reference to Stalin's greatness. Every achievement of the USSR was credited to Stalin. Such was his all-pervasive presence that Soviet communism became personalised around him. On occasion, in private, Stalin protested that he did not seek the glorification he received but, significantly, he made no effort to prevent it.

Khrushchev's role

Ironically, in view of his later denunciation of Stalin, it was Khrushchev who did as much as anyone to promote the image of Stalin as a glorious hero. At the trial of Zinoviev and Kamenev in August 1936, Khrushchev cursed the defendants as 'Miserable pigmies!' and went on: 'Stalin is hope, Stalin is expectation; he is the beacon that guides all progressive mankind. Stalin is our banner! Stalin is our will! Stalin is our victory!'

Khrushchev was the first to coin the term 'Stalinism' in 1936 when he spoke of the 'Marxism–Leninism–Stalinism that has conquered one-sixth of the globe'. At the eighteenth congress of the CPSU in March 1939, Khrushchev lauded the Soviet leader as 'our great inspiration, our beloved Stalin', extolling him as 'the greatest genius of humanity, teacher and *vozhd* who leads us towards communism'.

Stalin's transcendence

It is one of the many paradoxes of Soviet history that the Communist movement, which in theory drew its authority from the will of the masses, became so dependent on the idea of the great leader. Such was Stalin's standing and authority that he transcended politics. Since he represented not simply the party but the nation itself, he became the personification of all that was best in Russia. This was an extraordinary achievement for a Georgian and it produced a further remarkable development. It became common to assert that many of the great achievements in world history were the work of Russians.

The claims developed a surreal quality: that Shakespeare was really a Russian, that Russian navigators had been the first Europeans to discover America and that Russian mathematicians had discovered the secrets of relativity long before Einstein. Eventually Stalin overreached himself. He ordered his scientists to produce a popular soft drink to match the US capitalist Coca-Cola. They tried but finally had to admit that, while Soviet science could achieve marvels, miracles were beyond it.

Propaganda

The cult of personality was not a spontaneous response of the people. It did not come from below; it was imposed from above. The image of Stalin as hero and saviour of the Soviet people was manufactured. It was a product of the Communist Party machine which controlled all the main forms of information – newspapers, cinema and radio. Roy Medvedev, a Soviet historian, who lived through Stalinism, later explained that Stalin did not rely on terror alone, but also on the support of the majority of the people, who 'deceived by cunning propaganda, gave Stalin credit for the successes of others and even in fact for "achievements" that were in fact totally fictitious'. A striking example of building on the fictitious was the Stakhanovite movement (see page 100).

Worship of Stalin

Despite the Soviet attack on the Church, the powerful religious sense of the Russian people remained and it was cleverly exploited by the authorities. Traditional worship, with its veneration of the saints, its icons, prayers and incantations, translated easily into the new regime. Stalin became an icon. This was literally true. His picture was carried on giant flags in processions. A French visitor watching at one of the **May Day** celebrations in Moscow's Red Square was staggered by the sight of a flypast of planes all trailing huge portraits of Stalin. 'My God!', he exclaimed. 'Exactly, Monsieur', said his Russian guide.

However, even May Day came to take second place to the celebration of Stalin's birthday each December. Beginning in 1929, on his fiftieth birthday, the occasion was turned each year into the greatest celebration in the Soviet calendar. Day-long parades in Red Square of marching troops, rolling tanks, dancing children and applauding workers, all presided over by an occasionally smiling Stalin high on a rostrum overlooking Lenin's tomb, became the high moment of the year. It was a new form of tsar worship. Stalin's wisdom and brilliance were extolled daily in *Pravda* and *Isvestiya* (*The Times*), the official Soviet newspapers. Hardly an article appeared in any journal that did not include the obligatory reference to his greatness. There were no books on any subject that did not extol his virtues as the master-builder of the Soviet nation, inspiration to his people and glorious model for struggling peoples everywhere. Eulogies of Stalin poured off the press, each one trying to outbid the others in its veneration of the leader. Every political gathering was a study in the advancement of the Stalin cult. The exaggeration and the sycophantic character of it all are clear in the following extract from a speech given by a delegate to the seventh congress of soviets in 1935.

SOURCE H

From a speech by A.O. Avdienko, 1 February 1935, quoted in T.H. Rigby, *Stalin*, Prentice-Hall, 1966, p. 111.

Thank you, Stalin. Thank you because I am joyful. Thank you because I am well. Centuries will pass, and the generations still to come will regard us as the happiest of mortals, because we lived in the century of centuries, because we were privileged to see Stalin, our inspired leader. Yes and we regard ourselves as the happiest of mortals because we are the contemporaries of a man who never had an equal in world history. The men of all ages will call on thy name, which is strong, beautiful, wise and marvellous. Thy name is engraved on every factory, every machine, every place on the earth and in the hearts of all men. And when the woman I love presents me with a child the first word it will utter shall be: Stalin.

Konsomol

A particularly useful instrument for the spread of Stalinist propaganda was **Konsomol**, a youth movement which had begun in Lenin's time but became

? From your own knowledge, can you think of reasons why the speaker in Source H may not have been as sincere in his praise of Stalin as he appears to be?

a formal body in 1926 under the direct control of the CPSU. Among its main features were:

- It was open to those aged between 14 and 28 (a Young Pioneer movement existed for those under the age of fourteen).
- It pledged itself totally to Stalin and the CPSU.
- Membership was not compulsory but its attraction to young people was that it offered them the chance of eventual full membership of the CPSU, with all the privileges that went with it.
- It grew from 2 million members in 1927 to 10 million in 1940.

The idealism of the young was very effectively exploited by Stalin's regime. *Konsomol* members were among the most enthusiastic supporters of the Five-Year Plans, as they proved by going off in their thousands to help build the new industrial cities such as Magnitogorsk (see page 96). It was *Konsomol* which provided the flag wavers and the cheerleaders and which organised the huge gymnastic displays that were the centrepieces of the massive parades on May Day and Stalin's birthday.

Stalin's popularity

It is difficult to judge how popular Stalin was in real terms. The applause that greeted his every appearance in public or in cinema newsreels may have been as much a matter of prudence as of real affection. There was no way in which criticism or opposition could be openly expressed. The gulag was full of comrades who had spoken out of turn. The intense political correctness that prevailed required that Stalin be publicly referred to as the faultless leader and inspirer of the nation.

A fascinating insight into Stalin's standing with his own people was provided in 1937 by **Leon Feuchtwanger**, who was misled into exaggerating Stalin's economic successes but who remained a shrewd observer of Soviet attitudes. He described 'the worship and boundless cult with which the population surrounds Stalin' and went on to explain the particular character of Stalin's popularity.

SOURCE I

From Leon Feuchtwanger, *Moscow 1937*, Victor Gollancz, 1937, p. 137.

The people were grateful to Stalin for their bread and meat, for the order in their lives, for their education and for creating their army which secured this new well-being. The people have to have someone to whom to express their gratitude, and for this purpose they do not select an abstract concept, such as 'communism', but a real man, Stalin. Their unbounded reverence is consequently not for Stalin, but for him as a symbol of the patently successful economic reconstruction.

 KEY FIGURE

Leon Feuchtwanger (1884–1958)

A Jewish novelist and literary critic who was exiled from Nazi Germany in the 1930s.

In Source I, what does the writer mean by saying that the people's reverence for Stalin is 'for him as a symbol'?

However, Sheila Fitzpatrick, a distinguished researcher from a later generation, aware of how little Stalin had done to improve the conditions of the Soviet people, offers a different slant.

SOURCE J

? How is Stalin's popularity measured in Source J?

From Sheila Fitzpatrick, *Everyday Stalinism*, Oxford University Press, 1999, p. 100.

Despite its promises of future abundance and the massive propaganda that surrounded its current achievements, the Stalinist regime did little to improve the life of its people in the 1930s. Judging by the NKVD's soundings of public opinion, the Stalinist regime was relatively, though not desperately, unpopular in Russian towns. (In Russian villages, especially in the first half of the 1930s, its unpopularity was much greater.) Overall, as the NKVD regularly reported, the ordinary 'little man' in Soviet towns, who thought only of his own and his family's welfare, was 'dissatisfied with Soviet Power', though in a somewhat fatalistic and passive manner. The post-NEP situation was compared unfavourably with NEP, and Stalin – despite the officially fostered Stalin cult – was compared unfavourably with Lenin, sometimes because he was more repressive but often because he let people go hungry.

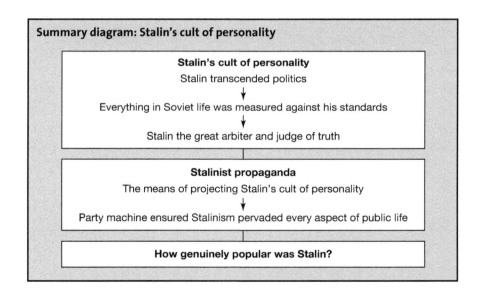

Summary diagram: Stalin's cult of personality

Stalin's cult of personality

Stalin transcended politics

↓

Everything in Soviet life was measured against his standards

↓

Stalin the great arbiter and judge of truth

Stalinist propaganda

The means of projecting Stalin's cult of personality

↓

Party machine ensured Stalinism pervaded every aspect of public life

How genuinely popular was Stalin?

4 Stalin's foreign policy 1933–41

▶ *How did Stalin adapt his foreign policy to meet the perceived threats to the Soviet Union?*

Stalin's attitude to foreign relations

There is an important distinction to be made between the theory and the practice of Soviet foreign policy under Stalin:

- Judged by its propaganda, the USSR was pledged to the active encouragement of worldwide revolution. The Comintern existed for this very purpose (see page 44).
- However, in practice, Stalin did not regard Soviet Russia as being strong enough to sustain a genuinely revolutionary foreign policy. His first task was to ensure the survival of the revolution in Russia itself, with him as its leader.

The Comintern continued to have a role under Stalin but it was limited to protecting the USSR. Far from being the vanguard of international communism, the Comintern became a branch of the Soviet foreign office.

'Socialism in one country'

Stalin conducted his foreign policy in accordance with his basic principle of 'socialism in one country'. The defence of the Soviet Union came before all other considerations. He had defeated Trotsky in the power struggle by emphasising that his opponent's call for the Soviet Union to spearhead international revolution put the nation at risk. Having gained power, Stalin kept to that principle.

The Nazi threat

Stalin's defensiveness made him slow initially to understand the threat posed by Nazi Germany. Even after Hitler came to power in 1933, Stalin tried to maintain the Treaties of Rapallo and Berlin, existing Soviet–German alliances (see page 47). However, the following developments combined to convince Stalin that Nazi Germany was a deadly menace:

- violent Nazi attacks on the **KPD**
- the signing of a German–Polish treaty in 1934, which increased the threat to the USSR's western borders
- open talk among German diplomats of their country's intention of expanding into the USSR
- Nazi propaganda against Soviet communism, which was as rabid as its anti-Semitism.

For the next six years Soviet foreign policy was primarily concerned with finding allies to nullify the German danger. One of the earliest opportunities

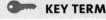 **KEY TERM**

KPD The German Communist Party.

for the USSR to lessen its isolation came with its acceptance into the **League of Nations** in 1934. The League provided a platform for the Soviet Union to call for the adoption of the principle of **collective security** in international affairs. One of the fruits of this was an agreement in 1935 between the USSR, France and Czechoslovakia, promising 'mutual assistance' if one of the partners suffered military attack.

However, in the 1930s collective security was more impressive in principle than in practice. The reason was that Europe's two most powerful states, France and Britain, were not prepared to risk war in order to uphold the principle. Without their participation there was no possibility of collective security becoming a reality.

Stalin and China

In 1935 in China, the Chinese Communist Party (CCP) led by Mao Zedong, having established its base at Yanan, became locked into what amounted to a civil war with the Nationalists (Guomindang), led by Chiang Kai-shek. In addition, the CCP was subjected to attacks from Japanese forces that had begun to occupy large parts of China. Yet throughout the years 1935–45, Stalin, declining to act in a spirit of Communist brotherhood, gave little help to Mao and the CCP. Stalin's primary aim was make the Chinese Communists obey Soviet instructions and conform to Soviet notions of Marxist revolution. That was why Mao was engaged in a continuous struggle to prevent his party from being taken over by the pro-Moscow members of the CCP. His success in resisting Soviet pressure reduced Stalin to disparaging Mao and his followers as being Communists only in name; 'they are "white" at heart, even though they wear "red" jackets'.

It was also for reasons of national self-interest that Stalin declined to give the CCP full support in its war with the Japanese. Believing that the Chinese Communists were far weaker than the Nationalists, Stalin gave his main backing throughout the 1930s to Chiang Kai-shek. This was not out of any sense of goodwill towards China. Stalin's hope was that by encouraging Guomindang resistance to the Japanese occupation of China that began in earnest in 1937, Russia would be less likely itself to be the object of **Japanese expansionism**. Broadly, this policy worked. There were a series of Russo-Japanese incidents in the late 1930s that led to fighting on the Manchurian border, but these were resolved in 1941 with the signing of a non-aggression pact between the Soviet Union and Japan. This held good until 1945 when, in keeping with a commitment given to the Allies at Yalta in February 1945, the USSR declared war on Japan only days before the Japanese surrender in August of that year.

Anti-Comintern Pact 1936

The USSR's hopes of sheltering under collective security were dashed in 1936 with the creation of an international alliance, the **Anti-Comintern Pact**, aimed directly against the Soviet Union. This carried a clear threat of a two-front attack on the USSR's European and Far Eastern borders. The danger that this represented had the effect of redoubling Stalin's efforts to obtain reliable allies and guarantees. However, in his attempts to achieve this, Stalin was labouring under a handicap, largely of his own making. The plain fact was that Soviet Russia was not trusted. Enough was known of the Stalinist purges to make neutrals in other countries wary of making alliances with a nation where such treachery or such tyranny was possible.

Spanish civil war 1936–9

If Stalin made it difficult for neutrals to sympathise with the defence needs of the Soviet Union, he also put barriers in the way of those on the political left in other countries who should have been his natural supporters. His pursuit of defence agreements with the capitalist powers led to compromises that alienated many Soviet sympathisers. This was especially so with regard to Stalin's attitude towards the **Spanish civil war**. The struggle in Spain was a complex affair, but outsiders tended to see it in simple terms as a struggle between the republican left and the fascist right, a reflection of the basic political divide in Europe. Stalin and the Comintern, in keeping with the Soviet policy of encouraging anti-fascist **popular fronts**, sent agents into Spain to organise an alliance of pro-Republican forces.

Stalin's motives and policies were mixed. By focusing on Spain he hoped to divert foreign attention away from the current Soviet purges. The sending of Soviet military equipment to the republican side was not simple generosity. In payment, the Spanish republic had to transfer the greater part of its gold reserves to the USSR. Furthermore, the popular front policy meant in practice that the Soviet Union required all the republican contingents to put themselves under Soviet direction. The Spanish left came to resent the Soviet Union's attempt to dominate and to doubt whether Stalin really wanted the victory of the Spanish republic. They were correct; Stalin was anxious not to see a major victory for Marxism in Spain. The explanation of this paradox lies not in Spain, but in Europe at large. Stalin feared that, if communism were installed in south-western Europe, this would so frighten France and Britain that they might well react by forming an anti-Soviet front with Germany and Italy, the very consequence which Soviet foreign policy was struggling to avoid.

Appeasement: the Munich settlement 1938

Stalin's greatest anxiety yet in foreign affairs came in the autumn of 1938 with the signing by France, Britain, Italy and Germany of the Munich agreement, the climax to the Czechoslovak crisis. Hitler had demanded that the Sudetenland,

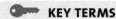

an area which in 1919 had been incorporated into Czechoslovakia, be allowed to become part of Germany. He had threatened invasion if his demands were not met. Neither Britain nor France was prepared to resist him militarily; instead they chose appeasement. In the Munich agreement they granted all his major demands.

In the Western world the Munich settlement has customarily been seen as an act of 'appeasement', a policy for avoiding war by making concessions to the aggressor. That was not the interpretation put on it by Stalin. For him, Munich was a gathering of the anti-Soviet nations of Europe, intent on giving Germany a free hand to attack a diplomatically isolated USSR. To forestall this, Stalin intensified his efforts to reach agreement with France and Britain. In the year after Munich, the Soviet foreign ministry delivered a series of formal alliance proposals to the French and British governments. These went unanswered. France and Britain could not bring themselves to trust Stalin. Blanked out in this way, Stalin then made a remarkable decision. He entered into an agreement with Nazi Germany.

SOURCE K

In what way does the cartoon in Source K suggest Stalin's sense of isolation from the world stage?

'**What, No Chair For Me?**' Low's cartoon of September 1938 accurately captured Stalin's response to the Munich settlement, which formally accepted Germany's demand for possession of the Sudeten region of Czechoslovakia. Stalin stands on the far right. The other people represented from left to right are Hitler, Neville Chamberlain of Britain, Daladier of France and Mussolini, fascist leader of Italy.

The Nazi–Soviet Pact 1939–41

In August 1939, the impossible happened. The two deadly enemies, Nazi Germany and Communist Russia, came together in a formal agreement, the

Nazi–Soviet Pact, in which both countries gave a solemn pledge to maintain peaceful relations with each other for a minimum of ten years. Of equal significance was a 'secret additional protocol', in which it was agreed that the USSR would take over the **Baltic States** and that Poland would later be divided between Germany and the USSR. At the beginning of September 1939, German forces began to occupy Poland. Within a month, Germany and the Soviet Union had carved up Poland between them.

The Nazi–Soviet Pact seemed to defy history and logic. But there was a rationale to this remarkable change in Soviet foreign policy. Given the real threat that Germany presented and the indifference of France and Britain to his offers of a defensive alliance, Stalin felt he had been left no alternative. He attempted to obviate the danger from Germany by the only move that international circumstances still allowed – an agreement with Germany. By 1941, within two years of the pact, Soviet Russia had regained all the territories it had lost as a result of the First World War. This, added to the ten-year guarantee of peace with Germany, seemed to justify the praise heaped on Stalin inside the Soviet Union for his diplomatic masterstroke. Bitter disillusion was to follow in June 1941 when Hitler tore up the treaty and launched a massive invasion of the Soviet Union (see page 141).

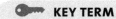

KEY TERM

Baltic States Estonia, Latvia and Lithuania.

Summary diagram: Stalin's foreign policy 1933–41

Soviet policy essentially defensive throughout 1930s

Stalin concerned to find allies to offset the threat from Nazi Germany
↓
USSR joined League of Nations in 1934
↓
Anti-Comintern Pact in 1936 quickened Stalin's desire to find allies
↓
Stalin saw Munich Agreement of 1938 as a Western plot against USSR
↓
France and Britain unwilling to ally with USSR
↓
Nazi–Soviet Pact 1939

Terms of the Nazi–Soviet Pact

Ten-year non-aggression agreement
Secret clauses on Baltic states and Poland

Results

Hailed as diplomatic triumph for Stalin
Lulled him into false sense of security
Gave Germany free rein in Western Europe
Left USSR exposed to German attack in June 1941

Chapter summary

The means by which Stalin chose to consolidate his political control of the Soviet Union were the purges. With the NKVD as the chief instrument of enforcement, Stalin organised the repression in three stages: the purge of the party, of the armed forces and of the people. So extensive was this coercive system that the USSR became a terror state. Despite the danger of this undermining any chance of genuine social cohesion, Stalin pressed on unrelentingly, backed by a *nomenklatura* that saw in the purges the opportunity to become the new Soviet establishment. Stalin extended his political grip to include all aspects of Soviet culture.

Contrary to the expectation that had inspired the original 1917 revolution, the lot of ordinary Russians did not improve under Stalin's rule, a reality that was masked by the intensity of Stalin's cult of personality which portrayed him as a uniquely gifted leader solving all the problems facing the Soviet Union and its people. Fearing for the Soviet Union's security, Stalin adopted an essentially defensive foreign policy seeking protective alliances. When these could not be obtained with France and Britain, he took the extraordinary step of making a pact with his greatest enemy, Nazi Germany.

Refresher questions

Use these questions to remind yourself of the key material covered in this chapter.

1 Why was Stalin able to extend the purges on such a huge scale?

2 In what sense did the post-Kirov purges mark 'Stalin's victory over the party'?

3 What was the connection between the 'Stalin enrolment' and the purges?

4 Was there any logic behind the Great Terror?

5 Why was there so little effective resistance to the purges?

6 How was Soviet culture manipulated to strengthen Stalin's power?

7 Why was religion persecuted under Stalin?

8 What role did education play in consolidating Stalin's authority?

9 What was the importance of the Lysenko affair?

10 How did the status of women in the Soviet Union change under Stalin?

11 How effectively did the Soviet Union develop a public health service?

12 What were the main characteristics of Stalin's cult of personality?

13 How was state propaganda used to promote Stalin's image?

14 How popular was Stalin in the Soviet Union?

15 How did the principle of 'socialism in one country' apply to Stalin's conduct of foreign affairs?

16 Why was Stalin reluctant to give full support to Mao and the CCP in China?

17 What form of threat to Stalin was the Anti-Comintern Pact?

18 How did Stalin view the Munich settlement?

19 Why was the Soviet Union willing to sign a non-aggression pact with Nazi Germany in 1939?

20 What were the consequences of the Nazi–Soviet Pact for the USSR?

Question practice

ESSAY QUESTIONS

1 'Stalin resorted to the purges as a method of control in the Soviet Union because he was paranoid about being toppled from power.' Assess the validity of this view.

2 How far was Soviet culture transformed under Stalin in the 1930s?

3 How successful were the Soviet attempts to improve education and health provision between 1929 and 1941?

4 To what extent were the lives of Soviet women transformed in the years 1929–41?

INTERPRETATION QUESTION

1 Using your understanding of the historical context, assess how convincing the arguments in Sources A (**page 109**), I (**page 131**) and J (**page 132**) are in relation to their analysis of Stalin's character.

SOURCE ANALYSIS QUESTION

1 With reference to Sources B (**page 112**), D (**page 114**) and H (**page 130**) and your understanding of the historical context, assess the value of these sources to the historian studying Stalin's methods of establishing political control of the Soviet Union.

CHAPTER 6

The Great Patriotic War and high Stalinism 1941–56

Although unprepared for the German invasion in 1941, Stalin recovered to lead the USSR to victory in the Great Patriotic War. As undisputed master of the USSR, he tightened his grip still further during the period of high Stalinism from 1945 to 1953. Despite now being a world statesman, he remained suspicious of his former wartime allies and used the Soviet control of Eastern Europe to build a defensive barrier against the West. His uncompromising attitude was a contributory factor in the development of the Cold War. This chapter studies these developments under the following headings and ends with a key debate:

★ Stalin as a war leader

★ The impact of the war on the USSR

★ High Stalinism in the USSR 1945–53

★ High Stalinism: the USSR's international position 1945–53

★ Stalin's legacy in 1953

The key debate on *page 171* of this chapter asks the question: Did Stalin fulfil or betray Lenin's revolution?

Key dates

1941	Operation Barbarossa	1948	Soviet blockade of Berlin
1941–5	Great Patriotic War	1949	Leningrad Affair
	USSR allied with USA and Britain in the Grand Alliance		USSR backed Red China's demand for a place in the UN
1944–8	Mass deportations of Soviet people		USSR detonated its first atomic bomb
	Soviet formation of the Eastern bloc	1950–3	Stalin backed Communist North in Korean War
1945	Yalta and Potsdam Conferences		
1947	The Truman Doctrine and the Marshall Plan	1953	Doctors' plot
			Death of Stalin

Stalin as a war leader

▶ *How did Stalin respond, as leader, to the invasion and occupation of the USSR?*

Outbreak of war with Germany

Since coming to power in Germany in 1933, Adolf Hitler had made no secret of his aggressive intentions towards the Soviet Union. In an attempt to offset this threat, Stalin had entered into a pact with Nazi Germany in August 1941 (see page 136). The extravagant claim made for the Nazi–Soviet Pact in Stalinist propaganda was that it had safeguarded Soviet security by a guarantee of freedom from Western attack. Stalin appears to have believed his own propaganda. It is one of the inexplicable things about him that he remained oblivious to the fact that Hitler's ultimate aim was the invasion and occupation of Russia and that the pact made the German invasion of Russia more likely to come sooner rather than later. He was thus wholly unprepared for the German attack when it came less than two years after the signing of the pact.

Operation Barbarossa 1941

On 22 June 1941, Germany launched Operation Barbarossa, the codename for the invasion of the Soviet Union. The invasion was on such a huge scale that preparations for it could not be concealed. For many months before it was unleashed, Soviet observers had known of its likelihood; millions of German troops had been moved to the Soviet borders. A week before the attack, the Kremlin received information from **Richard Sorge**, a Comintern agent in Japan, which provided hard evidence that Germany was about to mount a massive assault on western Russia. Stalin, however, refused to believe it, writing dismissively on Sorge's message 'This is German disinformation.'

On the following day Stalin was given confirmation of Sorge's story, this time from **Pavel Fitin**, the head of Soviet security, informing him that a reliable source in the German air force had warned, 'Preparations for an armed invasion of the USSR are fully complete and the attack may be expected at any time.' Stalin's reaction was to write angrily to Fitin's boss, **Merkulov**, the minister for state security: 'You can tell your "source" in German air force headquarters to go fuck himself. He's not a "source", he's a disinformer.'

Why Stalin refused to accept the truth remains a puzzle. Perhaps he could not bring himself to admit that the Nazi-Soviet Pact had failed. Perhaps he genuinely believed that German aggression could still be bought off. This might explain why in 1941 he had offered Soviet military and economic concessions to Germany. Yet however baffling Stalin's reasoning, its consequences were abundantly clear. Because he was unwilling to admit the reality of the situation in June 1941, none of his underlings could take the initiative. For days after the

 KEY FIGURES

Richard Sorge (1895–1944)
A German double-agent working for the USSR.

Pavel Fitin (1907–71)
Chief of the NKVD's foreign intelligence.

Vsevolod Merkulov (1895–1953)
Head of Soviet security and associate of Beria.

German invasion had started, Stalin sat in his *dacha*, refusing to speak or give instructions. The result was that in the first week of the Second World War on the eastern front, German forces advanced easily into a Soviet Union that was without effective leadership or direction.

Hitler had declared that the world would hold its breath when it witnessed Barbarossa. It was certainly a huge enterprise, unprecedented in the history of warfare. Germany put into the field:

- 3 million troops
- half a million motorised vehicles
- 4000 tanks
- 3000 aircraft.

Yet it was not this great array that gave the invaders the initial advantage. Indeed, in terms of simple logistics, the Soviet Union had the larger forces. It matched Germany in the number of troops, had four times the number of tanks, and three times the number of aircraft. What made the Soviet Union incapable of effective defence in the early days of the war was Stalin's mental paralysis.

Stalin's recovery

Once Stalin had thrown off his hysterical inertia, he began to show the strength of leadership for which he became renowned for the rest of the war. A remarkable aspect of the Barbarossa campaign was that in many areas along the front the local Soviet population at first welcomed the invaders. Some were even willing to join the German forces. This was not from love of Germany but from hatred of Stalinism. Had the German high command grasped the significance of this it might have enlisted the people of the occupied areas in a great anti-Stalin crusade. However, blinded by Nazi racial theory, which taught that the Slav peoples of the Soviet Union were inferior human beings, the Germans treated the areas they overran with calculated savagery. The consequence was described by Otto Brautigam, deputy leader of the German Ministry for the Occupied East.

SOURCE A

According to Source A, what has been the result of the German treatment of the occupied peoples of the USSR?

From an official memorandum by Otto Brautigam, 25 October 1942, quoted in William Shirer, *The Rise and Fall of the Third Reich*, Pan Books, 1960, pp. 1119–20.

In the Soviet Union we found on our arrival a population weary of Bolshevism. The population greeted us with joy as liberators and placed themselves at our disposal. The worker and the peasant soon perceived that Germany did not regard them as partners of equal rights but considered them only as the objective of her political and economic aims. It is no longer a secret that thousands of Russian prisoners of war have died of hunger in our camps.

Our policy has forced both Bolsheviks and Russian nationalists into a common front against us. The Russian fights today with exceptional bravery and self-sacrifice for nothing more or less than recognition of his human dignity.

Germany was eventually to pay the price for this. The Soviet people responded to German brutality by rallying under Stalin and committing themselves to a desperate struggle for survival which earned the title, the Great Patriotic War. After his initial paralysis of will, Stalin again began to exercise his formidable powers of leadership. In his first radio broadcast of the war on 3 July 1941 (Source B), Stalin appealed to the people to defend 'Mother Russia' by adopting the scorched-earth methods of warfare that had always saved the nation in its glorious past.

SOURCE B

From a radio broadcast by Stalin, 3 July 1941, quoted in Martin McCauley, *Stalin and Stalinism*, Longman, 1983, pp. 98–99.

*Comrades, citizens, brothers and sisters, men of our Army and Navy! The issue is one of life and death for the peoples of the USSR. We must mobilise ourselves and reorganise all our work on a new wartime footing. All, who by their panic mongering and cowardice hinder the work of defence, no matter who they may be, must be immediately hauled before a military tribunal. There can be no mercy to the enemy. In areas occupied by the enemy, sabotage groups must be organised to combat enemy units, to foment **guerrilla warfare** everywhere, to blow up bridges and roads, damage telephone and telegraph lines, to set fire to forests, stores and transports. In occupied regions, conditions must be made unbearable for the enemy. They must be hounded and annihilated at every step.*

The military struggle 1941–5

The USSR's struggle against Germany was a simple one in its essentials. It was a **war of attrition**. The early initiative lay with the German invader; Moscow and Leningrad were both besieged. However, the longer the war went on, the greater the opportunities became for the Soviet Union not merely to avoid defeat but to triumph over the German forces. From near defeat in 1941 following the German invasion, the Soviet forces drew the German armies deeper and deeper into Russia until the invaders were overstretched and vulnerable. The Red (Soviet) armies then counterattacked, winning the critical battles of Stalingrad and Kursk and pushing the enemy back into Germany until Berlin itself fell in May 1945.

> ### Key battles and campaigns
> - Operation Barbarossa: launched June 1941
> - Siege of Leningrad: September 1941 to January 1944
> - Siege of Moscow: October 1941 to January 1942
> - Battle of Stalingrad: July 1942 to February 1943
> - Battle of Kursk: July 1943
> - Operation Bagration: June to August 1944
> - Battle of Berlin: April to May 1945.

In what sense is Stalin's speech in Source B an attempt to make up for his initial lack of leadership when Germany invaded?

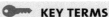 **KEY TERMS**

Guerrilla warfare A style of fighting in which mobile troops, who live off the land, harass the enemy with surprise attacks while avoiding pitched battles.

War of attrition A grinding conflict in which each side hopes to win by wearing the other down.

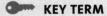

KEY TERM

Geneva Convention
International agreements in 1906 and 1929 that laid down the humane ways in which prisoners of war should be treated.

Soviet casualties were prodigious. In the worst years, 1941–2, the Red Army lost an average of 15,000 men each day. In the course of the war overall, more than 5.25 million Soviet troops became prisoners of war (POWs). Four million of these were shot or died in captivity. Since the USSR had not signed the **Geneva Convention**, Soviet prisoners had no protection, although it is doubtful, given the savagery with which the war was fought on the eastern front, whether either side would have honoured the convention. Nor was it merely a matter of death at the hands of the Germans. Despite the public accolades heaped on the gallant soldiers in the official Soviet press and in Stalin's radio broadcasts, the Soviet leader and his military high command treated their troops with indifference or deliberate brutality. Any Soviet soldier who fell into German hands, far from being regarded with sympathy, was deemed to be a traitor.

The character of the war

Two particular battles illustrate the character of the Soviet resistance and explain Germany's eventual defeat.

The Battle of Stalingrad 1942–3

As part of their push south-eastward to seize the oil fields of the Caucasus, the German forces besieged the city of Stalingrad. The city was not of major strategic value, but it bore Stalin's name. Defining it as a symbol of Russian resistance, Stalin demanded that his city be defended to the death. Hitler's response was perfectly matched. It was recorded in the official high command report: 'The *Führer* orders that on entry into the city the entire male population be done away with.'

But having entered Stalingrad, the Germans met such a ferocious resistance that they were forced on to the defensive. The besiegers became the besieged. Ignoring the appeals of his generals at the front, who urged a withdrawal, Hitler instructed his army to retreat not one millimetre. They were 'to fight to the last soldier and the last bullet'. The result was that the German forces, deprived of supplies and reinforcements, were battered and starved into submission. Their surrender on 31 January 1943 was a blow from which Germany never recovered, as the following figures indicate:

- 200,000 German troops died in the battle.
- Another 91,000 became prisoners at its end; of these, only 6000 would survive their captivity.
- Hitler's Sixth Army, which had been the most successful of all Germany's forces since the start of the war, had been destroyed.

The Soviet forces themselves had suffered terribly. In the battle that occupied the winter months of 1942–3 over a million Soviet troops were killed. The life expectancy of a soldier at the front was 24 hours. Yet Stalingrad was singly the most important conflict of the war in Europe. It proved that Hitler's armies were

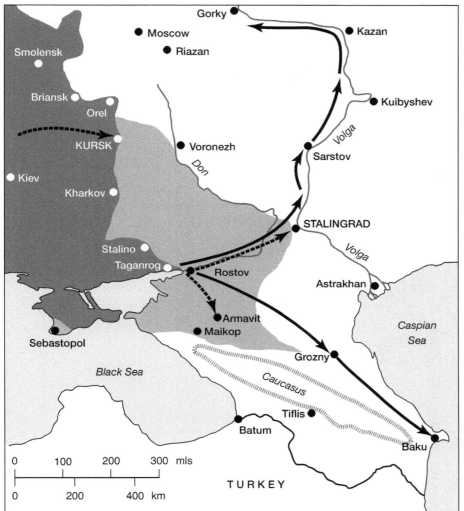

The position of Stalingrad and Kursk. Solid arrowed lines show the intended German offensives. Dotted arrowed lines show the actual German attacks. © Sir Martin Gilbert, 2007

not invincible and gave real promise of final victory to the Western Allies. The Soviet newspaper *Red Star* summed up the significance of it all when it stated: 'What was destroyed at Stalingrad was the flower of the German *Wehrmacht* [army]. Hitler was particularly proud of the 6th Army and its great striking power – And now it does not exist.'

The Battle of Kursk, July 1943

It was in an effort to regain his army's prestige that Hitler backed a plan by his generals, who had noted that a large bulge had appeared where the Soviet forces had overextended their defensive line in the region of Kursk. If the Germans were to launch a full-scale **Panzer** attack they could break through the Soviet line and so regain the initiative on the eastern front. So it was that in 5 July 1943 **Operation Citadel** was begun. It produced the largest tank battle in history. The Soviet commanders, with astonishing speed, poured their forces into the Kursk **salient**. The numbers of troops and armaments deployed are shown in Table 6.1.

Table 6.1 Troops and armaments at the Battle of Kursk

Combatant	Troops	Tanks	Aircraft
German	700,000	2400	1800
Soviet	1,300,000	3400	2100

It was superior numbers that mattered. After twelve days of savage attack and counterattack, the German forces still had not broken through. Mindful of Stalingrad, Hitler decided to save his armies from another devastating defeat by calling off the whole operation. The Soviet Union justifiably hailed it as another great victory. Kursk had confirmed what Stalingrad had first revealed; the Soviet forces were winning the war. And so it proved. Over the next two years

Reasons for Soviet victory

- German forces overstretched themselves.
- The vastness of Russia geographically, which created constant supply problems for the German armies.
- The exceptionally bitter winters, particularly 1941–2, which destroyed Germany's initial military advantage.
- Racial theory blinded German occupiers to the opportunity to enlist the support of the Russian people in an anti-Stalin crusade.
- Hitler's strategic error in dividing his forces on the eastern front.
- Hitler's fatal decision to make Stalingrad a fight to the death, which ultimately destroyed the previously ever-victorious Sixth Army.
- Hitler's stubbornness in refusing to contemplate retreat to save his armies.
- The sheer tenacity and resilience of Soviet resistors.
- Stalin's leadership, which proved inspiring after his initial paralysis.
- Survival of Moscow and Leningrad preserved the integrity of the USSR as a state.
- Transporting of Soviet industry to the Urals (see page 148).
- Lend–lease kept the USSR supplied with desperately needed resources at critical moments (see page 149).
- Ability and ruthlessness of Soviet generals, such as Zhukov (see page 147).

the Soviet army went over to the offensive. **Operation Bagration** in Belorussia in the summer of 1944 saw the defeat of the 1.2 million-strong German Army Group Centre, and opened the way for the Soviet forces to invade Germany itself and head for Berlin. In the spring of 1945, a battered, occupied, devastated Germany surrendered.

Stalin's wartime prestige and reputation

The USSR's triumph in the Great Patriotic War of 1941–5 did much to perpetuate the image of Stalin as national hero. Whatever doubts might have been whispered about him before the war became scarcely possible to consider, let alone utter, after 1945. The Soviet Union's triumph over Germany was a supreme moment in Russian history. Under Stalin, the nation had survived perhaps the most savage conflict in European history. This gave him a prestige as the nation's saviour, with the consequence that the Soviet people held him in even greater awe and feared him even more than before. As the tsars had always known, it does not matter whether a regime is loved as long as it is feared.

In wartime, it was the gravity of the situation, not his oratory, for he was an unimpressive speaker, that gave Stalin's broadcasts their power. Perhaps it was his recognition of his limitations in this regard that explains why after 1945 he made only three public speeches, each only a few minutes long. Yet in an odd way Stalin's remoteness was a strength. Seen as a distant figure on a high rostrum, or in the selected views of him in the official newsreels, he retained a powerful mystique.

In the Soviet celebrations at the end of the war, Stalin gave instructions that his role in the nation's military triumph be given the highest place. Paintings, portraying him as a warrior leader, planning the victory of the Soviet Union, adorned all public buildings. It was a continuation of his cult of personality. But Stalin had been no Hitler. Although he was brutally unforgiving of those in the military he regarded as failures, he showed judgement in allowing his generals, such as **Georgi Zhukov**, real freedom to direct the war. At the great victory parade held in Moscow's Red Square in 1945 it was Zhukov, mounted on a white charger, who reviewed the troops. He made an impressive figure. Stalin had originally intended to take the review himself but had changed his mind out of fear that he would be unable to control his horse.

KEY TERM

Operation Bagration
The 58-day battle that cost a combined total of 765,000 casualties.

KEY FIGURE

Georgi Zhukov (1896–1974)
The ablest of the Red Army generals, the most momentous of his many military successes being the Soviet forces' taking of Berlin in 1945.

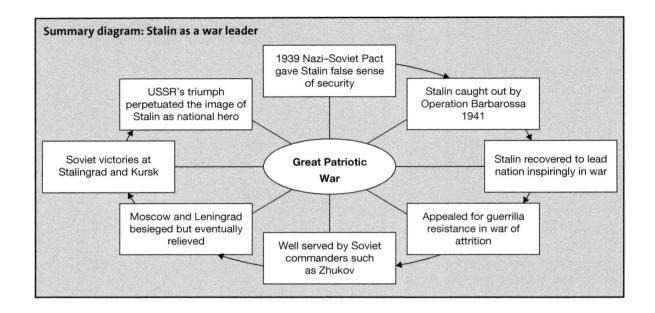

Summary diagram: Stalin as a war leader

- 1939 Nazi–Soviet Pact gave Stalin false sense of security
- Stalin caught out by Operation Barbarossa 1941
- USSR's triumph perpetuated the image of Stalin as national hero
- Stalin recovered to lead nation inspiringly in war
- Great Patriotic War
- Soviet victories at Stalingrad and Kursk
- Moscow and Leningrad besieged but eventually relieved
- Appealed for guerrilla resistance in war of attrition
- Well served by Soviet commanders such as Zhukov

2 The impact of the war on the USSR

▶ *How did the Soviet economy adjust to the demands of war?*

▶ *In what ways did the war increase the suffering of the Soviet people?*

The intensity of the Great Patriotic War placed great strains on the Soviet economy and brought great suffering to the Soviet people.

The wartime economy

Under the first three Five-Year Plans (see page 99), Soviet industrial expansion had been mainly sited west of the **Urals**, the area which proved most vulnerable to German attack after 1941. To offset the losses caused by German occupation, extraordinary efforts were made to transfer whole sectors of Soviet industry to the relative safety of areas east of the Urals. All adults not involved in essential war work were conscripted into the armed forces. This, together with the huge number of casualties, amounting to 4 million in the first year of the war, rapidly reduced both the agricultural and industrial workforce. Women and children had to fill the vacant places.

Work on the land became an almost totally female activity. Arms production received top priority. By 1942 over half of the national income was being devoted to military expenditure. This was the highest proportion by far of any of the

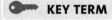

KEY TERM

Urals The mountain range dividing European and Asiatic Russia.

countries involved in the Second World War. In such circumstances the pre-war levels of production could not be maintained. Figure 6.1 indicates the degree of industrial disruption in the Soviet Union caused by the German occupation during the first two years of the war.

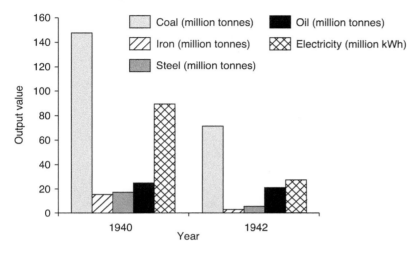

Figure 6.1 Industrial production in the USSR for 1940 and 1942.

In what ways does the chart in Figure 6.1 indicate the impact of the war on the USSR's main areas of production?

The lowest point in Soviet economic fortunes came in 1942. But from then on, as things began to improve on the military front, there was a corresponding improvement in the economy. The new factories in the Urals began to come into production. The 17 million tonnes of war materials sent by the USA to the USSR under a **lend–lease** programme bolstered the Soviet's home-produced supply of weapons and motor transport. Of special significance was the recovery and expansion of the Soviet railway system, which enabled troops and supplies to be moved strategically. With the retreat of the German armies on a broad front, following their defeats in 1943 at Stalingrad and Kursk, the USSR began to regain its lost industrial sites. The scale of economic recovery that followed can be seen in the data in Table 6.2, which illustrate the achieving of huge armaments production at a time of acute shortages in plant, materials and labour.

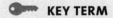 **KEY TERM**

Lend–lease The importing by the USSR of war materials from the USA with no obligation to pay for them until after the war.

Table 6.2 Wartime productivity in the USSR (calculated to a base unit of 100 in 1940)

Output	1941	1942	1943	1944
National income	92	66	74	88
Total industrial output	98	77	90	104
Armaments production	140	186	224	251
Fuel production	94	53	59	75
Agricultural output	42	38	37	54

How does Table 6.2 indicate the prodigious response of the USSR to the demands of war?

The ferocity and scale of the four-year fight to the death meant that everything in the Soviet Union was subordinated to the sheer need to survive. Stalin's insistence during the previous thirteen years that the Soviet economy be put on a war footing began to show certain benefits. Centralised authority was of great value when it came to organising the war effort. Furthermore, the harshness of the conditions under which the Soviet people had laboured in the 1930s had prepared them for the fearful hardships of war. The raw courage and resilience of the Russian people proved a priceless asset.

The suffering of the Soviet people in wartime

How much the Soviet people suffered can be expressed in simple figures. At the end of 1941, after only six months of war, the following losses had been sustained:

- Half the Soviet population was under German occupation.
- A third of the nation's industrial plants were in German hands.
- Iron and steel production had dropped by 60 per cent.
- Forty per cent of the railway system was no longer usable.
- Livestock had been reduced by 60 per cent.
- Grain stocks had been reduced by 40 per cent.

The USSR's survival by 1945 was achieved at the expense of even greater privation for the Soviet people than they had already borne during collectivisation and industrialisation (see pages 87 and 95). The following factors explain the scale of the suffering:

- the long German occupation of the most fertile land
- the shortage of agricultural labour
- the reimposition of state grain and livestock requisitions
- the breakdown of the food distribution system.

All these combined to transform the chronic Russian food shortage into famine. Over a quarter of the estimated 25 million fatalities suffered by the Soviet Union during the war were the result of starvation. A chilling example of what was endured is evident in the statistics relating to Leningrad, which was under German siege for 900 days from September 1941 to January 1944:

- A million people, one in three of the city's population, died from wounds, hunger or cold.
- Over 100,000 German bombs fell on the city.
- Over 200,000 shells were fired into the city.
- The police arrested 226 people for cannibalism, a token gesture at controlling what became a widespread practice.

As the Soviet military struggle drew to its successful close in May 1945, Stalin declared: 'We have survived the hardest of all wars ever experienced in the history of our Motherland. The point is that the Soviet social system has proved to be more capable of life and more stable than a non-Soviet system.' He chose not to admit that much of the suffering had been caused by his own policies, not least his mania for deporting whole peoples whose loyalty he doubted.

The deportations

The wartime deportations were an extension of the purges on a massive scale. Fearing that the national minorities would try to gain their independence by joining the German invaders, Stalin, during the course of the war, had the following peoples deported: Chechen Ingush, Meskhetians, Crimean Tatars, Kalmyks, Karachai and Volga Germans (see the map on page 152). The brutality with which the deportations were enforced, with people being dragged from homes and transported in airless cattle trucks, caused great suffering and many thousands died. In all, by 1945 some 20 million Soviet people had been uprooted.

The impact of war on Soviet women

The death toll of men at the front and the desperate need to keep the armaments factories running meant that women became indispensable to the war effort. So demanding and intense was the Soviet struggle that in 1945 half of all Soviet workers were female. In 1936 there had been 9 million women in the industrial workforce; by 1945 this had risen to 15 million. Without their effort the USSR could not have survived. Yet women received no comparable reward. Despite their contribution to the Five-Year Plans and to the war effort, women's pay rates in real terms dropped between 1930 and 1945.

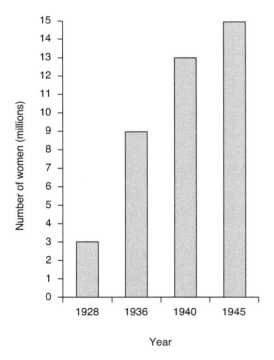

Figure 6.2 The number of women in the Soviet industrial workforce.

What trend in women's industrial employment is evident from the chart in Figure 6.2?

? In what ways does the map indicate the scale and character of the Stalinist deportations, 1941–5?

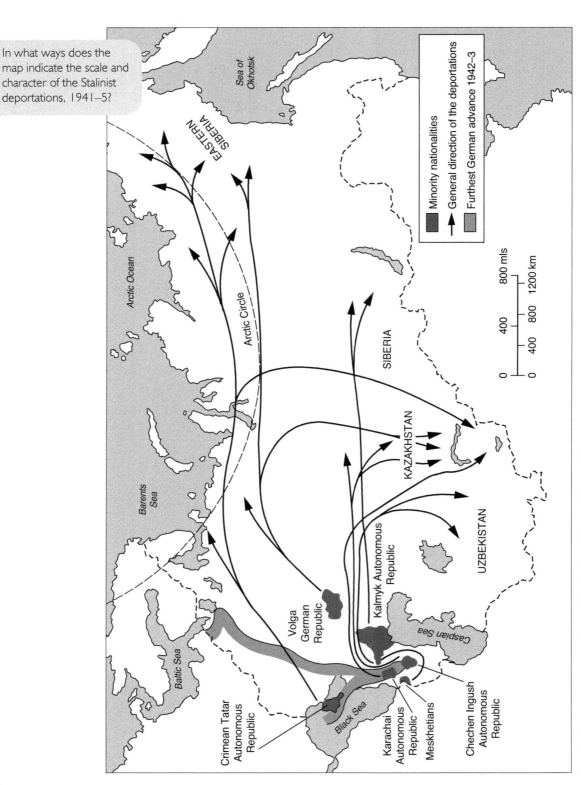

Stalin's deportation of nationalities 1941–5. © Sir Martin Gilbert, 2007

An equally striking statistic is that during the war over half a million women fought in the Soviet armed forces. However, rather than improving the status of women, this left them more vulnerable to mistreatment. It has come to light from recently opened Soviet records and the confessions of Red Army veterans that female soldiers were routinely sexually abused, especially by the senior officers. Although much official praise was lavished on the heroic wartime efforts of Soviet women, Stalin made no significant moves after 1945 to reward them for their contribution.

The impact of war on the Churches

The war, which began for the USSR in June 1941, brought a respite in the persecution of the Churches. Stalin was aware of how deep the religious instinct was in the great majority of Russians. While official policy was to denigrate and ridicule religion, there were occasions when it proved highly useful to the authorities. Stalin was shrewd enough to enlist religion in fighting the Great Patriotic War. Churches were reopened, the clergy released and the people encouraged to celebrate the great religious ceremonies. The majestic grandeur of the Orthodox liturgy provided a huge emotional and spiritual uplift. A Russian church congregation in full voice is a magnificent sound. Those besieged in Leningrad recorded that while worship did not lessen their hunger or soften the German bombardment, it lifted their morale and strengthened their resolve to endure the unendurable.

What is particularly fascinating and revealing is that for the period of the war the Soviet authorities under Stalin played down politics and emphasised nationalism. Talk of the proletarian struggle gave way to an appeal to defend holy Russia against the godless invaders. The Church leaders responded as Stalin had intended. Bishops and priests turned their services into patriotic gatherings. Sermons and prayers expressed passionate defiance towards the Germans and the people were urged to rally behind their great leader, Stalin, in a supreme war effort. The reward for the Church's co-operation was a lifting of the anti-religious persecution. The improved relations between the Church and the state continued after the war. By the time of Stalin's death in 1953, 25,000 churches had reopened, along with a number of monasteries and **seminaries**.

However, this did not represent any real freedom for the Orthodox Church. The price for being allowed to exist openly was its total subservience to the regime. In 1946, Stalin required that all the Christian denominations in the Soviet Union come under the authority of the Orthodox Church, which was made responsible for ensuring that organised religion did not become a source of political opposition.

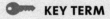 **KEY TERM**

Seminaries Training colleges for the clergy.

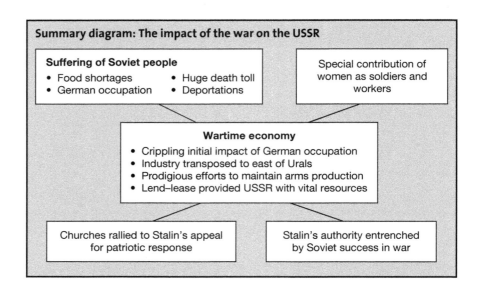

Summary diagram: The impact of the war on the USSR

Suffering of Soviet people
- Food shortages
- German occupation
- Huge death toll
- Deportations

Special contribution of women as soldiers and workers

Wartime economy
- Crippling initial impact of German occupation
- Industry transposed to east of Urals
- Prodigious efforts to maintain arms production
- Lend–lease provided USSR with vital resources

Churches rallied to Stalin's appeal for patriotic response

Stalin's authority entrenched by Soviet success in war

 3 # High Stalinism in the USSR 1945–53

▶ *What form did post-war Soviet reconstruction take under Stalin?*

High Stalinism is a term used to describe the last period of Stalin's rule after 1945, when his control at home was absolute and he had become a major influence on world affairs. It had two main features:

- the further consolidation of Stalin's personal power in the Soviet Union through his post-1945 domestic policies
- the transformation under his leadership of the USSR's international position from 1945 to 1953.

Stalin's post-war consolidation of power

As before 1941, Stalin used his economic policy after 1945 to increase his political control.

Economic reconstruction

Triumph in war did not lessen the suffering of the Soviet people or make them freer. Stalin's grip on the country became still tighter. When Stalin turned to the question of Soviet economic reconstruction after the ravages of war, it was with no thought of rewarding the people for their efforts. Instead, he called on the nation to redouble its efforts. Defence and the expansion of heavy industry were again to be the priorities. Little had changed in his economic thinking since 1928; his basic strategy remained the same.

The post-war Five-Year Plans

At the end of the war, the Soviet Union was in a potentially strong economic position. The recovery of all its occupied territory, its own occupation of eastern Germany and its hold over the rest of Eastern Europe had considerably increased its resources. But, against that had to be set the severe disruption caused by the war. The fourth FYP (1946–50) was aimed at restoring production to the 1941 level. Even allowing for inflated claims, this seems to have been largely achieved within three years. But, as had been the case with the earlier FYPs, the goals were reached only in the traditional areas of heavy industry. The Soviet economy itself remained unbalanced. In those sectors where unskilled and forced labour could be easily used, as in war-damage clearance and the rebuilding of abandoned factories and plants, the results were impressive.

Stalin's 'Grand Projects of Communism'

Stalin continued to favour large-scale construction projects. Bridges, dams, refineries and power-generating plants took pride of place in the FYP, but with little thought being given to their integration into an overall economic strategy. Their construction often involved the wasting of vital financial and material resources that could have been invested more productively elsewhere. These show pieces, collectively termed 'Stalin's Grand Projects of Communism', had more to do with propaganda than economic planning.

The same consideration applied to the successful detonation in 1949 of the Soviet Union's first atomic weapon (see page 166). Undeniably an impressive scientific achievement in itself, Soviet nuclear development imposed demands that the economy could bear only by diverting resources away from vital domestic areas. One of Stalin's most lasting economic legacies was to leave the Soviet Union burdened with a nuclear-based defence programme whose costs meant that little attention could be paid to improving the conditions of the ordinary Russians.

Weakness of the post-war Five-Year Plans

By 1950, the fourth FYP had realised it aims in regard to heavy industrial growth; the output of iron and steel, oil and electrical power had been doubled. The major weakness, as with the pre-war plans, was the failure to increase agricultural production or to raise the living standards of the workers. Lip service was paid to these two objectives in both the fourth and fifth FYPs, the latter (1951–5) outliving Stalin. Yet, in practice, hardly anything was done. Agriculture continued to be undercapitalised and regarded as secondary to the needs of industry. When Khrushchev (see page 185) was given special authority by Stalin to investigate problems on the collective farms, he spent more time enforcing political control in the countryside than in improving food yields.

Rationing

Food rationing was formally ended in 1947 but this was not a real sign that the chronic problem of shortages had been overcome. Indeed, it was only the existence of a widespread **black market**, which was officially condemned but secretly encouraged by the authorities, that enabled the workers to supplement their meagre food supplies. Moreover, accommodation was scarcer, living quarters more crowded and working conditions poorer than they had been in wartime. Wages were controlled so that they hardly rose above subsistence level and the rigours of the **Labour Code** were not relaxed. When Stalin died in 1953, the lot of the Soviet workers was harsher than at any time since 1917.

The later purges 1941–53

The purges that had taken place during Stalin's early rule continued with the coming of peace in 1945. They had become an integral part of the Stalinist system of government. Victory had not softened Stalin. He emerged from the war harder in attitude towards the Soviet people. This was clear from his treatment of Soviet troops who had deserted to the enemy during the war. When peace came, Stalin used the desertions to justify a large-scale purge of the Soviet armed forces. The ironic aspect of this was that he was helped by the Western Allies. At the **Yalta and Potsdam Conferences** in 1945 (see page 159), the victor nations had agreed that all released POWs should be returned to their country of origin. In central and eastern Europe these included many Soviet citizens who had fought for Germany against the USSR in an attempt to break free of Stalin. Terrified at the prospect of what awaited them, they pleaded with their Allied captors not to be sent back. However, in the face of Stalin's insistence, the Allies gave in and forcibly repatriated the prisoners they held. There were disturbing scenes as British troops forced Soviet prisoners at rifle and bayonet point to board the waiting trucks.

The consequences were as devastating as the prisoners had anticipated. Mass executions took place on Stalin's orders. What deepened the horror was that the victims were not only fighting-men. On the grounds that whole communities had supported Hitler's forces, whole communities were made to suffer. It was at this time that the Cossacks as a people were virtually destroyed in retribution for their support of the German armies during the war. Stalin was no gentler to the Soviet POWs who returned from German captivity. Asserting that their survival was proof of their collaboration with their captors, he ordered that returning POWs were to be transferred directly to Soviet labour camps.

Zhdanovism

The purges continued on the cultural front. In 1946, Andrei Zhdanov, who had been active as a prosecutor during the purges of the 1930s (see page 110), became the commissar responsible for imposing artistic conformity. All writers, artists and performers were placed under strict controls and censorship was imposed to stamp out free expression, which was condemned as 'subservience to Western capitalist values'. It was a reinforcement of the Soviet notion of 'socialist realism' (see page 120). The aim was clearly to prevent any form of political opposition developing under the guise of art and culture. Zhdanovism became the term used to describe the severity of this regime. Notable victims included the editors of Moscow's literary journals and art magazines and the internationally renowned poet Anna Akhmatova, all of whom were expelled from the Soviet Union of Writers. By the time of Zhdanov's death in 1948, the system that bore his name had extended its authority over all forms of intellectual life, including the Soviet universities, which were subjected to intense scrutiny to ensure that they behaved with absolute political correctness.

The Leningrad Affair

As he grew older Stalin became more still more suspicious of those around him. After 1947 he dispensed with the Central Committee and the Politburo, thus removing even the semblance of limitation on his authority. In 1949, he initiated another party purge, the 'Leningrad Affair', comparable in scale and style to those of the 1930s. Leading party and city officials, including those who had previously been awarded the title 'Hero of the Soviet Union' in honour of their courageous defence of Leningrad during the war, were arrested, tried on charges of attempting to use Leningrad as an opposition base, and then shot.

Deportations continued

Stalin's vindictiveness was also evident in the continuation of the deportations begun in the war. To prevent nationalist risings, the decree shown in Source C was issued. At the time of Stalin's death over 3 million people had been forcibly relocated under its terms.

SOURCE C

From an order of the Supreme Soviet, 26 November 1948, quoted in Richard Sakwa, *The Rise and Fall of the Soviet Union 1917–1991*, Routledge, 1999, p. 303.

Germans, Kalmyks, Ingush, Chechens, Balkars, Crimean Tatars and others have been deported to distant regions forever, and their unauthorised departure from place of settlement is punishable by hard labour for up to twenty years.

In 1948 in connection with the 'Leningrad case' practically the entire leadership of the Estonian party organisation was repressed.

On 22–23 May 1948 11,345 families of active participants in the armed nationalist underground and kulaks were deported from Lithuania, totalling 39,766 people (men 12,370, women 16,499 and children under fifteen, 10,897).

> What does Source C indicate about the scale and intensity of the deportations? **?**

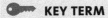

KEY TERM

Pogrom Traditional Russian state-organised persecution, going back to tsarist times, involving physical attacks on Jews and destruction of their property.

The Doctors' plot

Soviet Jews were the next section of the population to be selected for purging. Stalin ordered what amounted to a **pogrom** for no better reason than that his daughter, Alliluyeva, had had an affair with a Jew of whom he disapproved. Anti-Semitism was long established in Russia and it was a factor in the last purge that Stalin attempted. Early in 1953, it was officially announced from the Kremlin that a 'Doctors' plot' had been uncovered in Moscow; it was asserted that the Jewish-dominated medical centre had planned to murder Stalin and the other Soviet leaders. Preparations began for a major assault on the Soviet medical profession, comparable to the pre-war devastation of the Red Army. What prevented those preparations being put into operation was the death of Stalin in March 1953.

Summary diagram: High Stalinism in the USSR 1945–53

Post-war economic reconstruction
- Fourth and fifth FYPs a continuation of centralised economic control
- Stalin's 'Grand Projects'
- Weakness of Stalin's industrial strategy
- Further privations of Soviet people

Intensifying of Stalin's political control
- Purges renewed
- Brutal recriminations against returning Soviet POWs
- Further deportations
- Zhdanovism
- Leningrad Affair
- Doctors' plot

 # High Stalinism: the USSR's international position 1945–53

▶ *How did Stalin's post-war foreign policies alter the USSR's international status?*

The victory of the USSR over Nazi Germany was portrayed in Soviet propaganda as the triumph of Stalin's great anti-fascist crusade. However, the truth was that Stalin had not entered the war against Germany willingly. As the Nazi–Soviet Pact had shown, the object of Stalin's policy before 1941 had been to reach a compromise with Nazism, not fight against it. The USSR became a wartime ally of Britain and the USA not through choice but through circumstance. Before being attacked in June 1941, the Soviet Union had made no effort to assist Britain in its struggle with Germany that had begun in September

1939. Still less was the Soviet–American alliance a natural one. It came into being only after Germany, as an ally of Japan, declared war on the USA following the Japanese assault on **Pearl Harbor** in December 1941.

The Grand Alliance

Hitler's declaration of war on the USA was a momentous act since, perforce, it united the USA, Britain and the USSR against a common enemy. The coming together of the three anti-German allies became known as the **Grand Alliance**. However, a more accurate description might be 'the marriage of convenience'. What bound them together was their desire to defeat Germany. They had little else in common. In public, frequent tributes were made to the war efforts of their glorious allies, but behind the scenes there was constant bickering and tension between the Soviet Union and its two Western partners.

As the war drew towards its end, the ideological differences between the USSR and the other allies, which had been largely submerged because of the need for wartime co-operation, began to resurface. The Soviet fear was that Britain and the USA would attempt to enlist Germany in a war against the USSR. The fear on the Western side was that the Soviet advance into Eastern Europe and Germany heralded the start of a new period of Communist expansion.

The Yalta Conference, February 1945

The underlying hostility explains why, when Stalin, Churchill and Roosevelt met again at Yalta (a seaside resort in the Crimea) in February 1945 to plan the post-war settlement, there was mutual suspicion behind the official cordiality. As a result, the agreements they reached were temporary compromises that did not settle the larger issues. These agreements were as follows:

- On the question of the treatment of defeated Germany, it was agreed that the country would be divided into four zones, to be separately administered by the USA, the USSR, France and Britain.
- Attempts to arrive at agreement on the scale of the German payment of war reparations proved fruitless. Denied the right at Yalta to exact financial reparations, Stalin took consolation by seizing 60 per cent of German plant and resources in the Soviet-occupied areas.
- The victors agreed that all POWs be returned to their own countries. It soon became apparent from the news coming out of Eastern Europe that this meant death or imprisonment for all those Soviet citizens who had fought for Germany. Nonetheless, having made the original commitment the Allies kept to it for fear of antagonising Stalin.

The Polish issue

Among the most significant of the issues discussed at Yalta was the settlement of Poland. Towards the end of the war, the USSR had occupied Poland and had installed a pro-Soviet provisional government, with the promise of future

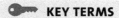

democratic elections. Britain and the USA did not trust Stalin, and feared that Poland would simply become a Soviet puppet. However, the presence of the Red Army in Poland and the readiness of the Western Allies to appease Stalin on some issues in order to gain concessions elsewhere led Churchill reluctantly to grant Stalin's wishes.

The United Nations

The differences that emerged between the powers over Poland and Eastern Europe weakened such agreements as were reached at Yalta. There was deep suspicion between East and West. This was indicated by the Soviet Union's hesitation in joining the United Nations (UN). It was fear of being outnumbered by the capitalist powers that led to Stalin's insistence, as a condition of the USSR's joining, on the **single-member veto** in the proposed **UN Security Council**, the body responsible for peace keeping.

Stalin's position at the Potsdam Conference, July 1945

The conference at Potsdam was essentially a continuation of Yalta. The issues under discussion were the same, and produced the same disagreements between the Soviet Union and the other allies. Stalin's attitude at Potsdam was even more uncompromising than it had been at Yalta. He was not prepared to concede on any of the major issues. He was strengthened in this by the fact that he was undoubtedly the dominant statesman at the conference. Both the USA and Britain had new leaders, Truman and Attlee, respectively, whereas Stalin had attended both conferences. Such continuity worked to his advantage in negotiations. The concessions over Poland and Eastern Europe that he had extracted from Britain and the USA at the Yalta Conference remained substantially unaltered.

Stalin and the Japanese war

At Yalta and Potsdam, the general expectation had been that the war against Japan would continue for a number of years. It was in the light of this that Stalin did a secret deal with Roosevelt. In return for the USSR's entering the war, large areas of Chinese territory would be ceded to it after Japan had been defeated. Ironically, the USA was to have no need of Soviet help in the war against Japan. The **atomic bombs** used against Japan brought a swift end to the Pacific War. This did not prevent Stalin's keeping to the letter of the original agreement. Immediately on receiving confirmation of the Hiroshima bombing, the USSR declared war on Japan. On 14 August, when Japan formally surrendered, Stalin duly proceeded to claim the Soviet Union's territorial rewards in the Far East.

Soviet–American rivalry

The tension between the USSR and the USA during and after the war had an ideological base. Two deep fears conditioned East–West relations:

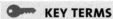

KEY TERMS

Single-member veto The right of an individual member to block the majority decisions of the others.

UN Security Council Composed of the USSR, the USA, France, Britain and Nationalist China.

Atomic bombs Dropped on Hiroshima on 6 August 1945 and on Nagasaki three days later.

- On one side was the Western anticipation that the Soviets, through such organisations as the **Cominform**, were still intent on overthrowing Western capitalist governments.
- On the other was Stalin's conviction that the West, led by the USA, was hell-bent on the crushing of Soviet communism. These mutual terrors were not ended by East–West co-operation in the war against Germany. Indeed, in many respects the profound disagreements over the strategy and purpose of the war increased the tensions.

Stalin and the Soviet satellites

In its push westwards in the final stages of the war, the USSR had liberated the nations of central and Eastern Europe from German control. It then imposed its own authority over them as **satellites**. As in the case of Poland, Stalin refused to withdraw the Red Army from these areas until they had set up pro-Soviet governments. Force and threats was used to achieve this. Some elections were permitted, but they were rigged so as to return large Communist majorities. The methods by which Stalin ruled in Russia were then enforced on the satellites, frequent purges being used to make sure that the national Communist parties were loyal to the USSR. The one exception was Yugoslavia, whose leader, **Marshal Tito**, never allowed his country to fall under Soviet domination.

Stalin's treatment of the satellites was in direct defiance of a joint 'Allied Declaration on Liberated Europe', which committed the victorious powers, including the USSR, to follow a democratic path in the areas they occupied. But Stalin's interpretation of democracy was very different from that of the other allies. The position he took was a simple one. He was determined to create a large buffer against any future German aggression, which he now equated with Western anti-communism. He was not prepared to withdraw Soviet forces from the countries of Eastern Europe unless Communist regimes subservient to Moscow had been installed. The Eastern bloc would have to pay the price for Soviet security.

The Turkish and Persian crises

Beginning in 1946, the USSR had massed troops on Turkey's borders with the aim of intimidating the Turks into allowing Soviet naval bases to be set up along the Dardanelles. Britain, fearing that this was a move towards Soviet expansion into the Middle East with Persia (present-day Iran) as the main objective, admitted to the USA that British forces were not strong enough to protect either Turkey or Persia. The Americans responded by drawing up military plans to repel any Soviet incursion into either country. When Stalin learned of the US determination, he backed down and ordered the withdrawal of Soviet forces.

KEY TERMS

Cominform As a gesture of goodwill towards its wartime allies, the USSR had abolished the Comintern in 1943, but in the post-war tensions it was reformed in 1947 under a new name.

Satellites A Western metaphor denoting the various countries orbiting around the sun (the USSR) and held in its magnetic grip.

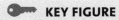

KEY FIGURE

Josef Broz Tito (1892–1980)

Yugoslav revolutionary leader and statesman.

? What territorial gains had the war and its aftermath brought the USSR?

Soviet expansion 1939–49. The term 'iron curtain' was used by Winston Churchill to describe the frontier lines dividing the Eastern bloc from the West.

The Greek crisis

Greece was another area where the resolution of the two **Cold War** sides was put to the test. In the post-war period, a civil war had broken out in Greece where the monarchy, supported, as elections showed, by nearly 70 per cent of the people, was challenged by Communist guerrillas. Stalin, eager to extend the Soviet bloc into the Balkans, backed the Communists, while British forces countered this by fighting on the government's side. Realising how stretched British resources were, the Americans were again prepared to become involved.

The Truman Doctrine

It was in promising to undertake the defence of Greece and Turkey that US President Truman made the famous statement that became known as the Truman Doctrine. In 1947, he publicly announced that the USA regarded it as its duty 'to support free peoples who are resisting attempted subjugation by armed minorities or by outside pressures'. The USSR was not expressly named as an aggressor, but Truman pointedly referred to a world divided between democracy and totalitarianism. The implication could not have been clearer. To Stalin, the doctrine was an act of bad faith, finally destroying what remained of the wartime alliance, and representing the renewal of US imperialism.

The Marshall Plan 1947

Stalin's worries regarding the Truman doctrine were deepened by his anxieties about US moves on the economic front. The abiding concern of the USA after 1945 was that Europe, enfeebled by war, would easily fall prey to an expansionist Soviet Union. Already many countries were experiencing severe economic problems. To prevent these becoming worse, the USA in 1947 introduced the Marshall Plan, which offered large amounts of US capital (in total some $15 billion) to Europe to enable it to undertake post-war reconstruction. The Western European nations accepted the plan, and their recovery began.

The USA's intention was expressed by General Marshall when he introduced his plan in June 1947. He declared that US policy was directed not against any country or doctrine but against hunger, poverty and chaos. The plan's purpose was 'the revival of a working economy in the world, so as to permit the emergence of political and social conditions in which free institutions can exist'. That was not how Stalin saw it. He condemned the plan as an extension of the Truman Doctrine. Both were a cover for US imperialism. His reaction was angrily voiced at the UN by Vyshinsky, the Soviet representative (Source D).

SOURCE D

From Andre Vyshinsky's address to the UN, September 1947, http://astro.temple. edu/~rimmerma/vyshinsky_speech_to_un.htm.

As is now clear, the Marshall Plan constitutes in essence merely a variant of the Truman Doctrine adapted to the conditions of post-war Europe. It is becoming more and more evident to everyone that the implementation of the Marshall Plan will mean placing European countries under the economic and political control of the United States.

Moreover, this plan is an attempt to split Europe into two camps and, with the help of the United Kingdom and France, to complete the formation of a bloc of several European countries hostile to the interests of the democratic countries of Eastern Europe and most particularly to the interests of the Soviet Union.

An important feature of this plan is the attempt to confront the countries of Eastern Europe with a bloc of Western European states including Western

According to Source D, why does Vyshinsky regard the Marshall Plan as 'hostile to the interests of the … Soviet Union'?

Germany. The intention is to make use of Western Germany and German heavy industry (the Ruhr) as one of the most important economic bases for American expansion in Europe, in disregard of the national interests of the countries which suffered from German aggression.

The Eastern bloc's economic plight made Marshall Plan aid a tempting offer, particularly to the poverty-stricken satellites. Stalin for a brief period considered accepting it. But in the end, as Vyshinsky's speech illustrated, he felt that he could not risk the Eastern bloc's becoming financially dependent on the USA. The political dangers were too great. To accept Marshall aid from the USA would be an admission of Soviet weakness. Instead, in 1949, under Soviet direction, the Eastern bloc formed **COMECON**. This was meant as a counter-weight to the Marshall Plan and to the various economic organisations, such as **OEEC**, formed by the Western European nations. Since it lacked Marshall aid funding, COMECON was always a pale shadow of its Western counterpart. It became in practice a mechanism by which the Soviet Union controlled its satellites.

NATO and the Warsaw Pact

It is arguable that Cold War suspicions rendered an economic arrangement between East and West impossible. Distrust of the intentions of the USA was further justified in Soviet eyes by the formation of **NATO** in 1949. In the West this was represented as a defensive alliance, entered into by the nations of Western Europe and North America for their mutual protection. For Stalin, it was a further stage in the spread of US imperialism, begun by the Truman Doctrine. He responded in kind by building a military alliance from the Eastern bloc. This eventually took the form, two years after Stalin's death, of the **Warsaw Pact**, whose members agreed to consult collectively and come to the aid of any member state should it be involved in conflict. The pact declared that each member state was sovereign and independent, but from the beginning it was dominated by the USSR.

Crisis over Germany

The suffering of the Russian people under German occupation during the Great Patriotic War conditioned the Soviet attitude towards Germany after 1945. Stalin was determined that never again should Germany be in a position to threaten the USSR, hence his refusal to contemplate the reunification of Germany. In its push westwards in the closing stages of the war, the USSR had occupied one-third of Germany. Within that area was the capital, Berlin, lying 160 km (100 miles) inside what became the Russian zone at the end of the war. In accordance with the Yalta agreements, Berlin, as with greater Germany, was divided into four **occupation zones**.

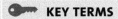

KEY TERMS

COMECON Council for Mutual Economic Assistance.

OEEC Organisation for European Economic Co-operation.

NATO The North Atlantic Treaty Organisation, created in 1949 of ten West European countries plus the USA and Canada.

Warsaw Pact Created in 1955, its member states were Albania, Bulgaria, Czechoslovakia, East Germany, Hungary, Poland, Romania and the USSR.

Occupation zones Administered separately by Britain, USA, France and the USSR. Berlin was similarly divided into four sectors administered by the same four powers.

Within a short time, the three areas of the city occupied by the Western Allies had amalgamated as West Berlin, which thus became a Western island in a Communist sea. This was why Stalin became so sensitive and uncooperative over the German question, always regarding Western suggestions for a settlement as the thin end of a wedge being driven into Soviet security. All future German questions had Berlin at their centre. It became a potent symbol of the Cold War divide.

At Yalta it had been accepted that the four occupying powers would withdraw from their zones once stability had been restored. Stalin, however, soon let it be known that the Soviet Union would not withdraw so long as Germany was regarded as a potential menace to Russia; in effect, this meant indefinitely. What Stalin wanted was to see the Russian zone develop as a buffer between Soviet-controlled Eastern Europe and the West.

The Berlin blockade 1948–9

Stalin's tough line produced a crisis over Berlin in 1948. The glaring gap between the rapidly recovering Western Germany and the bleak eastern region was becoming a serious propaganda weakness to the USSR. When the Western powers in June 1948 introduced the new German currency into West Berlin, the Soviet Union claimed that this was a breach of the Potsdam agreements, and retaliated by imposing a blockade. All fuel and power supplies to West Berlin were cut off, and all road, rail and canal links to West Germany were closed.

Stalin's objective was four-fold:

- to restore damaged Soviet prestige by obliging the Western powers to abandon their plans for a separate German state
- to end the affront to Soviet security of a Western outpost 160 km (100 miles) inside Soviet-controlled East Germany
- to break West Berlin economically
- to test how far the Western powers were prepared to go in support of Berlin.

The Western powers decided to relieve the siege by a massive airlift of essential supplies using the narrow air corridors. If the Soviet Union chose to intercept the planes, it would be an act of war. Over a period of 318 days, the USA and Britain mounted an airlift of supplies to the 2.5 million West Berliners. An average of over 600 individual flights per day provided West Berlin with 1.25 million tonnes of food and fuel. Accepting that his bluff had been called, Stalin ordered the blockade to be abandoned in May 1949. Some historians regard the successful Berlin airlift as marking the end of the first stage of the Cold War. The formal separation of Germany into the **FDR** and the **DDR** that followed represented the onset of **bipolarity**. At Stalin's death, Berlin and Germany remained unresolved questions.

 **KEY TERMS**

FDR West German Federal Republic.

DDR East German People's Republic.

Bipolarity The division of the world between East and West.

The beginnings of an arms race

It was during the Potsdam Conference in July 1945 that the news of the successful US detonation of a nuclear device was passed by Truman to Stalin. The Soviet leader already knew; Russian spies had passed the information to him. He reacted calmly, but he immediately resolved that his own country must now become a nuclear power. Defence experts in the USA had calculated that this would probably take decades. In the event, Stalin's Russia required only four years. In September 1949, Soviet scientists detonated an atomic bomb. They had been considerably aided by the information sent to them by spies in the West. But this was a mere detail beside the astounding realisation that in just four years, the USSR had caught up with the USA. It was now a nuclear nation. As the Stalinist propaganda machine was swift to point out, the USSR under its great leader had elevated itself to the status of superpower.

The success of the Russian atomic programme gave the USA added incentive to expand its own weapons programme, with the result that the world moved into the thermonuclear age. An arms race had begun that would last throughout the Cold War. By 1953 the Soviet Union had again caught up with its adversary by manufacturing a **hydrogen bomb**. Both powers proceeded to produce and stockpile weapons of ever-increasing destructiveness.

The China question

By chance, the Soviet acquisition of nuclear power in 1949 coincided with another equally remarkable development in world affairs. Only a week after the Soviet nuclear achievement, the news came through of the establishment in October of the People's Republic of China (PRC) under **Mao Zedong** – China was now a Communist state. The sense of shock among the Western nations was profound. Not only was the USA's great adversary now a nuclear power, but, in Western eyes, it was now part of a vast Communist alliance stretching from Eastern Europe to the China seas. Events were to prove this a false perception, but the fears generated by Cold War attitudes made it appear a reality.

Stalin and the UN

Relations between the USA and the USSR were not eased by their contacts in the UN. Both the General Assembly and the Security Council provided platforms for propaganda and point scoring. In the Security Council, discussion of the major international problems of the post-war world became a constant battleground between the USSR, regularly using its veto against the non-Communist members. Outnumbered as it was, Soviet Russia viewed the veto not as a last resort but as the instrument for redressing the anti-Soviet imbalance of the Security Council.

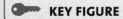

KEY TERM

Hydrogen bomb
A thermonuclear device that uses the atomic bomb as a detonator.

KEY FIGURE

**Mao Zedong
(1893–1976)**

The peasant revolutionary leader who ruled the PRC between 1949 and 1976.

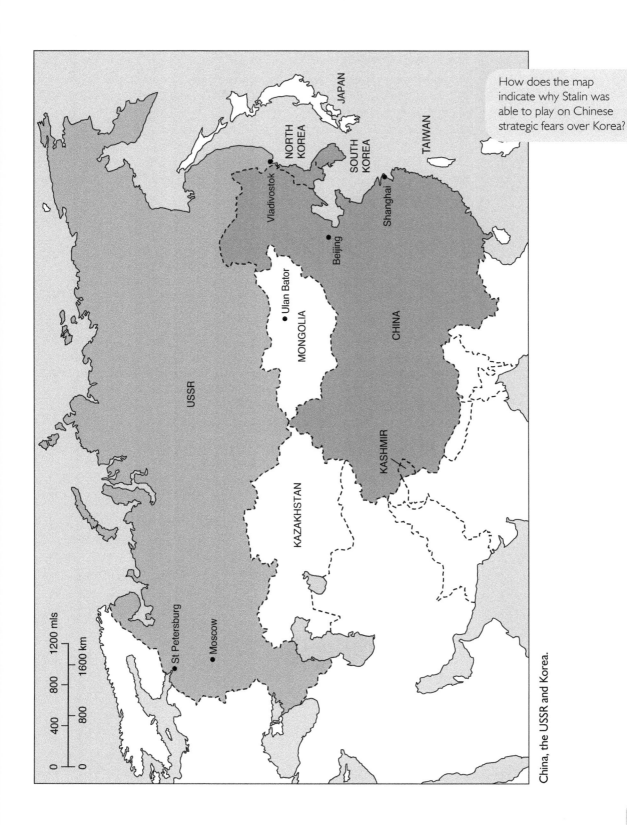

How does the map indicate why Stalin was able to play on Chinese strategic fears over Korea?

China, the USSR and Korea.

The Taiwan question

Soviet–American rivalry in the UN was particularly pronounced over Taiwan. In 1949, the Communists under Mao had driven their main enemy, the Nationalists under **Chiang Kai-shek**, from the Chinese mainland, forcing them to take refuge on the offshore island of Taiwan (Formosa). Nonetheless, the USA chose to continue recognising the defeated Nationalists as the real China and committed itself to the economic assistance and military defence of Taiwan. Stalin's response was to demand that Mao's Communist PRC replace Nationalist China at the UN and on the Security Council.

The Korean War 1950–3

It was the China issue that led to the war in Korea between 1950 and 1953. After Japan's defeat in 1945, Korea had been partitioned between a US-dominated south and a Soviet-dominated north. In 1950 the North Koreans crossed the dividing line of the 38th parallel with the intention of establishing Communist control over the whole country.

It was once believed that the crisis had been initiated by Mao in collusion with Stalin. However, what commentators now suggest is that Stalin had colluded with Kim Il Sung, the North Korean leader, in organising the venture, and that he called on the Chinese to give support only after the fighting had started. Having been convinced by Kim that the North Koreans were capable of sustaining a major war effort against the Americans, Stalin calculated that:

- the USA would be humiliated by being sucked into a conflict in Asia it could not win
- the Soviet Union would gain a very powerful position in the Far East at very little cost to itself since Soviet forces would not be directly involved.

The Soviet Union always denied that it was involved militarily in Korea. It was true that Soviet forces did not take part, although masses of Soviet weapons were used, and Soviet advisers acted on the North Korean side. The war, which ended in stalemate in 1953, did not fulfil Stalin's hopes. Korea remained divided with no prospect of a Communist takeover in the south. A further consequence was that the USA pledged itself to the defence of Taiwan and to the continued support of Nationalist China's membership of the UN, a position that was maintained until 1971.

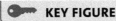

KEY FIGURE

Chiang Kai-shek (1887–1975)

Revolutionary Nationalist leader who held power in mainland China before being overthrown by Mao in 1949.

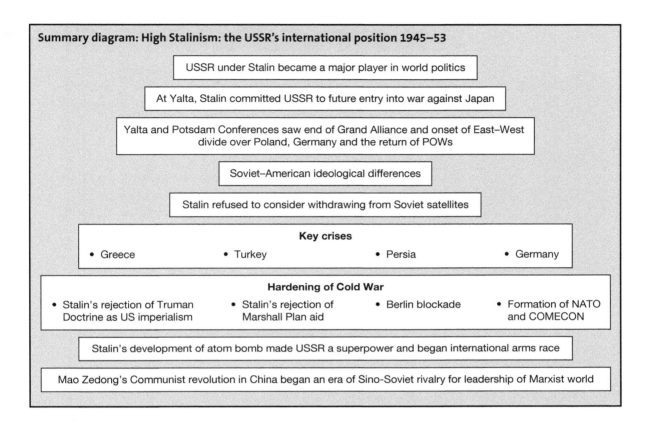

Summary diagram: High Stalinism: the USSR's international position 1945–53

USSR under Stalin became a major player in world politics

At Yalta, Stalin committed USSR to future entry into war against Japan

Yalta and Potsdam Conferences saw end of Grand Alliance and onset of East–West divide over Poland, Germany and the return of POWs

Soviet–American ideological differences

Stalin refused to consider withdrawing from Soviet satellites

Key crises

- Greece
- Turkey
- Persia
- Germany

Hardening of Cold War

- Stalin's rejection of Truman Doctrine as US imperialism
- Stalin's rejection of Marshall Plan aid
- Berlin blockade
- Formation of NATO and COMECON

Stalin's development of atom bomb made USSR a superpower and began international arms race

Mao Zedong's Communist revolution in China began an era of Sino-Soviet rivalry for leadership of Marxist world

5 Stalin's legacy in 1953

▶ *What was Stalin's legacy to the Soviet Union in 1953?*

▶ *What mark did Stalin leave on international relations?*

Defenders of Stalin suggest that, whatever the criticisms of his character and methods, it cannot be denied that he fulfilled the basic duty of any national leader – he preserved the security and independence of the nation he led. More than that, by the time of his death in 1953, he had preserved the integrity of the Soviet Union in a hostile capitalist world and had turned his nation into a superpower, capable of matching the USA. At his death, Stalin's reputation in the Soviet Union could not have been higher. He was the great leader who had:

- fulfilled the socialist revolution begun by Lenin
- purged the USSR of its internal traitors and enemies
- turned the USSR into a great modern economy through collectivisation and industrialisation
- led the nation to victory over fascism in the Great Patriotic War
- elevated the USSR to the status of superpower with its own nuclear weapons

- created an Eastern Communist bloc that rivalled the West in the Cold War
- made himself an outstanding world statesman.

These, of course, were achievements that Stalin claimed for himself through his propaganda machine. A more neutral estimate would have to include the negative side of Stalin's quarter century of power. His domestic legacy judged in this way might include:

- the use of terror as a state policy
- the authoritarian one-party rule by the CPSU
- a misguided belief in the supremacy of Communist economic planning (Stalin's policy of collectivisation was so disruptive that it permanently crippled Soviet agriculture and left the USSR incapable of feeding itself)
- his policy of enforced industrialisation, which achieved a remarkable short-term success but prevented the USSR from ever developing a truly modern economy
- the abuse and deportations suffered by the ethnic peoples of the Soviet Empire, which left them with a burning resentment that would eventually help to bring down the USSR
- the economic poverty of the Eastern bloc, largely due to the USSR's draining of its resources and Stalin's refusal to allow it to receive Marshall aid.

Foreign affairs

It is worth stressing that Stalin was the only statesman to have been at the helm continuously from 1941 when the Grand Alliance was formed, through to his death in 1953. He was involved in some way in every crisis that occurred in those twelve years. If any one individual can be said to have shaped, indeed to have personified, the Cold War, it was Joseph Stalin. His legacy in foreign affairs includes the following:

- the Soviet occupation of Eastern Europe
- the Cold War and the intensity of Cold War divisions
- international economic rivalry
- conflict with China for the leadership of world communism
- the iron curtain, with its suppression of democracy in the satellites
- the unresolved problem of Germany and Berlin
- Soviet ambitions and threats in the Middle East
- the nuclear arms race
- a record of unyielding refusal to trust the West
- the use of subterfuge in Asia
- a form of uncompromising diplomacy that embittered international relations.

Stalin's responsibility for the Cold War

Some commentators have suggested that Stalin's most enduring legacy was the Cold War, a product of his obduracy in foreign affairs. It has been argued that

Stalin never fully understood the Western position. Yet, this is not the whole story. The misunderstanding was two-way. There was a Soviet perspective that the West never fully appreciated. Despite the Soviet victory over Germany and the emergence of Stalin as an outstanding world statesman, the USSR in 1945 felt more vulnerable than at any time since the Bolshevik Revolution in 1917. Economics lay at the heart of Stalin's anxieties. Although the Soviet Union had managed to sustain itself through four years of total war, the strain involved had exhausted the economy by 1945. Since the USSR could not hope to compete on equal economic terms with the USA, Stalin calculated that the only policy available to him after 1945 was to withdraw the Soviet Union behind its new defensive barrier, provided by the wartime acquisition of Eastern Europe.

Soviet foreign policy under Stalin was sometimes complex in its operation, but it was essentially simple in its design. He set himself the primary task of defending his country's interests in a hostile world. Having, in any practical sense, abandoned the notion of leading an international Marxist revolution, he settled for the less ambitious but equally demanding task of safeguarding national security. He never lost his deep fear of a Western invasion. No matter how powerful he and the Soviet Union became, Stalin never ceased to regard his nation as vulnerable. The paranoia that characterised his domestic policies also shaped his approach to foreign affairs.

Summary diagram: Stalin's legacy in 1953

Stalin as a world statesman had made the USSR a superpower

⇩

Domestic legacy

- Cult of personality
- Terror as a state policy
- Authoritarian one-party rule

- Misguided economic planning prevented the USSR from modernising
- Abuse of ethnic peoples of Soviet empire ultimately destroyed the USSR

⇩

Foreign legacy

- Soviet occupation of Eastern Europe
- Cold War
- Conflict with China

- Iron curtain
- Unresolved problem of Germany and Berlin
- Nuclear arms race

Key debate

▶ *Did Stalin fulfil or betray Lenin's revolution?*

From the time he took power, Stalin insisted that he was the true heir to Lenin. He consistently claimed that Leninism and Stalinism were interlocked as one, and that the principal features of Soviet Russia under him – collectivisation, industrialisation, 'socialism in one country', cultural conformity – were 'Marxism–Leninism in action'. Trotsky rejected this: he claimed that Stalin had laid his dead bureaucratic hand on Russia, thus destroying the dynamic revolution that Lenin had created.

For decades scholars have debated this issue. Isaac Deutscher and Roy Medvedev, both of whom suffered personally under Stalin, followed Trotsky in suggesting that Stalin had perverted the basically democratic nature of Leninism into a personal dictatorship and thus prevented the development of genuine socialism in the Soviet Union. Robert McNeal, an American scholar, neatly summarises this interpretation in the following extract.

EXTRACT 1

From Robert McNeal, 'Trotskyist Interpretations of Stalinism', quoted in Robert Tucker, editor, *Stalinism*, Transaction Publishers, 1999, p. 30.

'Stalinism is the syphilis of the workers' movement.' Thus did Trotsky sum up the phenomenon that had defeated not only his political aspirations but also his attempts to comprehend it. It is a cry of anguish from a man who deeply believed in human progress, most particularly in the progressive meaning of his life as a revolutionary, and could not come to terms with the cruel irony that confronted him in Stalin's Russia.

However, Trotsky's view was challenged by Alexander Solzhenitsyn, a leading dissident Soviet writer who underwent long years of imprisonment in the gulag. Far from accepting that Stalin had diverged from Lenin's path, Solzhenitsyn regarded Stalin as the 'blind, mechanical executor of Lenin's will'. In 1974, Solzhenitsyn wrote that the current Soviet authorities and their sympathisers in the West were eager to identify Stalinism as unique to Stalin since it enabled all the mistakes of the Soviet past to be blamed on him rather than on the Soviet system itself which Lenin had founded.

EXTRACT 2

From Alexander Solzhenitsyn, *The Gulag Archipelago*, Collins, 1978, p. 80.

*They shift onto Stalinism the whole bloody burden of the past to make their present position easier. It is no less necessary to those broad **Left-liberal circles** in the West which in Stalin's lifetime applauded highly coloured pictures of Soviet life. But close study of our [Soviet] modern history shows there never was any such thing as Stalinism. Stalin was a very consistent and faithful heir to the spirit of Lenin's teaching.*

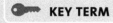

KEY TERM

Left-liberal circles
Westerners sympathetic towards Stalin and the USSR.

Solzhenitsyn's analysis was backed by Western commentators such as Edward Crankshaw and Robert Conquest, who described Stalin's tyranny as simply a fully developed form of Lenin's essentially repressive creed of revolution. Dmitri Volkogonov, the Russian biographer of Lenin and Stalin and Trotsky, went further. He suggested not only that was there a direct line of continuity between

Lenin and Stalin but also that the methods they used to impose communism on Russia meant that the Soviet Union could never become a truly modern state.

EXTRACT 3

From Dmitri Volkogonov, *Stalin: Triumph and Tragedy*, Weidenfeld & Nicolson, 1991, p. 547.

Stalinism was one extremely negative way of realizing the ideas contained in Marxist doctrine. But well before the revolution, Lenin attacked other Marxists who interpreted the doctrine in their own way as heretics. Marxism thus acquired the character of a political doctrine that sought not to adapt itself to changing conditions but to adapt conditions to fit its postulates [theories]. Stalinism turned into indifference towards the needs of real people in real time.

Such interpretations were given powerful support by the opening up of the Soviet state archives in the 1990s following the fall of communism and the break-up of the USSR. Building on the work of such analysts as Richard Pipes and Walter Laqueur, Robert Service, in his authoritative biography of Lenin, published in 2004, pointed to an essential link between Lenin and Stalin. He produced compelling evidence to establish his claim that Stalin, far from corrupting Lenin's policies, had fulfilled them. He confirmed that all the main features of the tyranny that Stalin exerted over the Soviet state – one-party rule, the secret police, terror tactics, show trials – were already in existence by the time of Lenin's death. Stalin simply refined them.

Chapter summary

Initially traumatised by Hitler's invasion of Russia in June 1941, Stalin recovered to become an inspiring war leader. But the desperate struggle of 1941–5 brought great suffering to the Soviet people, a suffering intensified by Stalin's relentlessly coercive political and economic measures. Yet victory in 1945 further consolidated Stalin as *vozhd* and international statesman. His increasing paranoia was evident after 1945 in his continuation of the purges against supposed enemies.

This same suspicious attitude informed Stalin's approach to foreign affairs; refusing to accept the right of the Western powers to dictate the post-war settlement, he remained obdurate in creating an Eastern bloc of Soviet-controlled satellites. In his eyes he was forming a buffer against Western expansion.

The manufacture by Soviet scientists of an atomic bomb in 1949 marked the beginning of an East–West arms race. The race was one of the features of the mounting Cold War which spread to the Middle East and Asia. Declining to accept Marshall Aid, Stalin attempted to reconstruct the Soviet economy employing the same top-down policies of the 1930s. The distorted economy was part of the Stalinist legacy over which historical controversy continues.

Refresher questions

Use these questions to remind yourself of the key material covered in this chapter.

1 Why did Stalin refuse initially to accept that a German invasion of the Soviet Union had taken place in 1941?

2 How much suffering did the Soviet people undergo during the war?

3 How did the war of 1941–5 alter Stalin's attitude towards the Church?

4 Why did the Stalinist purges continue into the war and the post-war period?

5 What policy did Stalin follow towards Eastern Europe?

6 What factors led to the introduction of the Truman Doctrine and the Marshall Plan in 1947?

7 Why did Stalin reject the Marshall Plan?

8 Why was Stalin unwilling to accept the reunification of Germany after 1945?

9 Why did Stalin order a blockade of West Berlin in 1948?

10 What influence did the development of nuclear weapons have on the Cold War?

11 Why were Soviet–American relations strained in the UN?

12 What was Stalin's involvement in the Korean War?

13 How far did Stalin achieve his hopes over Korea?

14 How responsible was Stalin for the onset of the Cold War after 1945?

15 What role did ideology play in the Soviet–Western divide?

 Question practice

ESSAY QUESTIONS

1 'Soviet industry was able to adapt to the demands of the Great Patriotic War 1941–5 because of Stalin's totalitarian control.' Assess the validity of this view.

2 How successful was Stalin as a wartime leader?

3 'The Great Patriotic War provided Stalin with greater opportunities to oppress the Soviet people.' Assess the validity of this view.

4 To what extent was Stalin personally responsible for the development of the Cold War by 1953?

INTERPRETATION QUESTION

1 Using your understanding of the historical context, assess how convincing the arguments in Extracts 1, 2 and 3 (pages 172–3) are in relation to their assessment of the historical relationship between Lenin and Stalin.

SOURCE ANALYSIS QUESTION

1 With reference to Sources B (page 143), C (page 157) and D (page 163), and your understanding of the historical context, assess the value of these sources to a historian studying Stalin's response to what he saw as the threats to the Soviet Union between 1941 and 1953.

CHAPTER 7

Khrushchev and de-Stalinisation 1953–64

The story of the USSR between 1953 and 1964 is as much about the legacy of Stalin as it is about Khrushchev. Aware of the impact his predecessor had made on the Soviet Union, Khrushchev attempted to reform Stalin's policies. His struggle to do so on both the domestic and foreign fronts ran into major difficulties and he was never able to wield the same power as Stalin had. Khrushchev's economic failures at home and his misjudgements over foreign affairs led to his fall in 1964. His policy of de-Stalinisation is examined under the following headings:

★ Khrushchev's rise to power 1953–8

★ De-Stalinisation and reform

★ Khrushchev and the Soviet economy

★ Khrushchev's fall 1964

Key dates

1953–6	Khrushchev emerged as leader of the USSR	1959	Khrushchev's Seven-Year Plan started
1954	'Virgin lands' policy introduced	1960	US spy-plane shot down over Soviet territory
1956	De-Stalinisation begun	1961	Berlin Wall erected
	Soviet crushing of Hungarian Rising	1962	Cuban Missile Crisis
1957	Sino-Soviet hostility began to develop	1963	USSR signed Nuclear Test-Ban Treaty
1958	Khrushchev's ultimatum to Western powers over status of DDR	1964	Khrushchev's fall

Khrushchev's rise to power 1953–8

 Why was Khrushchev able to outmanoeuvre his rivals in the power struggle following Stalin's death in 1953?

Kremlin power struggles have never been easy for the outsider to disentangle, but enough evidence has come to light to provide a reasonably reliable narrative of Khrushchev's rise to power. Following Stalin's death in March 1953, the collective leadership that emerged was made up of **Malenkov**, Molotov, **Bulganin** and Khrushchev (party secretary). Their initial anxiety was that Lavrenti Beria, Stalin's chief of the **MVD**, might use his organisation as a base for a power bid.

Beria's fall

The MVD certainly represented a major force in the Soviet Union, but Khrushchev was able to counter-balance it with the Red Army. The generals disliked Beria for his role in the Great Purge of the armed forces in the 1930s (see page 114), and felt that Khrushchev's war record gave him a special authority; he alone of the collective leaders had actually fought in the Great Patriotic struggle, and the Soviet commander-in-chief, Marshal Zhukov, had a particular admiration for him. This enabled Khrushchev to enlist the army's support. In June 1953, a contingent of troops surrounded Beria's apartment, blocking any possibility of the MVD's preventing his arrest. He was taken into custody, summarily tried, and then shot. This was one of the few executions during the post-Stalin power struggle. The blood-lettings of the 1920s and 1930s were not to be repeated. From now on the penalty for political defeat was to be demotion or dismissal. This was one aspect of the '**thaw**' that set in following Stalin's death.

Malenkov's weaknesses

It was due as much to Malenkov, the premier, as anyone that the thaw had begun. He had argued for the need for better relations with the outside world and had suggested that attention be given to the raising of Soviet standards of living at the expense of investment in heavy industry. However, his progressive thinking brought him no political benefits. Despite being tipped by many to become the next leader, he found himself being outmanoeuvred by Khrushchev. A major problem for Malenkov was that, despite being an able administrator, he was no match for Khrushchev in strength of personality. He lacked Khrushchev's forcefulness and persuasive ways. Another difficulty for him, similar to that which had faced the competitors to Stalin after 1924 (see page 68), was that Khrushchev was much better placed politically to sustain a power bid. Malenkov, as premier, was head of government. But Khrushchev, as party secretary, was the effective head of the party.

KEY FIGURES

Georgi Malenkov (1902–88)

Soviet premier (equivalent to prime minister) 1953–5.

Nicolai Bulganin (1895–1975)

Soviet premier, 1955–8.

KEY TERMS

MVD The secret police apparatus which had succeeded the *Cheka* and was later to become the KGB.

Thaw An easing of tension and restrictions following Stalin's death; a number of prisoners were released and censorship of writers and artists was relaxed somewhat.

Khrushchev's strengths

Khrushchev proceeded to undermine Malenkov's position in the Soviet system. He did this not by open attack but by using his influence with party members to criticise government ministers and their policies. Unscrupulously exploiting Malenkov's argument for shifting the economy away from heavy industry to suggest that he was intent on undermining the Soviet defence programme, Khrushchev frightened the Soviet military into dropping their support for Malenkov.

Khrushchev travelled widely about the countryside, something seldom done by Russian leaders either before or after the 1917 Revolution. He listened to complaints and made personal contact with a wide range of people and officials. It was a practice he continued after he came to power. He placed his own nominees in positions of authority, as Stalin had done, and began to establish a power base. By 1955 he was undoubtedly the dominant member of the collective leadership that had succeeded Stalin. It was in that year that Malenkov, publicly admitting that he was to blame for the current shortfall in grain production, resigned his premiership and gave up any thought of contending for power. He was replaced by Bulganin. For some time Bulganin and Khrushchev exercised what in appearance was a joint authority, but in reality Bulganin was very much the subordinate.

Dealing with the Stalin legacy

Conscious that to consolidate his growing authority he would have at some point to make it clear whether he intended to follow Stalin's policies, Khrushchev by 1956 felt strong enough to begin undermining Stalin's character and record. Initially he did not make an outright attack but spoke of the need for party reform and the decentralisation of policy in order to achieve greater administrative efficiency. By implication, this was a criticism of the government and methods that Stalin had bequeathed to the Soviet Union.

Khrushchev knew this was a risky strategy. The questioning of the Stalin legend disturbed party officials and made them fear for the future because, in one obvious sense, they were all Stalinists. They had all survived to hold their current positions because they had participated in, and benefited from, Stalin's terror. Many of them found it difficult to adapt to life without Stalin. They were perplexed and frightened by the implications of Khrushchev's attack on him. A line from a poem of the time expressed their feelings, 'We built upon granite, but now the stone crumbles, dissolves and melts at our feet.' It was around such men that an opposition to Khrushchev from within the party began to form. It included various disgruntled ministers and officials who feared for their positions if Khrushchev was intent on change.

SOURCE A

In what ways does the cartoon in Source A support the notion that reform is needed in the Soviet Union?

A Soviet cartoon from the period of collective leadership after Stalin's death. An official is given a dose of 'criticism'. The label on the bottle says it is a cure for 'gullibility, complacency, twaddle, conceit, bureaucratisation and other ailments'.

Opposition to Khrushchev

In February 1956, Khrushchev took his criticism of the former *vozhd* to its ultimate climax in a devastating secret report in which he laid bare Stalin's crimes against the party (see page 181). Throughout Soviet history, the main value of the party to its members had been as a provider of jobs. Anyone interfering with this, as Khrushchev now was, was bound to arouse opposition. Early in 1957, while Khrushchev was temporarily absent on one of his many visits abroad, the opposition plotted to remove him. Soon after his return, he had to face a concerted attack. Declaring that de-Stalinisation had gone too far and had been responsible for the recent anti-Soviet revolts in Poland and Hungary (see page 184), the Politburo voted by seven to four for his dismissal as party secretary.

Khrushchev proved equal to the challenge. Branding the opposition to him as the work of an 'anti-party group', he refused to accept the Politburo's decision unless it was backed by a vote of the full Central Committee of the party. Using his good relations with the army, he arranged to have his own supporters specially flown in from various parts of the USSR to attend the Moscow meeting. The gamble worked. The Central Committee voted to overrule the Politburo's decision. Molotov, **Kaganovich** and Malenkov were then censured for having been part of the 'anti-party group'. They duly resigned from their ministerial posts.

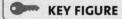 **KEY FIGURE**

Lazar Kaganovich (1893–1991)

A hard-line loyal Stalinist.

Nikita Khrushchev

1894	Born in southern Russia
1918–20	Served as a commissar in the Red Army
1931	CPSU district secretary in Moscow
1938	Party secretary in Ukraine
1942	Fought at Stalingrad
1949	Head of the CPSU in Moscow
1953–8	Rose to prominence in the post-Stalin power struggle
1956	Began process of de-Stalinisation
1958–64	Became dominant figure in USSR and an international statesman

Background

Khrushchev was born in 1894 into a poor peasant family in southern Russia. Having joined the Bolshevik Party in 1918, he became a Red Army commissar during the civil war. Throughout the 1920s Khrushchev was prominent in Ukrainian affairs and in the 1930s moved to Moscow. The Stalinist purges gave him the opportunity to rise by stepping into dead men's shoes. He knew that political survival required unswerving loyalty to Stalin; such commitment gained him membership of the Politburo in 1939. During the war years, 1941–5, he served as a political commissar in the army and fought at Stalingrad.

Rise

Khrushchev's reward was to be summoned by Stalin to Moscow in 1949, where he was appointed secretary to the General Committee and given responsibility for planning Soviet agriculture. The failure of one of his major schemes for developing agricultural centres in the countryside led to his being criticised in *Pravda*. At the time of Stalin's death in 1953, Khrushchev was an industrious but not outstanding member of the Politburo. His colleagues tended to underrate both his ambition and his ruthlessness, and yet by the late 1950s Khrushchev had come to dominate Soviet politics.

Soviet leader

As part of his de-Stalinisation programme, Khrushchev attempted to reform the Soviet economy, an enlightened policy but of only limited success since it met resistance from Soviet vested interests. His breezy, rumbustious style annoyed colleagues but made him popular abroad, where his *détente* approach was regarded as statesmanlike. Khrushchev never held absolute power; he remained answerable to the party in a way that Stalin never had been. The consequence was his political fall in 1964, removed on account of 'hare-brained' domestic and foreign policies, a reference to his brinkmanship over the 1962 Cuban Missile Crisis.

Khrushchev defeats the opposition

Having previously turned to the army as a saviour, Khrushchev now took steps to prevent its becoming a threat. Playing on internal jealousies within the high command, he undermined the position of his long-standing supporter, Marshal Zhukov, who was accused of creating his own 'cult of the individual'. Zhukov was forced to retire, to be replaced by **Malinovsky**. It only remained to demote Bulganin, which Khrushchev did by inducing him to confess to being involved with the 'anti-party group'. In March 1958, Bulganin resigned as premier and lost his place on the Central Committee. Shortly afterwards, Khrushchev took over that post himself. For the first time since Stalin's death, five years earlier, one man held the offices of prime minister in the government and first secretary in the party.

 KEY TERM

Détente A policy aimed at easing tensions between the rival international powers.

 KEY FIGURE

Rodion Malinovsky (1898–1967)

Marshal and commander-in-chief of the Soviet Union.

Summary diagram: Khrushchev's rise to power 1953–8

> As party secretary emerged from post-Stalin collective leadership to outmanoeuvre colleagues

Khrushchev's strengths
- Powerful personality which rivals could not match
- Had been close ally of Stalin
- As party secretary, understood the workings of CPSU politics
- Popular in the CPSU
- Foreign visits enhanced his reputation
- On good terms with the military

> Key move: used support of Marshall Khukov and the military to remove chief rival Beria

De-Stalinisation
- Khrushchev began to undermine Stalin legacy
- Embarked on policy of de-Stalinisation
- This aroused opposition from 'anti-party group'

Khrushchev defeated opposition
- Undermined anti-party group by refusing to accept Politburo's decision to remove him
- Persuaded Central Committee to reverse Politburo's decision
- Removed former ally and only possible rival, Zhukov

 # De-Stalinisation and reform

▶ *What were Khrushchev's motives in adopting a policy of de-Stalinisation?*

▶ *How did de-Stalinisation affect the relations of the USSR with its Eastern bloc satellites?*

Khrushchev's 'secret report', February 1956

The process of destroying Stalin's reputation reached its dramatic conclusion with Khrushchev's 'secret report' to the Twentieth Congress of the CPSU in February 1956. Although officially termed secret, all the evidence suggests that Khrushchev wanted the report to become widely known at home and abroad. In keeping with Khrushchev's subtle questioning of Stalin's strategies, signs had already appeared between 1953 and 1956 to suggest that Stalin's record might be reappraised by the new leaders of the Soviet Union. References in the press to his greatness and omniscience became less frequent and the economic changes in policy introduced by Malenkov were an implied criticism of Stalin's methods.

However, what was totally unexpected was the range and venom of Khrushchev's attack. In his report, which took hours to deliver, Khrushchev surveyed Stalin's career since the 1930s, exposing in detail the errors and crimes that Stalin had committed against the party. Stalin had been guilty of 'flagrant abuses of power'. He had been personally responsible for the purges, 'those mass arrests that had brought tremendous harm to our country and to the cause of socialist progress'. Khrushchev quoted a host of names of innocent party members who had suffered at Stalin's hands. Individual cases of gross injustice were cited and examples given of the torture used to extract confessions. Khrushchev's address was frequently interrupted by outbursts of amazement and disbelief from the assembled members as he gave the details of the Stalinist terror.

Khrushchev's report was not published in the USSR until 1989, but the foreign Communists who had attended the congress had within days leaked the details to the Western press; translations appeared worldwide. These provided a vivid picture of the report and the response it occasioned (see Source B).

SOURCE B

Adapted from Khrushchev's report to the Twentieth Congress of the CPSU, February 1956, quoted in Bertram D. Wolfe, *Khrushchev and Stalin's Ghost*, Praeger, 1957, pp. 124–6.

Of the 139 members and candidates of the Party Central Committee who were elected at the Seventeenth Congress, 98 persons, i.e. 70%, were shot, mostly in 1937–38. (Indignation in the hall) *The only reason why this 70% were branded enemies of the Party and of the people was that honest Communists were slandered, accusations against them were fabricated, and revolutionary legality was gravely undermined.* (Gasps from members)

The same fate befell not only the Central Committee members but also the majority of the delegates to the Seventeenth Party Congress. Of 1,966 delegates, 1,108 persons were arrested on charges of counter-revolutionary crimes. This very fact shows how absurd, wild and contrary to common sense were the charges of counter-revolutionary crimes made against a majority of the participants in the Congress. (Indignation in the hall)

The Seventeenth Party Congress is historically known as the Congress of the Victors. Delegates to the Congress were active participants in the building of our socialist state; many of them fought and suffered for Party interests during the revolutionary years and at the Civil War fronts. How then can we believe that such people could prove to be 'two-faced' and join the camp of the enemies of socialism during the era of the liquidation of the Zinovievites, Trotskyites and Rightists and after the great accomplishments of socialist construction? (Prolonged applause from members)

Why were members of the twentieth congress so shocked by the revelations in Khrushchev's report in Source B?

Khrushchev did not limit himself to the purges. He also attacked Stalin for his failures in foreign policy, particularly with regard to the Eastern bloc countries. He also ridiculed the idea of Stalin as a war hero. The special term that Khrushchev used to describe the Stalinism that he was condemning was 'the cult of personality'. He explained that by this he meant that all the mistakes perpetrated in the Soviet Union since the 1930s had been a consequence of Stalin's lust for personal power, his 'mania for greatness'.

It is significant that although Khrushchev read out a long list of Stalin's victims, who were now to be officially pardoned, it did not go back to before 1934 and did not include such names as Trotsky or Bukharin. Khrushchev's list was a selective one. His purpose was to blacken Stalin's name, not to criticise the Communist Party. It was important that the illegality and terror he was exposing should be seen as the crimes of one individual. In theory and in practice the party was the essential source of power in the Soviet system, and Khrushchev was anxious not to challenge the justification for his own authority.

Khrushchev's motives

Khrushchev's 'secret report' was an extraordinary event in Soviet history. For a quarter of a century before 1953, Stalin had exercised astonishing power. Revered as Lenin's heir, he had come to personify communism itself. To attack such a legend so soon after his death created a real danger of disruption within the Soviet Union and in the ranks of international communism. This raises the question of why Khrushchev took the risk. For him, de-Stalinisation had three basic aims:

- to justify the introduction of more progressive economic measures within the USSR
- to make coexistence with the West easier
- to absolve himself and the other Soviet leaders from complicity in Stalin's errors.

Protecting reputations

The third aim was of particular importance. Criticism of Stalin personally was the only way to explain the otherwise inexplicable failures of the Soviet system during the post-Lenin era. Khrushchev was taking a risk in undermining Stalin's reputation. He knew that he was laying himself open to the charge of having been an accessory to the offences that he was now condemning. After all, he had helped to carry out the purges in Moscow and the Ukraine. But Khrushchev calculated that, since all the Soviet leaders had climbed to their present positions by carrying out Stalin's orders, none of them had a clean record. Their shared guilt would prevent any serious challenge being offered to his denunciation of Stalin.

Limits of liberalisation

At the time, the populations of the Soviet satellites and many observers in the West interpreted de-Stalinisation as a sign that the USSR was moving towards political and social tolerance. They were mistaken. De-Stalinisation was never intended to be a genuine liberalising of Soviet society. It is true that large numbers of political prisoners were released from the gulag, the labour camps which had proliferated under Stalin. There was also some lifting of state censorship. However, these were gestures, not a wholesale abandonment of Soviet authoritarianism. At no time did Khrushchev denounce Stalin for having persecuted the Soviet people. The charge against him was always expressed in terms of crimes against the party. By concentrating his attack on Stalin's 'cult of personality', Khrushchev was placing the responsibility for the errors of the past on one man. The reputation and authority of the party were therefore undiminished.

De-Stalinisation and the Soviet satellites

In his launching of de-Stalinisation at the twentieth party congress in 1956, Khrushchev made great play of Stalin's mishandling of Tito and the **Yugoslav Communists**. Khrushchev contended that, had Stalin shown any real understanding of Tito and the national cause he represented, Yugoslavia would never have broken away from the Soviet bloc.

SOURCE C

Adapted from Khrushchev's report at the Twentieth Congress of the CPSU, February 1956, quoted in Bertram D. Wolfe, *Khrushchev and Stalin's Ghost*, Praeger, 1957, pp. 200–2.

Stalin, pointing to the copy of a letter lately sent to Tito, asked me 'Have you read this?' Not waiting for my reply, he answered 'I will shake my little finger and there will be no more Tito. He will fall'. This statement reflected Stalin's mania for greatness, but he acted just that way. 'I will shake my little finger and there will be no more Tito. I will shake my little finger and many others will disappear.'

But this did not happen. Tito did not fall. Why? The reason was that in this case of disagreement with the Yugoslav comrades Tito had behind him a state and a people who had gone through a severe school of fighting for liberty and independence, a people which gave support to its leaders. You see to what Stalin's mania for greatness led? He had completely lost consciousness of reality; he demonstrated his suspicion and haughtiness not only in relation to individuals in the USSR, but in relation to whole parties and nations.

In raising the Yugoslav issue, Khrushchev's main purpose appears to have been to ridicule Stalin's foreign policy failures. He was not calling for a revision of Eastern bloc communism. Nonetheless, that was how many of the Soviet satellites saw it. They read Khrushchev's attack on Stalin over Yugoslavia as an invitation to seek greater national independence for themselves. Khrushchev visited Tito in 1955 and 1956. This bestowal of Soviet favour strengthened the idea that, with Stalin gone, the Kremlin had accepted Yugoslavia's right to

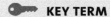
KEY TERM

Yugoslav Communists Yugoslavia under Tito had been the one Eastern European country to have successfully resisted Stalinist domination in the post-war period, remaining Communist but independent of the USSR.

According to Khrushchev in Source C, why had Stalin been unable to deal effectively with the problem of Yugoslavia?

develop its own brand of communism. If it was permissible for Yugoslavia, then why not for the other satellites?

Poland

Throughout the Eastern bloc there were stirrings of independence. The response was particularly marked in Poland and Hungary. In the former, strong demands were made for the Polish people to be left free to develop their own form of socialism. Facing mounting pressure, Khrushchev and the Kremlin leaders compromised for a time by allowing the popular Polish patriot **Gomulka**, who had been outlawed in Stalin's time, to return to political prominence. However, Gomulka had to promise to discourage **revisionism** in Poland and to renew the commitment of his country to the Warsaw Pact, the agreement signed in 1955 under direction from Moscow in which all the iron curtain countries committed themselves to the collective defence of Soviet Europe against 'Western imperialism' (see page 164). The pact was regarded as the touchstone of satellite loyalty to the USSR.

The Hungarian Rising 1956

How determined the USSR under Khrushchev was to maintain its grip was clearly revealed in its reaction to events in Hungary in 1956. In its early stages the Hungarian 'thaw' seemed to be acceptable to Moscow. **Imre Nagy** who, like Gomulka, had been denied public office during the Stalin years, was allowed to return as the new Hungarian leader. Appearances were deceptive. When the Nagy government began to tolerate popular anti-Soviet demonstrations, Khrushchev decided things had gone too far. Angered by the declared intention of the Budapest government to open politics to non-Communists and by Nagy's plan to withdraw Hungary from the Warsaw Pact, he ordered the long-threatened invasion. Russian tanks entered Budapest and the Hungarian 'liberal experiment' was crushed. Nagy was tried in secret and executed in 1958 on Soviet orders.

Khrushchev's heavy hand in Hungary was clear proof that de-Stalinisation had never been intended as a softening of the USSR's fundamental attitude. When the Soviet Union felt its own security threatened or its control of the Eastern bloc challenged, it was prepared to use force against its satellites. De-Stalinisation was a false dawn for those who thought it signified genuine independence for Eastern Europe. Khrushchev was as determined as his predecessor had been to assert the USSR's right to dictate to the Eastern bloc.

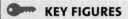

KEY FIGURES

Władysław Gomulka (1905–82)
Moscow-trained Polish Communist Party leader.

Imre Nagy (1896–1958)
Progressive Hungarian Communist, who led a non-Soviet government.

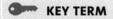

KEY TERM

Revisionism The Marxist word for political heresy, the failure to conform to revolutionary principles.

```
┌─────────────────────────────────────────────────────────────────────┐
│ Summary diagram: De-Stalinisation and reform                         │
│ ┌───────────────────────────────────────────────────────────────┐   │
│ │ Khrushchev's report                                           │   │
│ │ • Began process of destroying Stalin's reputation             │   │
│ │ • Attacked Stalin's cult of personality                       │   │
│ │ • Revealed Stalin's crimes against the party                  │   │
│ └───────────────────────────────────────────────────────────────┘   │
│                              ⇩                                        │
│ ┌───────────────────────────────────────────────────────────────┐   │
│ │ Khrushchev's motives                                          │   │
│ │ • To justify the introduction of more progressive economic    │   │
│ │   measures                                                     │   │
│ │ • To make coexistence with the West easier                    │   │
│ │ • To absolve himself and Soviet leaders from complicity in    │   │
│ │   Stalin's errors                                              │   │
│ └───────────────────────────────────────────────────────────────┘   │
│                              ⇩                                        │
│ ┌───────────────────────────────────────────────────────────────┐   │
│ │ Khrushchev sought better relations with Tito by ridiculing    │   │
│ │ Stalin's record                                                │   │
│ └───────────────────────────────────────────────────────────────┘   │
│                              ⇩                                        │
│ ┌───────────────────────────────────────────────────────────────┐   │
│ │ De-Stalinisation encouraged 'liberal experiments' in Soviet    │   │
│ │ satellites                                                     │   │
│ │ • But Khrushchev was swift to crush these and reassert Soviet  │   │
│ │   dominance                                                    │   │
│ │ • Khrushchev did not allow the 'thaw' at home to be misread as │   │
│ │   a weakening of government authority                          │   │
│ └───────────────────────────────────────────────────────────────┘   │
└─────────────────────────────────────────────────────────────────────┘
```

Khrushchev and the Soviet economy

▶ *What obstacles faced Khrushchev in his efforts to reform the Soviet economy?*

Believing that Stalin's programme of centralised state planning of the economy had led to stagnation, Khrushchev was determined to introduce reforms that would encourage rather than restrict growth.

Agriculture

It was not long after Stalin's death that the Soviet leaders began to admit that the collectivisation of agriculture had not solved the problem of food production and supply. In 1953 Khrushchev informed the Central Committee that grain stocks under Stalin had been lower than under the last tsar. Major changes were needed, he argued. Proud of his peasant origins, Khrushchev claimed a special knowledge of agriculture. He made a point of going to meet the peasants in their own localities to urge them to adopt more efficient techniques. His broad strategy was to encourage local decision-making.

● As an incentive to production, the state authorities began to pay higher prices to the peasants for their grain.
● Taxes on farming profits were reduced.

- Experts were sent from Moscow to work and advise at the local level.
- The machine tractor stations built in Stalin's time were sold to the farmers.

The relative success of this incentive scheme can be gauged from the statistic that between 1952 and 1958 farm-workers' incomes more than doubled. Although farm wages were still much lower than those of industrial workers, prospects of real economic advancement were greater than at any time since the NEP (see page 54).

The 'virgin lands' policy

The initiative most closely associated with Khrushchev at this time was the 'virgin lands' policy, introduced in 1954. This developed into a massive project for exploiting the previously unused areas of the Soviet Union for crop production. The regions earmarked for particular attention were Kazakhstan and southern Siberia. Over a quarter of a million volunteers, mainly drawn from *Komsomol* (the Young Communist League), were enlisted to work in these regions. Considerable financial and material investment was put into the scheme, most spectacularly in the provision of 120,000 motorised tractors. Two and half million hectares were freshly ploughed in the virgin lands in the first year of the scheme.

Failure of the 'virgin lands' policy

There was no doubting the enthusiasm that the policy aroused. But enthusiasm was not enough. Notwithstanding its occasional spectacular success, the 'virgin lands' scheme was flawed by a number of problems that proved insurmountable in the longer term:

- *Poor management*. Khrushchev was not well served by the officials responsible for turning his schemes into reality. The goodwill of the volunteers could not compensate for poor management and short-sighted planning. Too little allowance was made for local conditions. Crops were often sown in unsuitable soil and the effects of climate tended to be ignored. In the drive to convert to foodstuffs, successful crops such as cotton were replaced by those such as maize, which simply refused to grow. This occurred notably in Kazakhstan, where the **maize mania** often led to whole areas abandoning their traditional planting for the lure of a crop whose yield then proved so poor it was not worth harvesting.
- *Lack of fertilisers*. Fertilisers are essential to modern large-scale arable farming but these were seldom available in sufficient quantity in the Soviet Union, which had only 20 million tonnes of fertilisers for every 220 million hectares. This compared badly with the USA, for example, which boasted 35 million tonnes of fertiliser for every 120 million hectares. Khrushchev did initiate a belated crash programme for fertiliser production, but it proved too late to meet demand. The problem was that, while the speed with which crops had been sown and harvested in the 'virgin lands' had produced impressive yields

---

KEY TERM

Maize mania This was excited in part by Khrushchev's obsession with cornflakes, a maize cereal to which he had been introduced while in the USA. He believed that cornflakes could feed the nation.

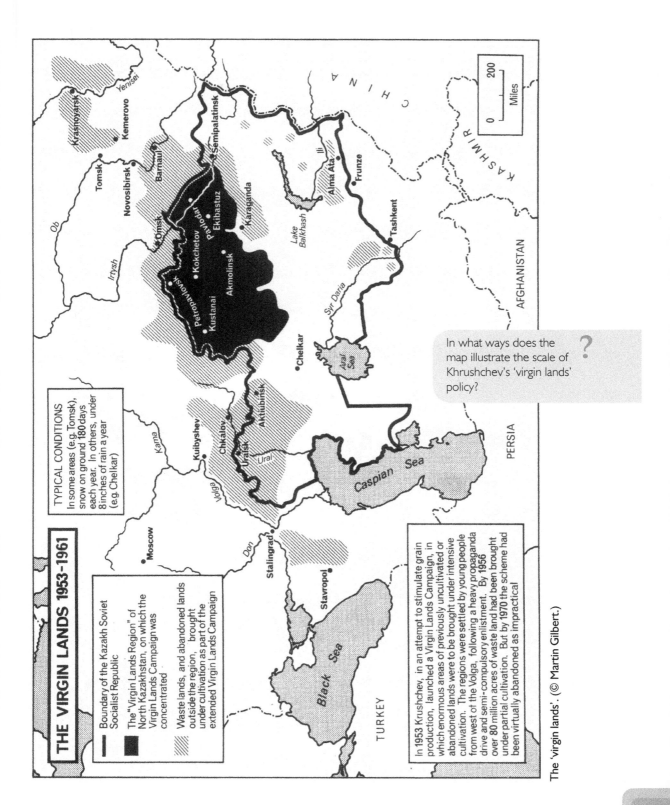

THE VIRGIN LANDS 1953–1961

— Boundary of the Kazakh Soviet Socialist Republic

⬛ The "Virgin Lands Region" of North Kazakhstan, on which the Virgin Lands Campaign was concentrated

▨ Waste lands, and abandoned lands outside the region, brought under cultivation as part of the extended Virgin Lands Campaign

TYPICAL CONDITIONS In some areas (e.g. Tomsk), snow on ground 180 days each year. In others, under 8 inches of rain a year (e.g. Chelkar)

In 1953 Krushchev, in an attempt to stimulate grain production, launched a Virgin Lands Campaign, in which enormous areas of previously uncultivated or abandoned lands were to be brought under intensive cultivation. The regions were settled by young people from west of the Volga, following a heavy propaganda drive and semi-compulsory enlistment. By 1956 over 80 million acres of waste land had been brought under partial cultivation. But by 1970 the scheme had been virtually abandoned as impractical

In what ways does the map illustrate the scale of Khrushchev's 'virgin lands' policy?

The 'virgin lands'. (© Martin Gilbert.)

initially, the process had quickly drained the soil of essential nutrients, which could not be replaced without a ready and adequate supply of fertilisers.

- *Poor storage facilities.* The failure to provide adequate drying and storage facilities frequently meant that crops became rotten or were eaten by pests before they could be distributed. One example is that of Kazakhstan, which produced 24 million tonnes of grain in 1959 but had adequate storage for only 10 million tonnes.

- *Inadequate farm machinery.* Despite the superficially impressive production of tractors, these were never enough to meet the demand that arose from the rapid expansion of land under cultivation. Furthermore, the expertise needed for their maintenance was lacking. Peasant farmers skilled in the handling of horse-drawn ploughs did not adapt quickly and easily to the new machines.

- *Labour shortage.* The living conditions of those who went to open up the 'virgin lands' were unattractively primitive. Life in shanty-towns lacking basic facilities in remote rural areas was intolerable to all but the most idealistic newcomers. Many left after only a short while. To quote one example, of the 25,000 agricultural experts who went to Kazakhstan in 1957 to develop the virgin lands, 14,000 had returned home three years later. The result of such reverse migrations was that there was a severe shortage of workers throughout the period of the 'virgin lands' venture.

- *Shortage of fodder.* Although there was an increase in Soviet grain production in the 1950s, this had fallen markedly by the 1960s. Official talk of record harvests could not disguise the fact that in few areas had production met the set targets. Lack of crops created an acute shortage of animal fodder. Unable to feed their animals, peasants were reduced to slaughtering them. The result was a sharp decrease in livestock. To avoid what threatened to become a famine, large quantities of North American and Australian grain had to be purchased. What had begun as a grand design to enable the USSR to overtake the Western countries in agricultural production was in the end sustained only by buying supplies from those countries.

Industry

Khrushchev intended to alter the direction of the Soviet economy by lessening dependence on heavy industry and giving greater prominence to light engineering and chemicals. He emphasised the need for sustained effort, but, whereas Stalin had applied coercion, Khrushchev offered incentives. Stalin's deliberate neglect of consumer goods was replaced by the promise of material rewards. In a radio broadcast, Khrushchev excited the interest of many Soviet women, and possibly some men, by suggesting that, if they continued to work hard, one day they would be able to buy nylon underwear.

Attack on bureaucracy

Contemptuous of the huge bureaucracy that had grown up under Stalin, Khrushchev was eager to see administration streamlined and decentralised. He hoped that by transferring decision-making from the centre to the localities, industrial planning would prove more realistic and progressive. However, the attempt to reduce central authority offended the entrenched bureaucrats. Those many party members and government officials who owed their positions to Stalin's preferment did not look kindly on reforms that threatened their privileges.

The Seven-Year Plan 1959

Stalin's Five-Year Plans had been intended to develop heavy industry, with no attention being given to consumer goods. When Khrushchev sought to redirect industry towards the production of consumer goods he had to break down the resistance of planners who had been trained to believe that a **consumer economy** contradicted Communist ideals. They still measured economic success by counting iron and steel output. This was a legacy of Stalin's concept of a siege or war economy. It is true that, even after Stalin, the USSR remained heavily committed to military development, but it was Khrushchev's genuine belief that if this could be lessened, the economic freedom it would give would provide the Soviet Union with the potential to catch up with the West. The USSR's lead in space technology, of which *Sputnik* was the outstanding example, was a remarkable but isolated achievement, not matched in any other aspect of its economy.

KEY TERMS

Consumer economy The basic and successful form of capitalism in the West, which shaped growth around satisfying people's natural desire to acquire the good things in life.

Sputnik Russian for 'satellite', the first man-made object to leave the atmosphere and orbit Earth; it was launched from Kazakhstan in 1957.

Why would the Soviet authorities issue a stamp such as that shown in Source D?

SOURCE D

A 1957 Soviet postage stamp showing the orbit of *Sputnik*. A striking feature of Soviet science was its rapid advance in space research, which for nearly two decades saw it ahead of the USA. In 1961, Yuri Gagarin, a Soviet cosmonaut, became the first man to go into space and orbit the Earth.

A new FYP was introduced in 1955, only to be scrapped as being too optimistic and replaced by a Seven-Year Plan in 1959. Under Khrushchev's instructions, this plan had been drawn up with the aim of promoting consumer goods, light industry, chemicals and plastics. In addition, the need for regional development was stressed. Less spectacularly than in agriculture, but no less significantly, Khrushchev was attempting to reverse a major feature of Stalin's policy. It was a recognition that the USSR could not develop as a modern state unless it brought a much greater degree of balance into its economy. An idea of how far Khrushchev's industrial policies succeeded during the period of his leadership can be gained from the performance figures shown in Table 7.1.

? What trends in output are observable in Table 7.1?

Table 7.1 A comparison between the targets in the Seven-Year Plan in 1959 with the actual performance by 1965

Output	Plan 1959	Actual 1965
Gross national income (based on 100 in 1958)*	162–165	158
Industrial goods (based on 100 in 1958)*	185–188	196
Consumer goods (based on 100 in 1958)*	162–165	160
Steel (millions of tonnes)	86–91	91
Oil (millions of tonnes)	230–240	242
Mineral fertilisers (millions of tonnes)	35	32
Grain (millions of tonnes)	164–180	121
Meat (millions of tonnes)	6.1	5.25
Workers employed (millions)	66.5	76.9
Total of available housing (millions of square metres)	650–660	72.9

* Based on a unit of 100 in 1958.

Set against the general success of the Seven-Year Plan, the obvious and serious failures were in underproduction of grain and meat, and in the inability to deal with the perennial Soviet problems of shortage of accommodation.

Khrushchev's economic record

At Stalin's death in 1953, the living standards of Soviet factory workers were barely higher than in 1928, while those of farm workers were actually lower than in 1913. Khrushchev attempted to improve conditions. He opted for:

- decentralised planning
- encouragement of local initiatives
- industrial diversification
- progressive techniques in agriculture
- wage incentives for workers and peasants.

Unfortunately, his measures were soundly conceived but poorly applied. In the relatively short time during which he was leader, he was unable to change the basic character of the Soviet economy.

At the time, Khrushchev received a bad press for the seeming failure of his agricultural policies. In hindsight, this appears undeserved. He was struggling to correct in a few years the neglect of a quarter of a century. Stalin's subordination of agriculture to the needs of industry had deprived the land of investment and resources. His collectivisation programme had so disrupted rural life that it would take generations for it to recover. Khrushchev's reforms were progressive and ambitious, but he was facing a task that was beyond the means at his disposal. The reintroduction of incentives and the huge project of bringing waste land into production were policies that needed time to develop before they could show returns. It was a problem that had beset agricultural reformers in tsarist days as well as in revolutionary Russia. Time was the one luxury they were never allowed.

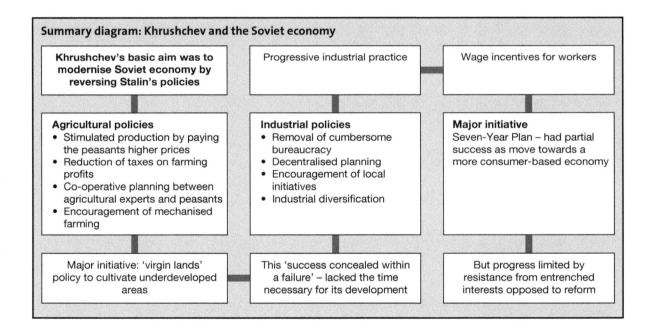

Summary diagram: Khrushchev and the Soviet economy

Khrushchev's basic aim was to modernise Soviet economy by reversing Stalin's policies	Progressive industrial practice	Wage incentives for workers
Agricultural policies • Stimulated production by paying the peasants higher prices • Reduction of taxes on farming profits • Co-operative planning between agricultural experts and peasants • Encouragement of mechanised farming	**Industrial policies** • Removal of cumbersome bureaucracy • Decentralised planning • Encouragement of local initiatives • Industrial diversification	**Major initiative** Seven-Year Plan – had partial success as move towards a more consumer-based economy
Major initiative: 'virgin lands' policy to cultivate underdeveloped areas	This 'success concealed within a failure' – lacked the time necessary for its development	But progress limited by resistance from entrenched interests opposed to reform

Khrushchev's fall 1964

▶ *What factors undermined Khrushchev's leadership of the USSR?*

In his memoirs, written in the late 1960s, Khrushchev claimed that it was as an international statesman that he had made his greatest contribution to the USSR. It is a claim that his Soviet contemporaries would have rejected. Indeed, it was his foreign policy as much as his perceived domestic failures that led to the opposition against him that eventually brought about his removal in 1964. Four major issues or crises dominated Khrushchev's foreign policy:

- the USSR's relations with the West
- the division of Germany
- the Cuban Missile Crisis
- the USSR's relations with China.

Relations with the West

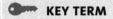

KEY TERM

Coexistence A mutual recognition and tolerant acceptance of the different political and social systems operating in the USSR and the West.

Khrushchev brought a fresh, more human, style to the conduct of Soviet foreign policy. As part of his de-Stalinisation programme, he followed a policy of **coexistence** with the West. This marked a major change in the Soviet attitude to the outside world. The revolutionaries of 1917 had seen themselves as warriors fighting an international class war. Although the realities of world politics had obliged Lenin and Stalin to suspend this objective, the commitment to international revolution had never been formally abandoned. Khrushchev, in his 'secret report' to the twentieth party congress in 1956, took the highly significant step of declaring that a violent conflict between the Communist and capitalist worlds was not inevitable in the way that Lenin had described. This declaration helped to prepare the way for coexistence.

This new Soviet approach was obviously welcome in the West, but for Khrushchev, coexistence was not simply or primarily a matter of goodwill. He pursued it because it offered greater protection for the Soviet Union and because peace would give some relief from the heavy costs of military defence.

Steps towards coexistence

The path towards better relations with the West had already been smoothed by a number of developments after Stalin's death:

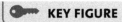

KEY FIGURE

President Eisenhower (1890–1969)

US president from 1952 to 1960.

- 1953 saw the end of the Korean War (see page 168).
- In 1954, the USSR joined the USA and Britain for talks at Geneva.
- In 1955, the Soviet Union signed a peace treaty with Austria and withdrew its army of occupation, stationed there since 1945.
- In 1955, a summit conference was held in Geneva during which Khrushchev and Bulganin met US **President Eisenhower** and the French and British prime ministers.

Accompanied by Bulganin, Khrushchev began a series of visits to countries outside the Eastern bloc, something that would have been unthinkable in Stalin's time. India, China, Yugoslavia, Britain and the USA were among the countries visited. On the whole, these travels were a propaganda success. He boasted of Soviet achievements in space and defended the Soviet system with passion and wit. He made a remarkable impact in the USA, where he became an instant celebrity. In Hollywood, he watched the filming of one of the dance sequences from *Can Can*, which by Soviet standards was a trifle saucy. When asked what he thought of it, Khrushchev said it was indecent, decadent and bourgeois – and could he see it again?

Khrushchev's cordial meetings with Eisenhower in 1959 at Camp David gave rise to the term 'the spirit of Camp David' as an expression of the improved Soviet–American understanding. However, it soon became clear how fragile this understanding was. In 1960, a Paris summit conference broke up in acrimony when Khrushchev announced that the USSR had shot down a US **U2 aircraft** detected over Soviet territory. He stormed out melodramatically.

Despite this episode, Khrushchev's continued willingness to negotiate with the West led to one of his greatest diplomatic successes, the signing by the superpowers of a Nuclear Test-Ban Treaty in October 1963, an agreement between the USA and the USSR to abandon nuclear detonations in the atmosphere. It was the Cold War's first major agreement on arms limitation.

Khrushchev and Germany

Khrushchev inherited a long-standing problem in the shape of the post-war division between West and East Germany (see page 164). Sustained by Marshall Aid, West Germany and West Berlin began to make a remarkable economic recovery, which contrasted sharply with East Germany and East Berlin, where a lack of resources and aid resulted in severe poverty. This glaring disparity became an embarrassment to the East German authorities and the Soviet Union. The freedom and open lifestyle of the West Berliners proved a powerful temptation to East Germans. In the eight years after 1949 over 2 million refugees fled from East Germany to the West, by way of West Berlin. Many of these were professional and skilled workers whom the DDR (East Germany) could ill afford to lose.

Khrushchev declared his intention of 'blocking up the drain'. His first move was to demand that the Western powers acknowledge the existence of a separate East German state, but by 1958 the DDR had still not gained Western recognition. To press the issue, Khrushchev delivered an ultimatum. He warned that, if within six months the West had not responded positively, the USSR would sign a separate peace treaty with the DDR. This would directly threaten the independence of West Berlin since, as a sovereign state, the DDR would have the right to claim the whole of its capital, Berlin.

KEY TERM

U2 aircraft A US reconnaissance-plane for spying over Soviet territory.

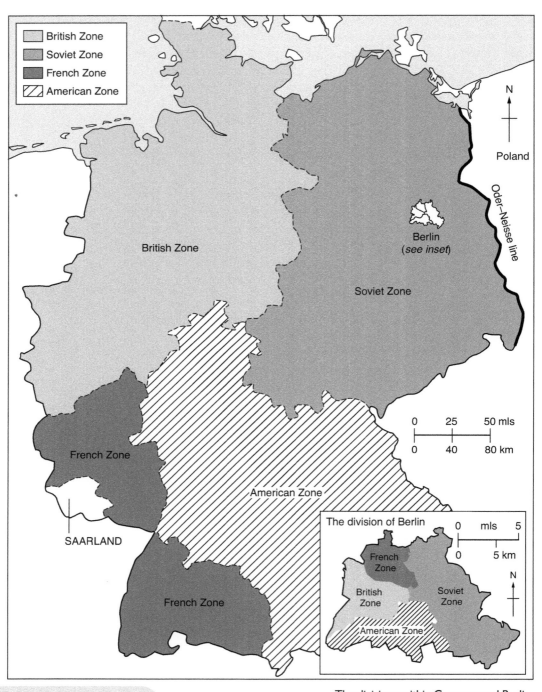

The divisions within Germany and Berlin.

In what ways does the map illustrate why West Germany and West Berlin were such contentious issues between the Soviet Union and the Western powers?

It was a bluff and the USA called it by reasserting the absolute freedom of West Berlin. Faced with this, Khrushchev withdrew the ultimatum and in a series of meetings, first with Eisenhower and then with **Kennedy**, modified his demands. Having tried the gentler approach, Khrushchev then returned to the attack. In June 1961, he met Kennedy again. This time he repeated his warning that the Western powers must be prepared to leave Berlin within six months. The effect of this threat was to increase the flight of refugees from East to West Berlin, 1000 a day leaving in the summer of 1961. Unable to staunch the haemorrhage, **Ulbricht**, the East German leader, ordered the building of the Berlin Wall, a grim construction of drab concrete that split the city in half.

The Berlin Wall in 1961 marked the failure of Khrushchev's attempt to get his way by pressure and threat of force. His last initiative on the German issue was in effect an acknowledgement of this. In 1963, he made formal contact with the West German government and let it be known that he was prepared to solve the Berlin issue by bypassing the East Germans and negotiating directly with **Bonn**. This drastic reversal of Soviet policy provoked an understandably bitter response from Ulbricht and the East Germans, who felt they had been betrayed.

In retrospect, it can be seen that Khrushchev's policy towards Germany was shaped as much by the pressures on him in the Soviet Union as by the intrinsic merits of the question. Khrushchev knew that he needed success to justify his leadership. Had he been able to resolve the Berlin issue on Soviet terms, this would have enhanced his position in the USSR, but at every stage he was thwarted by the strength of the USA's commitment to West Germany. His subsequent behaviour in 1962 in regard to Cuba may well represent his attempt to recover the prestige he had lost.

The Cuban Missile Crisis 1962

In 1960, **Fidel Castro**, the leader of Cuba, openly declared himself a Communist and began to take steps to end the USA's economic domination of the island. Seeing the possibility of a major Cold War coup, Khrushchev quickly arranged for the Soviet Union to buy up Cuba's **sugar crop** and offer a package of economic assistance. The Soviet Union hoped, and the USA feared, that the creation of a Russian-backed Marxist state in Cuba would be the prelude to the rapid spread of Soviet-style communism throughout Central and South America. Aware of the alarm in the USA over this, Khrushchev warned that the USSR would be prepared to act if the USA used force against Cuba. The Soviet Union's increasing involvement in Cuba culminated in the installation on the island of Soviet nuclear missiles, capable of reaching almost every state in the USA. Throughout the Cuban affair Khrushchev was involved in every aspect of the planning.

In a private conversation, Khrushchev spoke of 'putting one of our hedgehogs down the Americans' trousers'. However, his publicly stated justification for Soviet actions was that the nuclear devices were there to defend Cuba against

KEY FIGURES

President Kennedy (1917–63)

US president from 1961 to 1963.

Walter Ulbricht (1893–1973)

A German Communist who played a leading role in the creation of post-war East Germany.

Fidel Castro (1927–)

The revolutionary Cuban leader who had taken power in 1959 as a 'humanist' but not yet a Communist.

KEY TERMS

Bonn The post-war capital of West Germany.

Sugar crop The Cuban economy was heavily dependent on a single crop, sugar.

possible US intervention. But, since this claim followed a previous denial that the USSR had installed any missiles at all, the argument was unconvincing. Kennedy announced a naval blockade of Cuba until the missiles were removed, and let it be known that if any attempt were made to use them against the USA, he would order a retaliation in kind.

This was the most dangerous point reached in the Cold War. The world stood on the brink of nuclear destruction. However, faced by the USA's uncompromising stance, Khrushchev, putting reason before politics, chose not to risk a full-scale nuclear confrontation. He gave the order for the Soviet ships to put about and not to challenge the US naval blockade. With the tension broken, direct contacts by letter and telephone were made between Kennedy and Khrushchev. Their exchanges produced a compromise; Khrushchev agreed to the withdrawal of Soviet missiles from Cuba while Kennedy agreed to reduce the USA's bases in Turkey. This latter agreement was a significant gain for the USSR, but at the time it was overshadowed by what Soviet observers regarded as a major diplomatic victory for the Americans. It had been the USSR that had backed off. The USA had reasserted its paramount influence in the western hemisphere. This damaged the USSR's international standing and led to serious criticism of Khrushchev within the Soviet Union. At the time of his dismissal in 1964, the report of the CPSU's Central Committee included the passage quoted in Source E.

? On what grounds is Khrushchev censured in the report?

SOURCE E

From a CPSU Central Committee report, 1964, quoted in Dmitri Volkogonov, *The Rise and Fall of the Soviet Empire*, HarperCollins, 1998, p. 247.

Comrade Khrushchev declared that if the USA touched Cuba we would launch a strike against it. He insisted that our missiles be sent to Cuba. This provoked the most serious crisis, bringing the world to the brink of nuclear war; the organizer of this most dangerous venture himself was greatly alarmed. Having no other way out we were forced to accept all the demands and conditions dictated by the USA.

Khrushchev and China

The coming to power of the Chinese Communists under Mao Zedong in China in 1949 appeared to have created a great Marxist power-bloc that stretched eastwards from Europe to the Pacific. But appearances were deceptive. There was little real harmony between Moscow and Peking. Relations between the USSR and Communist China had not been easy in Stalin's time and did not improve under Khrushchev.

Reasons for Sino-Soviet hostility

The basic reason was that rather than being united, the two powers were rivals for the leadership of the Communist world. According to the Kremlin's traditional Marxist analysis, China, as a rural and agricultural society, could not be regarded as a fully developed proletarian state. Slighting Soviet references to the inferiority of the Chinese model angered the Maoists, who retaliated by accusing the USSR of betraying the cause of world revolution by pursuing coexistence with the capitalist West. There was the added problem that Mao took Khrushchev's de-Stalinisation personally. He regarded the assault on Stalin's 'cult of personality' as a scarcely veiled attack on his own personal leadership in China.

Despite occasional appearances of understanding, Sino-Soviet relations grew increasingly embittered in the 1950s. Mao made no effort to hide his contempt for what he regarded as Khrushchev's toadying to the West. Mao demanded that the USSR show greater commitment to liberation movements worldwide and abandon revisionism. In 1957 the Chinese were offered Soviet assistance in developing their own nuclear weapon, but in return Moscow wanted control of Peking's defence policy. The price was too high. Mao rejected the offer, opting for an independent Chinese nuclear programme. China was not prepared to play a subordinate role to the USSR.

These profound disagreements over foreign policy, nuclear power and ideology were deepened by disputes over territory. In the late 1950s and 1960s, the USSR and China stationed large numbers of troops along their joint border in central Asia. Incidents were frequent and threatened to lead to a major confrontation. The Sino-Soviet gap widened still further. In 1962, that gap became a gulf as a result of the Cuban Missile Crisis. China fiercely criticised the Soviet Union on two counts: first, for siting its rockets so clumsily that they were easily detected; and second, for its craven submission to the US ultimatum.

Khrushchev dismissed the Chinese Communists as 'petty bourgeois, not true proletarian revolutionaries'. Mao retaliated by dismissing the Soviet leaders as 'fascists, unworthy of the Marxist–Leninist inheritance'. There was a markedly personal element to all this. Khrushchev and Mao had developed a deep distaste for each other. Khrushchev referred to Mao as 'a living corpse', while Mao spoke of the Soviet leader as 'a decrepit old boot'. Behind the insults was a deadly serious battle for ascendancy in the Communist world. Instead of developing into the great monolith that the West had feared, China and the Soviet Union were engaged in a bitter competition for the loyalty of the rest of the Communist world. The public squabbling brought Khrushchev little credit and the scandal of Sino-Soviet disharmony weakened his position within the USSR.

Factors in the fall of Khrushchev

In October 1964, Khrushchev took a holiday at a Black Sea resort. During his absence from Moscow, the Politburo met and decided on his removal as leader. A meeting of the Central Committee was convened and Khrushchev was summoned to Moscow to appear before it. He was informed that he had retired through age and poor health and that he had been replaced. The news was announced on the radio and in *Pravda*. The other Moscow newspaper, *Izvestia*, whose editor was Khrushchev's son-in-law, was not allowed to appear that day. Accepting that he had been outmanoeuvred and had no allies, Khrushchev slipped away into obscure retirement. Some days later, *Pravda* published a lengthy editorial in which, without referring to him by name, it listed his weaknesses and errors.

SOURCE F

From *Pravda*, 28 October 1964.

The Leninist Party is the enemy of subjectivism, individualism and drifting in Communist construction, of hare-brained scheme-making, of half-baked conclusions and hasty decisions and actions taken without regard to realities. Bragging and phrase-mongering, bossiness, reluctance to take account of scientific achievement and practical experience are alien to it. It is only on the Leninist principle of collective leadership that it is possible to direct and develop the increasing creative initiative of the Party.

? What are the main charges levelled at Khrushchev in Source F?

Whatever his achievements may have been in the previous decade, it is clear that by the autumn of 1964 Khrushchev was politically friendless and isolated. The *Pravda* analysis provides a basis for summarising the main ways Khrushchev had upset the vested interests in party and government and thus unwittingly prepared the way for his own downfall:

- the cult of personality
- Khrushchev's public style
- decentralisation
- de-Stalinisation
- lack of support from the military
- foreign policy failures
- economic failures.

The cult of personality

It was an irony that Khrushchev, in choosing to attack Stalin's cult of personality, had provided the grounds for his own eventual dismissal. He had created the language that could be used to justify the removal of any subsequent leader whose personal authority grew too large. In Stalin's time, his subordinates were too frightened to oppose him. Khrushchev never engendered such fear. All Stalin's colleagues had owed their positions directly to his patronage. Khrushchev was never a master patron in that same way. It is true that some of the middle- and lower-rank officials were his *protégés*, but he never had the control of the party and governmental machine that Stalin had possessed.

Khrushchev's public style

In the earlier years of his leadership, Khrushchev's gregarious and jocular style made a welcome change from the joylessness of Stalin. But this attribute was of advantage only when things were going well. As the *Pravda* editorial made clear, when his reputation began to wane his style and manner were characterised as personal failings. Khrushchev was a very visible leader of the Soviet Union. He took a direct part in a wide range of domestic and foreign affairs. This close personal involvement had its obvious advantages, but it also made him vulnerable. When policies failed, he appeared responsible in a way that a less involved leader would not have been. There was no single event that caused his slide into disfavour. It was rather that as time went on his policy failures tended to outweigh his successes. Dissatisfaction accumulated.

Decentralisation

Khrushchev's attempts to streamline and decentralise many areas of party and government involved him in a continuous struggle with the forces of Soviet bureaucracy. Stalinism had been a heavily bureaucratic system. The party under Stalin had been the great dispenser of jobs and patronage. When Khrushchev sought to rationalise the system, he challenged the livelihood and privileges of a whole army of officials and functionaries.

De-Stalinisation

Khrushchev's de-Stalinisation initiative had been a calculated risk. After decades of Stalin worship, it was a huge psychological wrench for party members to admit that the great leader had been so wrong on so many counts. Some of the old guard, such as Molotov and Kaganovich, could not bring themselves to accept the total destruction of the Stalin legend. For expediency's sake, they went along with de-Stalinisation, but they remained fearful of what it might reveal about their own past complicity. They also thought that it threatened the reputation of the party. Moreover, the greater freedom of expression given to writers and artists in the post-Stalin 'thaw' seemed to them to be an added and unnecessary danger. The party die-hards did not easily forgive Khrushchev for placing such hazards in their path.

Lack of support from the military

In his rise in the mid-1950s, Khrushchev had been able to rely on the backing of the leaders of the armed forces, but by 1964 that support had been largely forfeited, mainly as a result of his wish to cut military expenditure. By the mid-1950s the USSR possessed the hydrogen bomb and was making significant advances in missile development. Khrushchev felt that this justified a cutback in conventional forces. In 1960, he proposed reducing the armed services by over a million men, a cut of one-third. Such developments, taken together with the loss of Soviet military prestige over Cuba, meant that by 1964 he had exhausted the goodwill of all the generals.

Foreign policy failures

Khrushchev suffered a similar decline in reputation in regard to foreign affairs. In personal terms there was no doubt that he had become a truly international statesman; his foreign travels and summit diplomacy were unprecedented in Soviet tradition. Despite this, the failures loomed larger than the successes:

- He had entered into a long and unresolved conflict with Mao's China.
- He had awakened hopes of independence in the Eastern bloc countries, only to dash them by invasion and the reimposition of Soviet control.
- He had fought a running Cold War battle with the West over Germany, but had been unable to deliver the peace treaty by which he had set such store.
- He had tried to recover Soviet prestige by installing Soviet missiles in Cuba, only to have to back down in the face of US determination.

These undeniable failures aroused bitterness in his Kremlin colleagues.

Economic failures

Khrushchev had promised a modernised Soviet economy, geared to the interests of the consumer but still capable of matching the West. It was an unrealistic boast. Advances were made, but the basic problems inherited from Stalin were still there in the mid-1960s. Ironically, his most far-sighted policy, the reclamation of the 'virgin lands', was the one which, in his own time, brought him the greatest criticism and discredit. Khrushchev's reputation also suffered badly in his final four years as leader when troubles grew among the Soviet workforce. Rising prices and the failure of his government reforms to improve conditions on a wide front led to strikes and demonstrations, the most serious occurring in 1962 in Novocherkassk, where 7000 strikers were dispersed only after being fired on by troops, who killed over twenty of the protesters.

Those involved in the plot to oust him in 1964 could be confident that the range of Soviet interests angered or disillusioned by Khrushchev's policies during the previous eight years was such that there would be little resistance to his removal. The view of one of his Soviet contemporaries provides an astute insider's assessment of Khrushchev's basic weakness (see Source G).

? How does the writer in Source G support his view that Khrushchev was 'too lightweight a figure'?

SOURCE G

From Dmitri Volkogonov, *The Rise and Fall of the Soviet Empire*, HarperCollins, 1998, p. 247.

It is normal for a leader to be feared or cursed or criticised, but when he is laughed at and made the butt of jokes, his time is up. After the sinister giants Lenin and Stalin, it seems that in the end Khrushchev was somehow too lightweight a figure for the public … As a reformer he was not understood, while many were simply not willing to forgive him for exposing the personality cult.

Summary diagram: Khrushchev's fall 1964

Factors that weakened Khrushchev

Domestic
- Attack on cult of personality rebounded against him
- De-Stalinisation regarded by party hardliners as betrayal
- Reforms threatened vested interests
- His public style criticised for inviting ridicule
- Loss of support from the military
- Limited success of economic reforms

Foreign policy
- Coexistence seen at home as appeasement of capitalist enemies
- Problems with Soviet satellites
- Failure to resolve German question on Soviet terms
- Humiliating Soviet climb-down in Cuban Missile Crisis
- Unresolved conflict with Mao's China

Khrushchev never possessed Stalin's degree of authority

Chapter summary

Having outwitted his rivals in the party manoeuvres that followed Stalin's death, Khrushchev resolved to use his leadership to introduce necessary reform into the Soviet Union. He saw Stalin's legacy as a main obstacle and embarked on a policy of de-Stalinisation aimed at undermining Stalin's reputation. The policy angered the CPSU's old guard, who feared that their vested interests were under threat. Khrushchev's disfavour with many in the party meant that he never exercised complete control in the way Stalin had. Nevertheless, he pressed ahead with reform in both domestic and foreign affairs. His 'virgin lands' policy for the transformation of Soviet agriculture was ambitious, but unsuccessful in the short term, as were his schemes for modernising industry through decentralised planning and the diversification of production.

By adopting a policy of coexistence with the West, Khrushchev had considerable initial success in easing international tension, but perennial problems, Berlin and China prominent among them, remained. Khrushchev's audacious placing of nuclear missiles in Cuba proved a step too far. Forced by the USA to remove them, he and the USSR lost face, a major factor in the party's dismissal of him in 1964, by which time his perceived failures had robbed him of political support.

Refresher questions

Use these questions to remind yourself of the key material covered in this chapter.

1 Why was Khrushchev able to outwit his opponents in the power struggle following Stalin's death?

2 How far did Khrushchev's economic reforms achieve their objectives?

3 What risks was Khrushchev taking in introducing a policy of de-Stalinisation?

4 What were the major weaknesses of Khrushchev's 'virgin lands' policy?

5 How successful was Khrushchev's Seven-Year Plan?

6 What were the major obstacles confronting Khrushchev in his attempts at economic reform?

7 How far was Khrushchev responsible for the East–West confrontation over Berlin?

8 In what sense did de-Stalinisation prove a false dawn for the Soviet satellite states?

9 Why did Khrushchev order the forcible suppression of the Hungarian Rising in 1956?

10 What was Khrushchev hoping to achieve by installing nuclear missiles in Castro's Cuba?

11 Why did the two Communist superpowers, Russia and China, fall out with each other?

12 What factors had undermined Khrushchev's leadership of the Soviet Union by 1964?

 # Question practice

ESSAY QUESTIONS

1 'Following the death of Stalin, Khrushchev was able to overcome his rivals in the leadership struggle because he was prepared to be more ruthless.' Assess the validity of this view.

2 'Khrushchev's "virgin lands" enterprise was a success concealed within a failure.' Assess the validity of this view.

3 How far was the Soviet economy transformed under Khrushchev between 1954 and 1964?

4 To what extent was Khrushchev's fall from power in 1964 the result of the foreign policies he had followed?

INTERPRETATION QUESTION

1 Using your understanding of the historical context, assess how convincing the arguments in Extracts A, B and C are in relation to Khrushchev's legacy to the Soviet Union.

EXTRACT A

From William J. Tompson, *Khrushchev: A Political Life*, St. Martin's Press, 1995, pp. 283–4.

Throughout the Brezhnev years and the lengthy interregnum that followed, the generation which had come of age during the 'first Russian spring' of the 1950s awaited its turn in power. As Brezhnev and his colleagues died or were pensioned off, they were replaced by men and women for whom the Secret Speech and the first wave of de-Stalinization had been a formative experience, and these 'Children of Twentieth Congress' took up the reins of power under the leadership of Mikhail Gorbachev and his colleagues. The Khrushchev era provided this second generation of reformers with both an inspiration and a cautionary tale.

EXTRACT B

From David Christian, *Imperial and Soviet Russia*, Macmillan, 1997, p. 374.

At the end of his life, Stalin's authority was so immense and so personal that his removal transformed the political situation. The system that emerged under his successors remained extremely centralized, but was less personal and less violent than that of Stalin. With Stalin removed, the party Secretariat reasserted its natural authority within the Soviet political system. Khrushchev, the dominant official within the Secretariat, used his power to win the struggle for the succession. The mild treatment he handed out to his rivals after the 'anti-party' plot of 1957 suggested that, while the party would remain highly centralized, it now felt confident enough to dispense with the murderous methods of the purge era. Khrushchev's peaceful removal, in 1964, showed that a party oligarchy had now replaced the personal authority of Stalin.

EXTRACT C

From Dmitri Volkogonov, *The Rise and Fall of the Soviet Empire*, HarperCollins, 1998, p. 247.

It is normal for a leader to be feared or cursed or criticised, but when he is laughed at and made the butt of jokes, his time is up. After the sinister giants Lenin and Stalin, it seems that in the end Khrushchev was somehow too lightweight a figure for the public. As a reformer he was not understood, while many were simply not willing to forgive him for exposing [Stalin's] personality cult. Khrushchev tried to speed up the rate of reform, but the engine failed to start. He knew that change in society was needed, but he tried to effect it using old Bolshevik methods, though his comrades saw his acts as a dramatic departure from Marxism–Leninism. He was completely isolated, even though he dwelt within a huge crowd of 'Leninists'.

AQA A level History

Essay guidance

At both AS and A level for AQA Component 2: Depth Study: Revolution and Dictatorship: Russia, 1917–1953, you will need to answer an essay question in the exam. Each essay question is marked out of 25:

- for the AS exam, Section B: answer **one** essay (from a choice of two)
- for the A level exam, Section B: answer **two** essays (from a choice of three).

There are several question stems which all have the same basic requirement: to analyse and reach a conclusion based on the evidence you provide.

The AS questions often give a quotation and then ask whether you agree or disagree with this view. Almost inevitably, your answer will be a mixture of both. It is the same task as for A level – just phrased differently in the question. Detailed essays are more likely to do well compared to vague or generalised essays, especially in the Depth Studies of Paper 2.

The AQA mark scheme is essentially the same for AS and the full A level (see the AQA website, www.aqa.org.uk). Both emphasise the need to analyse and evaluate the key features related to the periods studied. The key feature of the highest level is sustained analysis: analysis that unites the whole of the essay.

Writing an essay: general skills

- *Focus and structure.* Be sure what the question is asking and plan what the paragraphs should be about.
- *Focused introduction to the essay.* Be sure that the introductory sentence relates directly to the focus of the question and that each paragraph highlights the structure of the answer.

- *Use detail.* Make sure that you show detailed knowledge, but only as part of an explanation being made in relation to the question. No knowledge should be standalone; it should only be used in context.
- *Explanatory analysis and evaluation.* Consider what words and phrases to use in an answer to strengthen the explanation.
- *Argument and counter-argument.* Think of how arguments can be balanced so as to give contrasting views.
- *Resolution.* Think how best to 'resolve' contradictory arguments.
- *Relative significance and evaluation.* Think how best to reach a judgement when trying to assess the relative importance of various factors and their possible interrelationship.

Planning an essay

Practice question 1

To what extent was the success of the Bolshevik rising in October/November 1917 due to the weakness of the Provisional Government?

This question requires you to analyse why the Bolsheviks were successful in seizing power. You must discuss the following:

- How the weakness of the Provisional Government helped the Bolsheviks to seize power (your primary focus).
- The other factors that allowed this to happen (your secondary focus).

A clear structure makes for a much more effective essay and is crucial for achieving the highest marks. You need three or four paragraphs to structure this question effectively. In each paragraph you will deal with one factor. One of these *must* be the factor in the question.

A very basic plan for this question might look like this:

- Paragraph 1: the effects of the weakness of the Provisional Government.
- Paragraph 2: the effects of events beyond the control of the Provisional Government, such as the situation in the First World War and the problems inherited from the tsar's government.
- Paragraph 3: the dedication and growing organisation of the Bolsheviks, plus arrangements for the takeover.

It is a good idea to first cover the factor named in the question so that you don't run out of time and forget to do so. Then cover the other factors in what you think is their order of importance, or in the order that appears logical in terms of the sequence of paragraphs.

The introduction

Maintaining focus is vital. One way to do this from the beginning of your essay is to use the words in the question to help write your argument. The first sentence of question 1, for example, could look like this:

The Bolsheviks were successful in seizing power in October/November 1917 partly because of the weakness of the Provisional Government, but there were other factors as well to explain this.

This opening sentence provides a clear focus on the demands of the question, although it could, of course, be written in a more exciting style.

Focus throughout the essay

Structuring your essay well will help with keeping the focus of your essay on the question. To maintain a focus on the wording in question 1, you could begin your first main paragraph with 'weakness':

The weakness of the Provisional Government was one very important factor in allowing the Bolsheviks to seize power.

- This sentence begins with a clear point that refers to the primary focus of the question

(the Bolsheviks seizing power) while linking it to a factor (the weakness of the Provisional Government).
- You could then have a paragraph for each of your other factors.
- It will be important to make sure that each paragraph focuses on analysis and includes relevant details that are used as part of the argument.
- You may wish to number your factors. This helps to make your structure clear and helps you to maintain focus.

Deploying detail

As well as focus and structure, your essay will be judged on the extent to which it includes accurate detail. There are several different kinds of evidence you could use that might be described as detailed. These include correct dates, names of relevant people, statistics and events. In question 1, for example, you could use terms such as Dual Authority and Petrograd soviet. You can also make your essays more detailed by using the correct technical vocabulary.

Analysis and explanation

'Analysis' covers a variety of high-level skills including explanation and evaluation; in essence, it means breaking down something complex into smaller parts. A clear structure that breaks down a complex question into a series of paragraphs is the first step towards writing an analytical essay.

The purpose of explanation is to provide evidence for why something happened, or why something is true or false. An explanatory statement requires two parts: a *claim* and a *justification*.

In question 1, for example, you might want to argue that one important reason was the Provisional Government's failure to solve the food shortages. Once you have made your point, and supported it with relevant detail, you can then explain how this answers the question. You could conclude your paragraph like this:

So the Provisional Government's failure to act decisively on food shortages was important[1] because[2] the poor, especially the industrial city workers, increasingly lost faith in it and were more eager to turn to revolutionary parties such as the Bolsheviks[3] who were growing in strength in industrial areas.

1 The claim.
2 'Because' is a very important word to use when writing an explanation, as it shows the relationship between the claim and the justification.
3 The justification of the claim.

Evaluation

Evaluation means considering the importance of two or more different factors, weighing them against each other, and reaching a judgement. This is a good skill to use at the end of an essay because the conclusion should reach a judgement which answers the question. Your conclusion to question 1 might read as follows:

Clearly, the weakness of Provisional Government meant that many Russians, especially the poor in the cities, were looking to other alternatives. However, the return of Lenin to Russia in spring 1917 and the growing organisation of the party in Petrograd meant that it was well positioned to mount a coup. Therefore, the weakness of the government provided an opportunity for the Bolsheviks.

Words like 'clearly', 'however' and 'therefore' are helpful to contrast the importance of the different factors.

Complex essay writing: argument and counter-argument

Essays that develop a good argument are more likely to reach the highest levels. This is because argumentative essays are much more likely to develop sustained analysis. As you know, your essays are judged on the extent to which they analyse.

After setting up an argument in your introduction, you should develop it throughout the essay. One

way of doing this is to adopt an argument–counter-argument structure. A counter-argument is one that disagrees with the main argument of the essay. This is a good way of evaluating the importance of the different factors that you discuss. Essays of this type will develop an argument in one paragraph and then set out an opposing argument in another paragraph. Sometimes this will include juxtaposing the differing views of historians on a topic.

Good essays will analyse the key issues. They will probably have a clear piece of analysis at the end of each paragraph. While this analysis might be good, it will generally relate only to the issue discussed in that paragraph.

Excellent essays will be analytical throughout. As well as the analysis of each factor discussed above, there will be an overall analysis. This will run throughout the essay and can be achieved through developing a clear, relevant and coherent argument.

A good way of achieving sustained analysis is to consider which factor is most important.

Here is an example of an introduction that sets out an argument for question 1:

The Provisional Government that took over from Tsar Nicholas II inherited many problems to which there were no easy solutions.[1] Hence the condition of Russia deteriorated during the summer of 1917. However, this was not the only reason for the success of the Bolsheviks in October/November 1917.[2] The problems caused by the First World War were difficult to resolve as the new government needed to keep the support of its allies. But the most important reason why the Bolsheviks succeeded was the way in which Lenin and Trotsky took advantage of the special circumstances in Petrograd and Moscow in autumn 1917.[3]

1 The introduction begins with a claim.
2 The introduction continues with another reason.
3 Concludes with an outline of the argument of the most important reason.

- This introduction focuses on the question and sets out the key factors that the essay will develop.
- It introduces an argument about which factor was most significant.
- However, it also sets out an argument that can then be developed throughout each paragraph, and is rounded off with an overall judgement in the conclusion.

Complex essay writing: resolution and relative significance

Having written an essay that explains argument and counter-argument, you should then resolve the tension between the argument and the counter-argument in your conclusion. It is important that the writing is precise and summarises the arguments made in the main body of the essay. You need to reach a supported overall judgement. One very appropriate way to do this is by evaluating the relative significance of different factors, in the light of valid criteria. Relative significance means how important one factor is compared to another.

The best essays will always make a judgement about what was most important based on valid criteria. These can be very simple, and will depend on the topic and the exact question. The following criteria are often useful:

- Duration: which factor was important for the longest amount of time?
- Scope: which factor affected the most people?
- Effectiveness: which factor achieved most?
- Impact: which factor led to the most fundamental change?

As an example, you could compare the factors in terms of their duration and their impact.

A conclusion that follows this advice should be capable of reaching a high level (if written, in full, with appropriate details) because it reaches an overall judgement that is supported through evaluating the relative significance of different factors in the light of valid criteria.

Having written an introduction and the main body of an essay for question 1, a concluding paragraph that aims to meet the exacting criteria for reaching a complex judgement could look like this:

Thus, the reasons for Bolshevik success were complex with several interrelated factors. The success was not inevitable (in spite of the view of Marxist historians). It only became possible because of particular circumstances. The weakness of the Provisional Government provided an opportunity for an alternative government to seize power, but the Bolsheviks were a tiny party compared with the SRs and the Mensheviks. It was the total commitment and energy of the Bolshevik leaders, the organisation they established in the Petrograd soviet, and the detailed plans of Trotsky that allowed the Bolsheviks to seize the key buildings and announce to a surprised Russian people that Kerensky had fled and Commissar Lenin was their new leader.

Sources guidance

Whether you are taking the AS exam or the full A level exam for AQA Component 2: Depth Study: Revolution and Dictatorship: Russia and the Soviet Union, 1917–1929, Section A presents you with sources and a question which involves evaluation of their utility or value.

AS exam	A level exam
Section A: answer question 1 based on two primary sources. (25 marks)	Section A: answer question 1, based on three primary sources. (30 marks)
Question focus: with reference to these sources and your understanding of the historical context, which of these two sources is more valuable in explaining … ?	Question focus: with reference to these sources and your understanding of the historical context, assess the value of these three sources to a historian studying …

Sources and sample questions

Study the sources. They are all concerned with the background to the collapse of tsarist rule in February 1917.

SOURCE 1

From a speech made by Paul Milyukov, leader of the liberal Kadet Party to the *Duma* on 1 November 1916.

Today we are aware that with this government we cannot legislate, and we cannot, with this government, lead Russia to victory. We are telling this government, as the declaration of the [Progressive Bloc] stated: We shall fight you, we shall fight you with all legitimate means until you go.

When the Duma declares again and again that the home front must be organised for a successful war and the government continues to insist that to organize the country means to organize a revolution, and consciously chooses chaos and disorganization – is this stupidity or treason? We have many reasons for being discontented with the government. But all these reasons boil down to one general one: the incompetence and evil intentions of the present government. Cabinet members must agree unanimously as to the most urgent tasks. They must agree and be prepared to implement the programme of the Duma majority. They must rely on this majority, not just in the implementation of this programme, but in all their actions.

SOURCE 2

From a Petrograd *Okhrana* (secret police) report, January 1917.

There is a marked increase in hostile feelings among the peasants, not only against the government but also against all other social groups. The proletariat of the capital is on the verge of despair. The mass of industrial workers are quite ready to let themselves go to the wildest excesses of a hunger riot. The prohibition of all labour meetings, the closing of trade unions, the prosecution of men taking an active part in the sick benefit funds, the suspension of labour newspapers, and so on, make the labour masses, led by the more advanced and already revolutionary-minded elements, assume an openly hostile attitude towards the Government and protest with all the means at their disposal against the continuation of the war.

SOURCE 3

Nicolai Sukhanov, a Menshevik eyewitness, describes the situation in Petrograd in February 1917.

February 21st. I was sitting in my office. Behind a partition two typists were gossiping about food difficulties, arguments in the shopping queues, unrest among the women, an attempt to smash into a warehouse, 'Do you know,' declared one of these young ladies, 'if you ask me, it's the beginning of the Revolution.'

February 22nd and 23rd – the movements in the streets became clearly defined, going beyond the limits of the usual factory meetings.

February 24th, the movement swept over St. Petersburg like a great flood. Many squares in the centre were crowded with workers. Fugitive meetings were held in the main streets and were dispersed by the Cossacks but without energy or zeal and after lengthy delays.

AS style question

With reference to Sources 1 and 2, and your understanding of the historical context, which of these two sources is more valuable in explaining why the February Revolution broke out?

A level style question

With reference to Sources 1, 2 and 3, and your understanding of the historical context, assess the value of these sources to a historian studying the reasons for collapse of the tsarist system in February 1917.

The mark schemes

AS mark scheme

See the AQA website for the full mark schemes. This summary of the AS mark scheme shows how it rewards analysis and evaluation of the source material within the historical context.

Level 1	Describing the source content or offering generic phrases.
Level 2	Some relevant but limited comments on the value of one source *or* some limited comment on both.
Level 3	Some relevant comments on the value of the sources and some explicit reference to the issue identified in the question.
Level 4	Relevant well-supported comments on the value and a supported conclusion, but with limited judgement.
Level 5	Very good understanding of the value in relation to the issue identified. Sources evaluated thoroughly and with a well-substantiated conclusion related to which is more valuable.

A level mark scheme

This summary of the A level mark scheme shows how it is similar to the AS, but covers three sources. Also the wording of the question means that there is no explicit requirement to decide which of the three sources is the most valuable. Concentrate instead on a very thorough analysis of the content and evaluation of the provenance of each source.

Level 1	Some limited comment on the value of at least one source.
Level 2	Some limited comments on the value of the sources *or* on content or provenance *or* comments on all three sources but no reference to the value of the sources.
Level 3	Some understanding of all three sources in relation to both content and provenance, with some historical context; but analysis limited.
Level 4	Good understanding of all three sources in relation to content, provenance and historical context to give a balanced argument on their value for the purpose specified in the question.
Level 5	As Level 4, but with a substantiated judgement.

Working towards an answer

It is important that knowledge is used to show an understanding of the relationship between the sources and the issue raised in the question. Answers should be concerned with:

- provenance
- arguments used (and you can agree/disagree)
- tone and emphasis of the sources.

The sources

The two or three sources used each time will be contemporary – probably of varying types (for example, diaries, newspaper accounts, government reports). The sources will all be on the same broad topic area. Each source will have value. Your task is to evaluate how much – in terms of its content and its provenance.

You will need to assess the *value of the content* by using your own knowledge. Is the information accurate? Is it giving only part of the evidence and ignoring other aspects? Is the tone of the writing significant?

You will need to evaluate the *provenance* of the source by considering who wrote it, and when, where and why. What was its purpose? Was it produced to express an opinion or to record facts or to influence the opinion of others? Even if it was intended to be accurate, the writer may have been biased – either deliberately or unconsciously. The writer, for example, might have only known part of the situation and reached a judgement solely based on that.

Here is a guide to analysing the provenance, content and tone for Sources 1, 2 and 3.

Analysing the sources

To answer the question effectively, you need to read the sources carefully and pull out the relevant points as well as add your own knowledge. You must remember to keep the focus on the question at all times.

Source 1 (page 208)

Provenance:

- The source is from a speech by Paul Milyukov, leader of the Kadet Party. He will have a particular view on how Russia should be governed.
- It is taken from a speech to the *Duma* – it will therefore be addressing that particular audience for publicising the views of the Kadet Party.

Content and argument:

- The source argues that the government is incompetent.
- The country is chaotic and disorganised – the fault of the government.
- The government must do what the *Duma* majority keeps on proposing.

Tone and emphasis:

- The tone is assertive. Milyukov is demanding, on behalf of the *Duma,* action by the government, even though the Kadets only had one-eighth of the members.

Own knowledge:

- Use your knowledge to agree/disagree with the source, for example: details about why Russia was unable to achieve victory in the war, or evidence relating to why the author thought that the tsar's government was incompetent and with evil intentions.

Source 2 (page 208)

Provenance:

- The source is from a report made by the *Okhrana* – we do not know who by.
- It provides a contemporary account of what the *Okhrana* thought at the time.

Content and argument:

- The source argues that the peasants are increasingly hostile towards the government and other social groups.
- Those who would favour revolution are gaining more support because of the government's

suppression of peaceful forms of protest, for example through trade unions.

Tone and emphasis:

- The tone shows signs of fear if protests continue as they were at the time.

Own knowledge:

- Use your knowledge to agree/disagree with the source, for example: evidence about the extremely low morale of the industrial workers in Petrograd, or the attitude of the tsarist government towards freedom of speech.

Source 3 (page 209)

Provenance:

- The source is from an eyewitness of the events unfolding in Petrograd.
- It is written by a Menshevik who would want to see positive signs of an impending revolution.

Content and argument:

- The source sees the workers gaining more control of the city.
- The Cossacks lacked enthusiasm in acting against the workers.

Tone and emphasis:

- The writer is enthusiastic about the increasing chaos on the streets.

Own knowledge:

- Use your knowledge to agree/disagree with the source, for example: detailed knowledge about the situation on the streets, such as the bread queues, or knowledge about why some of the Cossacks were reluctant to act brutally against the strikers.

Answering AS questions

You have 45 minutes to answer the question. It is important that you spend at least one-quarter of the time reading and planning your answer. Generally, when writing an answer you need to check that you are remaining focused on the issue identified in the

question and are relating this to the sources and your knowledge.

- You might decide to write a paragraph on each 'strand' (that is provenance, content and tone), comparing the two sources, and then write a short concluding paragraph with an explained judgement on which source is more valuable.
- For writing about content, you may find it helpful to adopt a comparative approach, for example when the evidence in one source is contradicted or questioned by the evidence in another source.

At AS level you are asked to provide a judgement on which is more valuable. Make sure that this is based on clear arguments with strong evidence, and not on general assertions.

Planning and writing your answer

- Think how you can best plan an answer.
- Plan in terms of the headings above, perhaps combining 'provenance' with 'tone and emphasis', and compare the two sources.

As an example, here is a comparison of Sources 1 and 2 in terms of provenance, and tone and emphasis:

The two sources have different viewpoints. In terms of their provenance, Source 2 is a police report describing the growing disorder in Petrograd and the threat this poses to the government if the war, which the people are protesting against, continues in the same way. Source 1 is more studied in its analysis; however, it is taken from a speech when Milyukov would have been campaigning to get support for the Liberal Kadets who wanted peaceful change within an existing framework of government.

Then compare the *content and argument* of each source, by using your knowledge, for example:

Source 1 is arguing for a new government to work with the Duma. The situation with the war was critical at the time (with some details); Rasputin was extremely unpopular because he was reputed to control the government; and the Duma had no confidence in the ministers appointed by the tsar.

Source 2, however, focuses on the chaos which had become common on the streets of Petrograd, especially when 40,000 workers at the Putilov armaments factory went on strike and there were long queues in the street for bread. This source sees the increasing chaos as highly dangerous and warns that the repression of the workers is proving ineffective.

Which is *more valuable*? This can be judged in terms of which is likely to be more valuable in terms of where the source came from; or in terms of the accuracy of its content. However, remember the focus of the question: in this case, why the February Revolution broke out.

With these sources, you could argue that Source 2 is the more valuable because it was written closer to the actual revolution than Source 1, and it gives a real sense of the urgency on the streets, whereas Source 1 is more limited to debates within the *Duma* with less focus on the scene which actually led to the revolution.

Then check the following:

- Have you covered the 'provenance' and 'content' strands?
- Have you included sufficient knowledge to show understanding of the historical context?

Answering A level questions

The same general points for answering AS questions (see 'Answering AS questions') apply to A level questions, although, of course, here there are three sources and you need to assess the value of each of the three, rather than choose which is most valuable. Make sure that you remain focused on the question and that when you use your knowledge it is used to substantiate (add to) an argument relating to the content or provenance of the source.

If you are answering the A level question with Sources 1, 2 and 3 above:

- Keep the different 'strands' explained above in your mind when working out how best to plan an answer.
- Follow the guidance about 'provenance' and 'content' (see the AS guidance).
- Here you are *not* asked to explain which is the most valuable of the three sources. You can deal with each of the three sources in turn if you wish.
- However, you can build in comparisons if it is helpful – but it is not essential. It will depend to some extent on the three sources.
- You need to include sufficient knowledge to show understanding of the historical context. This might encourage cross-referencing of the content of the three sources, mixed with your own knowledge.
- Each paragraph needs to show clarity of argument in terms of the issue identified by the question.

Interpretations guidance

Section A of the exam for AQA Component 1: Breadth Study: Tsarist and Communist Russia, 1855–1964 contains extracts from the work of historians. This section tests your ability to analyse different historical interpretations so you must focus on the interpretations outlined in the extracts. The advice given here is for both the AS and the A level exams:

- for the AS exam, there are two extracts and you are asked which is the more convincing interpretation (25 marks)
- for the A level exam, there are three extracts and you are asked how convincing the arguments are in relation to a specified topic (30 marks).

An interpretation is a particular view on a topic of history held by a particular author or authors. Interpretations of an event can vary, for example, a historian might give weight to one particular factor and then largely ignore another.

Interpretations can also be heavily conditioned by events and situations that influence the writer, such as the interpretations on whether Stalin betrayed or fulfilled Lenin's revolution (see page 171). Someone writing about the event years after it has occurred may see it very differently to someone writing about it at the time.

The interpretations that you will be given will be largely from recent or fairly recent historians, and they may, of course, have been influenced by events in the period in which they were writing.

Interpretations and evidence

The extracts will contain a mixture of interpretations and evidence. The mark scheme rewards answers that focus on the *interpretations* offered by the extracts much more highly than answers that focus on the *information or evidence* mentioned in the extracts. Therefore, it is important to identify the interpretations:

- *Interpretations* are a specific kind of argument. They tend to make claims such as 'Trotsky's leadership was the most important reason why the Reds won the Civil War.'
- *Information or evidence* tends to consist of specific details. For example: 'Trotsky's methods were important in getting support for the Communists in the Civil War.'
- *Arguments and counter-arguments*: sometimes in an extract you will find an interpretation that is then balanced in the same paragraph with a counter-argument. You will need to decide with which your knowledge is most in sympathy.

The importance of planning

Remember that in the exam you are allowed an hour for this question. It is the planning stage that is vital in order to write a good answer. You should allow at least one-quarter of that time to read the extracts and plan an answer. If you start writing too soon, it is likely that you will waste time trying to summarise the *content* of each extract. Do this in your planning stage – and then think how you will *use* the content to answer the question.

Analysing interpretations: AS (two extracts)

The same skills are needed for AS and A level for this question. The advice starts with AS simply because it involves only two extracts rather than three.

> **With reference to these extracts and your understanding of the historical context, which of these two extracts provides the more convincing interpretation of the success of Stalin's economic policies? (25 marks)**

Extracts A and B are used for the AS question. Extracts A, B and C are used for the A Level question.

EXTRACT A

A view of Soviet industrial achievements in the 1930s. From an official history of the USSR, published in 1981. (From *Stalin and the Soviet Union*, S.J. Lee, Routledge, 1999, p. 52.)

While the economies of the capitalist countries were sinking ever deeper into recession the Soviet economy was humming. The laying of a firm foundation for a socialist economy created favourable conditions for the further progress of the country's national economy in the second Five Year Plan period, 1933–1937.

The key economic task of the second Five Year period – technical re-equipment of the national economy – was fulfilled. During the second Five Year Plan period, industrial output went up by 120 per cent. The USSR moved into first place in Europe and second in the world in gross industrial output.

EXTRACT B

A view of the Soviet economy in the 1930s. (From *Stalin: Biography*, Robert Service, Pan, 2004, p. 265.)

Disruption was everywhere in the economy. Ukraine, south Russia, and Kazakhstan were starving. The Gulag heaved with prisoners. Nevertheless the economic transformation was no fiction. The USSR under Stalin's rule had been pointed decisively in the direction of becoming an industrial, urban society. This had been his great

objective. His gamble was paying off for him, albeit not for millions of victims. Magnitogorsk and the White Sea Canal were constructed at the expense of the lives of Gulag convicts, Ukrainian peasants and even undernourished, overworked factory labourers.

EXTRACT C

The effects of industrialisation in Soviet Russia in the 1930s (only relevant for A level). (From *Stalinist Values: The Cultural Norms of Soviet Modernity Stalin*, David Hoffman, an American historian, Cornell, 2003, p. 111.)

Social change must be gradual and consensual if it is to succeed. Even if violence achieves superficial change, it does not permanently transform the way people think and act. Moreover in the Soviet case the means and ends were themselves in contradiction. State coercion by its very nature

could not create social harmony. The arrest and execution of millions of people only sowed hatred, mistrust and disharmony in Soviet society.

Analysing Extract A

From the extract:

- The Soviet economy was booming while other countries' were not.
- Firm foundations had been laid to allow the second Five-Year Plan to succeed.
- Statistics are presented to show the success of industrial production in the 1930s.

Assessing the extent to which the arguments are convincing:

- Deploying knowledge to corroborate that the Soviet economy thrived in the 1930s.
- Deploying knowledge to highlight the limitations of the achievements of the Five-Year Plans.
- Suggesting that the statistics at the end are highly selective, for example, industry in the USSR was starting from a very low base. 'Second in the world in gross industrial output' is a good claim to make, but it is not substantiated.

- The extract comes from an official history, written to show how the USSR developed into a major superpower, with Stalin as the hero of the time (even though he had been denounced by Khrushchev in 1956).
- The extract omits any reference to the sufferings outlined in Extract B.

Analysing Extract B

From the extract:

- The economy had been transformed, with the USSR on the way to becoming an industrial, urban society.
- Stalin's gamble of ruthlessly pushing forward had worked.
- However, there were millions of victims – in factories, on construction sites and in villages.

Assessing the extent to which the arguments are convincing:

- Deploying knowledge to agree with the assessment of success in terms of industrial production (and agreeing with Extract A).
- Deploying knowledge to highlight the phrase 'pointed decisively in the direction of becoming …'; for example, most of the population of the USSR still lived in a rural environment.
- Juxtaposing the achievements against the huge suffering of millions by providing more knowledge to substantiate the argument in the source.
- The extract comes from a respected British historian and was published in 2004, well after the fall of the Soviet Union and the release of secret records from the Stalinist era.

Comparing the analysis of each extract should give the direction of an overall conclusion and judgement about which of the extracts is more convincing. In this case it may be that Extract B is more convincing because it does try to present a balanced view.

The mark scheme for AS

The mark scheme builds up from Level 1 to Level 5, in the same way as it does for essays.

- Do not waste time simply describing or paraphrasing the content of each source.
- Make sure that when you include your knowledge that it is being used to advance the analysis of the extracts – not as knowledge in its own right.
- The top two levels of the mark scheme refer to 'supported conclusion' (Level 4) and 'well-substantiated conclusion' (Level 5).
- For Level 4, 'Supported conclusion' means finishing your answer with a judgement that is backed up with some accurate evidence drawn from the source(s) and your knowledge.
- For Level 5, 'well-substantiated conclusion' means finishing your answer with a judgement that is very well supported with evidence, and, where relevant, reaches a complex conclusion that reflects a wide variety of evidence.

Writing the answer for AS

There is no one correct way! However, the principles are clear. In particular, contextual knowledge should be used *only* to back up an argument. None of your knowledge should be standalone – all your knowledge should be used in context.

For each extract in turn:

- Explain the evidence in the extract, backed up with your own contextual knowledge, for Stalin's economic policies being successful.
- Explain the points in the extract where you have evidence that contradicts Stalin being a success.

Then write a conclusion that reaches a judgement on which is more convincing as an interpretation. You might build in some element of comparison during the answer, or it might be developed in the last paragraph only.

Analysing interpretations: A level (three extracts)

For the AQA A level exam, Section A gives you three extracts (see page 214), followed by a single question.

Using your understanding of the historical context, assess how convincing the arguments in each of these three extracts are in relation to Stalin's economic policies. (30 marks)

An analysis of Extracts A and B has already been provided for the AS question (see page 213).

Analysing Extract C (page 214)

From the extract:

- Stalin's major changes could not instantly change everyone's thoughts and behaviours.
- Social harmony could not be engineered by the state.
- The brutality of the 1930s created huge problems of hatred and mistrust.

Assessing the extent to which the arguments are convincing:

- Deploying knowledge to corroborate the extent of the brutality.
- Deploying knowledge to explain the divisions within Soviet society.
- Suggesting that this extract comes from an American writer whose language is nearer to sociology rather than history.
- The extract minimises the successes that Stalin actually achieved – in spite of brutality and opposition.

Writing the answer for A Level

First, make sure that you have the focus of the question clear – in this case, the focus is on Stalin's economic policies and how convincing the extracts are on that subject. Then you can investigate the three extracts to see how convincing they are.

You need to analyse each of the three extracts in turn. A suggestion is to have a large sheet of paper divided into nine blocks.

Extract's main arguments	Knowledge to corroborate	Knowledge to contradict or modify
A		
B		
C		

- In the first column list the main arguments each extract uses.
- In the second column list what you know that can corroborate the arguments.
- In the third column list what might contradict or modify (you might find that you partly agree, but with reservations) the arguments.
- You may find, of course, that some of your knowledge is relevant more than once.

Planning your answer

Decide how you could best set out a detailed plan for your answer:

- Briefly refer to the focus of the question.
- For each extract in turn set out the arguments, corroborating and contradictory evidence.
- Do this by treating each argument (or group of arguments) in turn.
- Make comparisons between the extracts if this is helpful. The mark scheme does not explicitly give credit for doing this, but a successful cross-reference may well show the extent of your understanding of each extract and add to the weight of your argument.
- An overall judgement is not required, but it may be helpful to make a brief summary, or just reinforce what has been said already by emphasising which extract was the most convincing.

The mark scheme for A level

For each of the three extracts, the mark scheme makes it clear that a good answer will:

- identify the arguments presented in each extract
- assess the extent to which the arguments are convincing, using own knowledge
- take every opportunity to make a balanced answer wherever this is appropriate, by corroborating and contradicting the arguments in each extract.

The full mark scheme can be found on the AQA website (www.aqa.org.uk). This summary of the mark scheme shows how it progresses upwards:

Level 1	General comments about the three extracts or accurate understanding of one extract.
Level 2	Some accurate comments on the interpretations in at least two of the three extracts, but with limited comments or with description.
Level 3	Some supported comments on the interpretations, putting them in their historical context. Some analysis of the content of the extracts, but little attempt to evaluate them.
Level 4	Good understanding of the interpretations provided in the extracts, with knowledge to give a good analysis and some evaluation.
Level 5	Very good understanding and strong historical awareness to analyse and evaluate.

Notice that there is no reference in the mark scheme to *comparing* the extracts or reaching a judgement about the most convincing.

Glossary of terms

All-Russian Congress of Soviets A gathering of representatives from all the soviets formed in Russia since February 1917.

All-Russian Constituent Assembly An elected parliament representing all the regions of Russia.

Amazons A special corps of female soldiers recruited by Kerensky.

American Relief Association Formed in 1921 by future US President Herbert Hoover to provide food and medical supplies for post-war Europe.

Anti-Comintern Pact Formed by Germany, Italy and Japan.

Anti-Semitism Hatred of the Jewish race; for centuries Russia had been notorious for its vicious treatment of the Jews.

Atomic bombs Dropped on Hiroshima on 6 August 1945 and on Nagasaki three days later.

Baltic States Estonia, Latvia and Lithuania.

Bipolarity The division of the world between East and West.

Black market Illegal buying and selling of rationed or scarce goods at inflated prices.

Bonn The post-war capital of West Germany.

Bourgeois experts A mocking reference to those workers whose skills had enabled them to earn higher wages and thus be less committed to building the new Russia.

Bourgeoisie The owners of capital, the boss class, who exploited the workers but who would be overthrown by them in the revolution to come.

British Communist Party Set up in 1921, it was always subservient to the Comintern, which provided the bulk of its funds.

Bureaucratisation The growth in power of the Secretariat, which was able to make decisions and operate policies without reference to ordinary party members.

Cadres Party members who were sent into factories and construction sites to spy and report back on managers and workers.

Capital The finance for investing in the purchasing of industrial machinery, plants and factories.

Capitalist methods of finance The system in which the owners of private capital (money) increase their wealth by making loans on which interest has to be paid later by the borrower.

Central Committee The decision-making body of the Bolshevik Party.

Cheka The All-Russian Extraordinary Commission for Fighting Counter-Revolution, Sabotage and Speculation: the secret police.

Class struggle A continuing conflict at every stage of history between those who possessed economic and political power and those who did not, the 'haves' and the 'have-nots'.

Coexistence A mutual recognition and tolerant acceptance of the different political and social systems operating in the USSR and the West.

Cold War The state of tension between the West (USA and its allies) and the Soviet bloc, which never escalated into full war; hence the word 'cold'.

Collective farms (*Kolkhozy* in Russian.) Run as co-operatives in which the peasants pooled their resources and shared their labour and wages.

Collective security Nations acting together to protect individual states from attack.

Collectivisation The state taking land and property previously owned by peasants, accompanied by the requirement that the peasants now live and work communally.

COMECON Council for Mutual Economic Assistance.

Cominform As a gesture of goodwill towards its wartime allies, the USSR had abolished the Comintern in 1943, but in the post-war tensions it was reformed in 1947 under a new name.

Comintern   Communist International, a body set up in Moscow in March 1919 to organise worldwide revolution.

Command economy   A system in which all the main areas of economic activity are under central government control and direction.

Commissar for Nationalities   Minister responsible for liaising with the non-Russian national minorities.

Commissars   Russian for ministers: Lenin chose the word because he said it 'reeked of blood'.

Consumer economy   The basic and successful form of capitalism in the West, which shaped growth around satisfying people's natural desire to acquire the good things in life.

Co-operatives   Groups of workers or farmers working together on a joint enterprise.

Cossacks   The remnants of the élite cavalry regiment of the tsars.

Council of People's Commissars   A cabinet of ministers, responsible for creating government policies.

Counter-revolution   A term used by the Bolsheviks to cover actions or ideas they regarded as reactionary and opposed to progress.

CPSU   The Communist Party of the Soviet Union, the new name for the Bolshevik Party from 1918 onwards.

Dacha   A country house used as a temporary retreat from the city.

DDR   East German People's Republic.

De facto   The real situation, as compared to what it should or might be in theory or in law.

Decree on Nationalisation   The takeover by the state of the larger industrial concerns in Russia.

Delayed revolution   According to Lenin, the gap between the workers' gaining consciousness of their latent power and their organised overthrow of their bourgeois oppressors.

'Deliver the votes'   To use control of the party machine to gain majority support in key divisions.

Democratic centralism   Lenin's insistence that democracy in the Bolshevik Party lay in the obedience of its members to its leaders, who were the only ones who truly understood the science of revolution.

Deportation   Removal to remote, barren areas.

Détente   A policy aimed at easing tensions between the rival international powers.

Dialectic   The dynamic force that drives the class struggle forward.

Dual authority   The coexistence of the provisional committee and the Petrograd soviet.

Economism   Putting the improvement of the workers' conditions before the need for revolution.

Emigrant internationalists   Russian revolutionaries living in exile.

Factionalism   The forming within the party of groups with a particular complaint or grievance.

Fait accompli   An established situation that cannot be changed.

FDR   West German Federal Republic.

Geneva Convention   International agreements in 1906 and 1929 that laid down the humane ways in which prisoners of war should be treated.

Georgian   People who inhabit the rugged land of Georgia. Strictly speaking, Stalin was Ossetian, a separate ethnic group living in northern Georgia. However, he always described himself as Georgian.

'German woman'   The description used by anti-tsarists to suggest that Alexandra was spying for Germany.

Gigantomania   The worship of size for its own sake.

Gold standard   The rouble had a fixed gold content, giving it strength when exchanged with other currencies.

Gosplan   The government body responsible for national economic planning.

Grand Alliance   The USSR led by Stalin, the USA led by Franklin Roosevelt, and Britain led by Winston Churchill.

Great Depression   A period of severe economic stagnation which began in the USA in 1929 and lasted until the mid-1930s, affecting the whole of the industrial world. Marxists regarded it as a portent of the final collapse of capitalism.

Greens   Largely made up of groups from the national minorities, struggling for independence.

Guerrilla warfare   A style of fighting in which mobile troops, who live off the land, harass the enemy with surprise attacks while avoiding pitched battles.

Gulag   An extensive network of prison and labour camps.

Haemophilia   A genetic condition where blood fails to clot, leaving the sufferer with painful internal bleeding, which can be life threatening.

Hydrogen bomb   A thermonuclear device that uses the atomic bomb as a detonator.

Icons   Paintings of Christ and Christian saints whose artistic beauty was one of the great glories of the Orthodox Church.

Industrialisation   The introduction of a vast scheme for the building of factories, which would produce heavy goods such as iron and steel.

Infant mortality   The number of children who die per 100 or per 1000 of all those in a particular age group.

Inflation   A decrease in the value and purchasing power of money.

Intelligentsia   People of influence in the intellectual world, for example, academics and writers.

International revolutionaries   Marxists who were willing to sacrifice national interests in the cause of a worldwide rising of workers.

Japanese expansionism   Stalin's concern was that imperialist Japan would exploit the USSR's problems on its European borders to encroach on Soviet territory in the Far East.

Konsomol   The Communist Union of Youth.

KPD   The German Communist Party.

Kulaks   Bolshevik term for rich, exploiting peasants.

Labour Code   Military-style, non-negotiable workplace rules imposed on workers, who faced severe penalties for disobeying them.

League of Nations   The body set up in 1919 with the aim of resolving international disputes and so maintaining world peace.

Left-liberal circles   Westerners sympathetic towards Stalin and the USSR.

Lend–lease   The importing by the USSR of war materials from the USA with no obligation to pay for them until after the war.

Leningrad   Petrograd had been renamed in Lenin's honour.

Maize mania   This was excited in part by Khrushchev's obsession with cornflakes, a maize cereal to which he had been introduced while in the USA. He believed that cornflakes could feed the nation.

Marshals of the Soviet Union   Equivalent to field marshals or five-star generals.

Marxism–Leninism–Stalinism   The concept of an ideological continuity between the founder of Marxism and its great interpreters, Lenin and Stalin.

May Day   Also known as 'Labour Day' – usually 1 May – traditionally regarded as a special occasion for honouring the workers and the achievements of socialism.

MVD   The secret police apparatus which had succeeded the *Cheka* and was later to become the KGB.

National minority governments   A number of Russia's ethnic peoples exploited the Provisional Government's difficulties by setting up their own governments and claiming independence.

NATO   The North Atlantic Treaty Organisation, created in 1949 of ten West European countries plus the USA and Canada.

Neopatriarchal   A new form of male domination.

Nepmen   Those who stood to gain from the free trading permitted under NEP, for example, rich peasants, retailers, traders and small-scale manufacturers.

Nomenklatura   The Soviet establishment, an élite set of privileged officials who ran the party and government.

Occupation zones Administered separately by Britain, the USA, France and the USSR. Berlin was similarly divided into four sectors administered by the same four powers.

October deserters Those Bolsheviks who, in October 1917, believing that the party was not yet strong enough, had advised against an uprising.

OEEC Organisation for European Economic Co-operation.

OGPU Succeeded the *Cheka* as the state security force. In turn it became the NKVD, the MVD and then the KGB.

Okhrana The tsarist secret police.

Operation Bagration The 58-day battle that cost a combined total of 765,000 casualties.

Operation Citadel The German codename for the Kursk campaign.

Orgburo The organisation bureau, which turned policies into practice.

Orthodox Church Russia's established state religion and traditionally one of the bulwarks of tsardom, supporting the idea that tsars ruled by divine right.

Packets Special benefits and privileges.

Panzer Fast-moving armoured tank unit.

Parliamentary-bourgeois republic A contemptuous term for the Provisional Government, which in Lenin's eyes had simply replaced the rule of the tsar with the rule of the reactionary *duma*.

Party card The official CPSU warrant granting membership to the holder. It was a prized possession in Soviet Russia since it entitled the holder to a wide range of privileges, such as quality accommodation, higher food rations, access to health care and education for the member's children.

Party democracy The right of all party members to express their opinion on policy.

Patronage The right to appoint individuals to official posts in the party and government.

Pearl Harbor A naval base in Hawaii where the US Pacific fleet was attacked by the Japanese in 1941.

Petrograd For patriotic reasons, the German name for St Petersburg was changed to the Russian form soon after the war began.

Pogrom Traditional Russian state-organised persecution, going back to tsarist times, involving physical attacks on Jews and destruction of their property.

Politburo The political bureau, responsible for major policy decisions.

Political commissars Dedicated party workers whose function was to accompany the officers permanently and report on their political correctness and loyalty.

Political expediency Pursuing a course of action with the primary aim of gaining a political advantage.

Popular front An alliance of socialist and progressive parties.

Pravda The Russian word for truth; the chief Bolshevik newspaper, dating from 1912.

Proletariat The exploited industrial workers who would triumph in the last great class struggle.

Red Guards Despite the Bolshevik legend that these were the crack forces of the revolution, the Red Guards, some 10,000 in number, were largely made up of elderly factory workers.

Reds Bolsheviks and their supporters.

Reparations Payment of the costs of war by the loser to the victor.

Requisitioning State-authorised seizure of property or resources.

Revisionism The Marxist word for political heresy, the failure to conform to revolutionary principles.

Revolution from below The CPSU consistently claimed that the 1917 revolution had been a genuine rising of the people rather than a power grab by the Bolsheviks.

Russian peasantry Agricultural workers, who made up over 80 per cent of the population.

Salient An area that protrudes into the enemy's lines, forming a bulge.

Satellites   A Western metaphor denoting the various countries orbiting around the sun (the USSR) and held in its magnetic grip.

Second revolution   The modernisation of the Soviet economy by means of state direction and central control.

Secretariat   The civil service that carried out the administration of policies.

Seminaries   Training colleges for the clergy.

Single-member veto   The right of an individual member to block the majority decisions of the others.

Socialist realism   The notion that all creative works must be representational, relating directly to the people and easily understood by them.

Soviet   Originally the Russian word for a representative council. It was appropriated by the Bolsheviks to describe themselves and the cause they espoused.

Soviet Union of Writers   The body which had authority over all published writers and had the right to ban any work of which it disapproved.

Sovnarkom   Russian for government or cabinet.

Spanish civil war   Fought principally between General Franco's fascist forces and the republicans. Franco was the eventual winner.

Sputnik   Russian for 'satellite', the first man-made object to leave the atmosphere and orbit Earth; it was launched from Kazakhstan in 1957.

State capitalism   The system, during the first year of Bolshevik rule, by which the main pre-revolutionary economic and administrative structures were maintained.

State farms   (*Sovkhozy* in Russian.) Contained peasants working directly for the state, which paid them a wage.

State grain procurements   Enforced collections of fixed quotas of grain from peasants.

Storming   An intensive period of work to meet a high set target. Despite the propaganda with which it was introduced, storming proved a very inefficient form of industrial labour and was soon abandoned.

Sugar crop   The Cuban economy was heavily dependent on a single crop, sugar.

System of dating   Until February 1918, Russia used the Julian calendar, which was thirteen days behind the Gregorian calendar, the one adopted in most Western countries by this time. This book uses the older dating for the events of 1917.

Tax in kind   The surrendering by the peasant of a certain amount of his produce, equivalent to a fixed sum of money. This replaced requisitioning, the seizure of all the peasant's stocks.

Testament   A set of reflections and comments that Lenin made on his fellow Communist leaders.

Thaw   An easing of tension and restrictions following Stalin's death; a number of prisoners were released and censorship of writers and artists was relaxed somewhat.

Triumvirate   A ruling or influential bloc of three people.

Troika   A three-man team.

Tuberculosis   A wasting disease often affecting the lungs, which was especially prevalent in Russia.

U2 aircraft   A US reconnaissance-plane for spying over Soviet territory.

UN Security Council   Composed of the USSR, the USA, France, Britain and Nationalist China.

Union of Municipal Councils   A set of patriotic urban local councils.

Union of Zemstva   A set of patriotic rural local councils.

United Opposition   The group led by Kamenev and Zinoviev, sometimes known as the New Opposition, which called for an end to NEP and the adoption of a rapid industrialisation programme.

Universal suffrage   All adults having the right to vote.

Urals   The mountain range dividing European and Asiatic Russia.

Urban workers   Factory workers who, while comprising only four per cent of the population, were economically and politically significant.

USSR   Union of Soviet Socialist Republics (often shortened to Soviet Union), the official title for Communist Russia, adopted in 1922.

Vesenkha   The Supreme Council of the National Economy.

Vozhd   A supreme leader; equivalent to *Führer* in German.

War commissars   Ministers responsible for military organisation.

War-credits   Money loaned on easy repayment terms, mainly by France and Britain, to Russia to finance its war effort.

War of attrition   A grinding conflict in which each side hopes to win by wearing the other down.

Warsaw Pact   Created in 1955, its member states were Albania, Bulgaria, Czechoslovakia, East Germany, Hungary, Poland, Romania and the USSR.

White Russian émigrés   Anti-Bolsheviks who fled from Russia during the years following the 1917 October Revolution.

White Sea Canal   In fact three canals linking Leningrad with the White Sea; built predominantly by forced labourers, who died in their thousands, the canal proved practically worthless since it was hardly used after construction.

Whites   The Bolsheviks' opponents, including tsarists and those parties that had been suppressed by the new regime.

Yalta and Potsdam Conferences   Meetings of the Allied powers held in February and July 1945, respectively, to discuss the settlement of the post-war world.

Yugoslav Communists   Yugoslavia under Tito had been the one Eastern European country to have successfully resisted Stalinist domination in the post-war period, remaining Communist but independent of the USSR.

Zemgor   The joint body which devoted itself to helping Russia's war wounded.

Zhenotdel   The Women's Bureau of the Communist Party.

Further reading

Books of overall relevance

David Christian, *Imperial and Soviet Russia* (Macmillan, 1997)
A very helpful combination of documents, commentary and analysis across the whole period

Michael Court, *The Soviet Colossus History and Aftermath* (M.E. Sharpe, 1996)
A clear informed narrative from the fall of tsardom to the fall of Khrushchev and beyond

Geoffrey Hosking, *Russia and the Russians* (Allen Lane, 2001)
A very readable coverage of the whole period by a leading authority

Stephen Kotkin, *Stalin: Paradoxes of Power 1878–1928*, Allen Lane, 2014
A detailed study on newly available Russian sources

Martin Malia, *The Soviet Tragedy: A History of Socialism in Russia, 1917–1991* (Free Press, 1994)
A survey of why the 74-year Soviet experiment failed

Martin McCauley, *Who's Who in Russian History since 1900* (Routledge, 1997)
An exceptionally helpful reference book of mini-biographies

Martin McCauley, *The Rise and Fall of the Soviet Union: 1917–1991* (Routledge, 2013)
Especially good on political and cultural developments

Alec Nove, *An Economic History of the USSR* (Penguin, 1992)
Established as the most reliable short account of economic developments across the period

Richard Sakwa, *The Rise and Fall of the Soviet Union 1917–1991* (Routledge, 1999)
An excellent selection of key documents, linked with a very well-informed commentary

Robert Service, *The Penguin History of Modern Russia: From Tsarism to the Twenty-first Century* (Penguin, 2009)
Informed coverage of the whole period by an outstanding Western historian

Dmitri Volkogonov, *The Rise and Fall of the Soviet Empire: Political Leaders from Lenin to Gorbachev* (HarperCollins, 1998)
Intrinsically valuable as an analysis and made more so by the fact that the Russian author lived and worked under Stalin

Website

http://www.marxists.org/history/ussr/events/revolution/index.htm
Soviet History Archive: a rich set of sources, starting with 1917 and covering politics, economics, culture and foreign affairs

Chapter 1

Edward Acton, *Rethinking the Russian Revolution* (Edward Arnold, 1990)
An interesting survey of many of the major interpretations of 1917

Sheila Fitzpatrick, *The Russian Revolution 1917–1932* (Oxford University Press, 1994)
A short stimulating survey by a celebrated expert in the field

Richard Pipes, *The Russian Revolution 1899–1919* (Collins Harvill, 1990)
Strongly critical of Lenin and the Bolsheviks, but a very detailed and readable account by a Polish-American historian

Ian D. Thatcher, editor, *Late Imperial Russia: Problems and Perspectives* (Manchester University Press, 2005)
A collection of stimulating essays by a group of leading scholars

Chapter 2

E.H. Carr, *The Russian Revolution from Lenin to Stalin 1917–1929* (Palgrave, 2004)
A much shortened version of a monumental study by a pioneer historian in Russian studies

Richard Pipes, *Russia under the Bolshevik Regime, 1919–24* (Collins Harvill, 1994)
A detailed study of the Bolshevik consolidation of power

Richard Pipes, *Three Whys of the Russian Revolution* (Pimlico, 1998)
A short but very useful summary of the major points in the previous book

Robert Service, *Lenin: A Biography* (Macmillan, 2000)
First part of a classic trilogy of the three great figures of the period

S.A. Smith, *The Russian Revolution: A Very Short Introduction* (Oxford University Press, 2002)
Despite its title, a brilliant analysis of the period between the October coup and NEP

Chapter 3

Isaac Deutscher, *Trotsky* (Oxford University Press, 1954–70)
A classic three-volume study of Stalin's great rival, written by a Trotsky admirer

Robert Service, *Trotsky: A Biography* (Macmillan, 2004)
Robert Service, *Stalin: A Biography* (Macmillan, 2009)
The second and third parts of the trilogy, dealing with the relations between Stalin and Trotsky

Dmitri Volkogonov, *Stalin: Triumph and Tragedy* (Weidenfeld & Nicolson, 1991)
Written from a Russian perspective with Stalin as the central figure

Chapter 4

Robert Conquest, *Harvest of Sorrow* (Macmillan, 1988)
A pioneering study of Stalin's shattering collectivisation programme

R.W. Davies, editor, *The Economic Transformation of the Soviet Union* (Cambridge University Press, 1994)
The most authoritative analysis of Stalin's economic reforms

Peter Gattrell, *Under Command: The Soviet Economy 1924–53* (Routledge, 1992)
Acknowledged as an outstanding study of Stalin's economic policies

Chapter 5

Anne Applebaum, *Gulag: A History of the Soviet Camps* (Penguin, 2003)
A detailed account of Stalin's repressive measures

Robert Conquest, *The Great Terror: Stalin's Purge of the Thirties* (Penguin, 1971)
The first book in the West to reveal the scale and character of the purges

Sheila Fitzpatrick, *Everyday Stalinism. Ordinary Life in Extraordinary Times: Soviet Russia in the 1930s* (Oxford University Press, 1999)
A leading Western scholar's absorbing study on the impact of Stalin's policies on ordinary Russians

J.A. Getty and R.T. Manning, *Stalinist Terror: New Perspectives* (Cambridge University Press, 1993)
Brings together informed thinking on the motives behind and the results of Stalin's terror programme

Simon Sebag Montefiore, *Stalin: The Court of the Red Tsar* (Knopf, 2004)
An absorbing study of Stalin's style of government

Lynne Viola, *The Unknown Gulag: The Lost World of Stalin's Special Settlements* (Oxford University Press, 2007)
A study that reveals the involvement in the terror of those below Stalin

Chapter 6

Sheila Fitzpatrick, editor, *Stalinism: New Directions* (Routledge, 2000)
A collection of scholarly revisionist essays analysing the character of Stalinism

David L. Hoffman, *Stalinist Values: The Cultural Norms of Soviet Modernity* (Cornell University Press, 2003)
Brings together many of the major ideas on Stalinism as a cultural phenomenon

Stephen Kotkin, *Stalin: Paradoxes of Power, 1878–1928* (Allen Lane, 2014)
The first volume of a planned trilogy which seems set to become a definitive modern study of Stalin

Roy Medvedev, *Let History Judge: The Origins and Consequences of Stalinism* (Oxford University Press, 1989)
The views of a Russian critic who suffered under Stalin

Alec Nove, *Stalinism and After* (Unwin Hyman, 1975)
A masterly survey of the impact of Stalinism

Richard Overy, *The Dictators: Hitler's Germany and Stalin's Russia* (Allen Lane, 2004)
Offers fascinating insights into Stalin's conduct of the Great Patriotic War

Robert C. Tucker, *Stalinism – Essays in Historical Interpretation* (Transaction Publishers, 1999)
Reflections and analysis by one of the major experts on the nature of Stalinism

Chapter 7

Martin McCauley, editor, *Khrushchev and Khrushchevism* (Indiana University Press, 1987)
A collection of studies of Khrushchev and his impact on the Soviet Union

R. Medvedev, *Khrushchev* (Oxford University Press, 1982)
An insider's account of the Khrushchev years

William Taubman, *Khrushchev: The Man and His Era* (Norton, 2003)
An interesting assessment of Khrushchev's contribution to the Soviet Union

William J. Tompson, *Khrushchev: A Political Life* (St. Martin's Press, 1995)
An informed account of Khrushchev's successes and failures

Index